MANAGING FOR NEGATIVE GROWTH

A Handbook for Practitioners

MANAGING FOR NEGATIVE GROWTH

A Handbook for Practitioners

Allan Easton
Hofstra University

CONSULTING EDITOR
Joseph L. Massie
University of Kentucky

RESTON PUBLISHING COMPANY, INC.
Reston, Virginia
A Prentice-Hall Company

Library of Congress Cataloging in Publication Data

658.4
E13

Easton, Allan
    Managing for negative growth.

    Bibliography.
    Includes index.
    1. Management.   2. Business losses.   I. Title.
    HD38.E15   658.4   75-43876
    ISBN 0-87909-479-6

© 1976 by
Reston Publishing Company, Inc.
A Prentice-Hall Company
Reston, Virginia 22090

10 9 8 7 6 5 4 3 2 1

Printed in the United States of America.

To Miriam

The study of contracting or constant size organizations has received little attention in the management or organization literature. Growth and expansion have tended to be the objectives of most organizations and the criteria by which success was judged. It is clear, however, that . . . we must be concerned with the management of organizations that are not growing . . . .

RICHARD M. CYERT, *Management of Non-Profit Organizations* (Pittsburg, Pa., Carnegie-Mellon University, 1974). An administrative paper. P. 33

Contents

Preface

This is not an ordinary "how-to" book in which a self-styled Delphic oracle dispenses business advice. Each business firm is unique. Each has its special flavor best understood by the people who have devoted their lives to it. No one is more capable of coping with the intricate details of the operation than those persons steeped in the firm's lore and past practices. No outsider can hope to match that depth of specific knowledge and understanding. No well-meaning stranger can comprehend the subtleties, the nuances, the complex interpersonal arrangements, the historical precedents, the unwritten agreements. Consequently, no uninformed outsider should offer flip, superficial, long-distance diagnoses which, more likely than not, are neither helpful in, nor applicable to, the real-world situation.

What this book does is to recount and examine some typical situations likely to be encountered by firms forced to contract in size. It suggests alternative courses of action that managers should not fail to explore.

It offers a variety of procedures for analyzing negative growth situations for the on-the-scene executive so that he will be less likely to overlook workable courses of action just because his field of perception is temporarily narrowed by the revulsion and shock of what he must do.

In the presence of the severe psychological stress inherent in negative growth situations, executives suffer changes in their values. Things deemed important in normal times are downgraded in priority. Survival and self-preservation transcend other less durable values. Behavior thought intolerable becomes increasingly accepted. Decisions that should take into account the welfare of many affected parties are made, instead, on the narrow grounds of individual, group, or organizational self-interest.

Many psychologists believe that when a person is unexpectedly placed in a highly stressful, threatening situation, he tends to regress to an earlier stage in his life. In his normal state, he is self-reliant, secure, generous, outgoing, happy, and decisive. In the face of extreme stress, however, he moves away from his normal behavior patterns. He regresses in time to when he could lean more on others; when decisions were made for him instead of by him; when he was bothered much more by feelings of insecurity and inadequacy. He tends to become grasping instead of generous, moody and depressed instead of happy, introverted instead of outgoing. Instead of being decisive, he vacillates. His liquor consumption climbs and he suffers psychosomatic symptoms. His home situation deteriorates and intrafamily conflict, easily contained in normal times, causes the family unit to fly apart.

An important purpose of this book is to aid the executive, who is traumatized by the unpleasant things that he is forced to do, in designing and carrying out an effective negative growth program for his firm. He alone is on the firing line. He alone must make the unpleasant decisions. He alone must face the unhappy consequences of inappropriate actions. This book is intended to help him design well-plotted change programs, to help him carry out negative growth strategies, and to help save much wear and tear on the executive psyche and soma. It can help minimize any unnecessary injuries that may be inflicted on the inevitable victims of the contraction, and can help make the shrinking process run perceptibly smoother—at much lower cost to all affected parties.

In this book, I have concentrated my attention on the retrenchment process and have not treated the problems of the post-contraction condition. I have made this choice because the business literature and the large body of contemporary material on organizational change deal very capably with the management of stable and growing companies. What has been neglected, possibly because few authors like to "think the unthinkable" or to write about the seamy side of business life, is the treatment of those nasty little problems encountered during the contraction process.

In doing the research for this book about negative growth, I have drawn liberally on my own experience as a business executive and as a teacher of business administration subjects at Columbia University's and Hofstra University's schools of business. In addition, I have interviewed business associates, students, and fellow faculty for their reminiscences and experiences in retrenching companies. I made one discovery at an early phase of the writing: Everybody loves to talk endlessly about his successes. No one is overly communicative about his associations with failure and decline.

Many of the mini-cases and examples cited in the text are drawn from life, but names are changed to protect the participants from embarrassment. Other examples are fictional, but in the sense that they are more real than true life. They are concocted to illustrate a particular point; if the event and behavior did not actually happen, it surely could have.

I have also, consciously and unconsciously, called upon my recollections of conversations with businessmen and of books, articles, and news stories that I have read throughout the years I have been interested in business. My sources are far too many and far too imperfectly recalled to give each a credit by name. To all the persons whose materials and ideas I have borrowed or who have influenced my thought and development, I herein give my thanks and I acknowledge my debt to them.

ALLAN EASTON

PART I

INTRODUCTION AND BACKGROUND

Thinking About
Negative Growth

PRELIMINARIES

The American business ethos assigns high positive valuation to growth. Just as children yearn to grow into adults, so do ambitious managers hunger to enlarge their operations or to move into large areas of responsibility, power, and influence. It is much more prestigious to be the general manager of a subsidiary employing 10,000 people than of one with a mere 1000. Much higher status accrues to the organization head who increases his sales and earnings at a twenty per cent annual rate than to the leader of the company of comparable size, but who maintains level or diminishing sales and earnings. A company president whose firm's sales, profits, size of plant, share of market, number of employees, or total assets are not increasing more or less regularly will undoubtedly be seen by himself, and by his peers, as being neither successful nor very dynamic.

This love for growth is also expressed in the securities markets, where investors typically assign higher price-to-earnings multipliers to the shares of companies that report growing earnings per share, than for those with level or diminishing year-to-year per-share earnings. For business managers whose compensation includes generous stock purchase deals, growth in company earnings produces euphoria, but contraction leads to dismay and feelings of failure. "Grow or die" is an accepted imperative in both the business and nonbusiness organizational world.

But conventional wisdom warns even the most optimistic of us, "A tree cannot grow to the sky." There are limits to growth and there will be times when growth is not possible. The life span of many long-lived organizations includes intervals of nongrowth as well as positive growth and, perhaps, even prolonged periods of contraction. All three stages present unique and difficult managerial challenges, but, of the three, dealing with the contraction phase is the least pleasant. Even if, to the indefatigable optimist, the contraction stage is seen as the precursor to renewed expansion, as, for example, in the typical "turn-around" situation, managers are likely to discover that coping with the shrinking of an organization is an extremely painful and frustrating experience. No matter how skillful the pruning job, no matter how considerate the manager, inevitably many persons suffer injury during a business contraction.

In those happier days when our prototypical firm was small and very, very profitable, its leaders reasoned that the operation could be made much more lucrative by making it grow and grow. Perhaps the transitional stage between the initial size and another stage of growth might have been less than profitable, but everybody understood why that could happen and forgave the temporary lapses. After a while, with application of diligence and skill, plus a bit of luck, a new plateau of sales and earnings was reached. It was such hard work, but what a good feeling it gave everyone on the team!

That most recent rise in the firm's fortunes gives everyone a still greater appetite for even more—a condition of mind the psychologists call "rising level of aspiration." "More, more, more" is the operative philosophy. For those firms where the opportunity for internally generated growth was lacking because of market saturation or stiff competition, managerial creativity, undaunted, found another way—the acquisitions route. And so on, upward and upward, almost (but not quite) to the sky.

Looking backward at the path of the firm's upward progress, one might reasonably ask, "We were profitable when we were smaller. Why can't we just retrace our steps, you know, reverse the process, and move backward to a previously profitable level of operation on a smaller scale than now? Isn't that possible?"

Clearly, it is possible and many firms have done just that. To a degree, the process is reversible. Many processes in nature and economic life are reversible; some are not. For example, the birth of a baby is obviously an irreversible process. And we recall, "All the king's horses and all the king's men couldn't put Humpty Dumpty together again." Some processes are reversible, although the reverse operation may be harder to do than the forward. In mathematics, for example, extracting a cube root is harder than cubing a number; integration is harder than differentiation; division is harder than multiplication, and so forth.

In a like sense, some business processes may be fully reversible; others may be partly or completely irreversible. We should not be surprised, therefore, that reversing positive growth is harder and more taxing than managing for positive growth. Contraction will be difficult for two reasons: (1) the reverse process is undoubtedly harder to perform, and (2) very few of today's managers and administrators have sufficient knowledge, experience, or training to cope effectively with business contraction. Today's managers are trained in another school where "grow or die" rules their hearts and minds.

Before they can reach their conclusion that a program of planned contraction is the best, or the only feasible, course of action, the executives of the firm destined to undergo negative growth go through a few preliminary stages in their reasoning process. At the outset, they are dissatisfied with the condition of the company. When they examine the cluster of symptoms, the leadership group makes a diagnosis of the firm's shortcomings, and becomes convinced that the company's faults can best be corrected by adopting a negative growth strategy. By implication, they reject two other alternatives: (1) make no changes, and (2) keep trying to expand.

Having arrived at the choice of the negative growth alternative, they complete the first step in a long, complicated decision sequence. This first phase is diagrammed in Fig. 1-1 and the following phase is shown schematically in Fig. 1-2.

WHY NEGATIVE GROWTH?

What circumstances can cause such intense dissatisfaction that the firm's leaders are moved to adopt so drastic an action as a planned contraction? Consider these cases:

— At Whittaker Corporation, a series of ill-conceived acquisitions during the 1960's makes necessary a program of divestitures, retrenchments, and reorganizations to restore the company to health. The company's annual reports repeatedly contain the item: "income

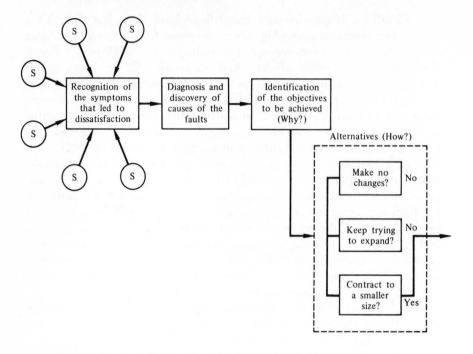

FIGURE 1-1.   Preliminary stages in the reasoning process that can lead to the adoption of a negative growth strategy.

(loss), net of taxes, of operations disposed of, or about to be disposed of." (Whittaker Corp. annual reports to stockholders.)

— Faced with continued unprofitable operations, the GAF Corp., a New York-based corporation, gives notice of its intention to discontinue operations of its Northern Vermont asbestos mine. One hundred eighty workers elect to purchase the mine from its owner, and they intend to operate it as the Vermont Asbestos Group, Inc. (*Business Week,* March 31, 1975, p. 21.)

— Very disappointing sales in the domestic market for automobiles present automobile manufacturers, their suppliers, and their retail outlets with uncertain prospects for survival. Although some industry spokesmen express confidence that sales will eventually return to predepression levels, all wonder what sizes and kinds of cars the public will be willing to buy. (*Wall Street Journal,* May 27, 1975, p. 14.)

— Once they enjoyed a booming business in supplying automobile manufacturers and the big replacement market with "buggy whip"

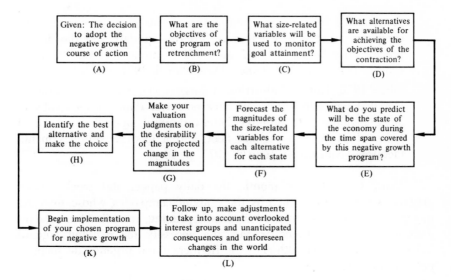

FIGURE 1-2.   The second stage in a negative growth program, beginning with a decision to implement negative growth and ending with implementation of the best way for achieving the firm's retrenchment objectives.

antennas. Suddenly, these suppliers see their original equipment manufacturers (O.E.M.) market collapse because auto-glass manufacturers incorporate the radio antenna into their windshields beginning with the 1972 automobile year.

— Cluett, Peabody & Co. has a textile plant in Saratoga Springs, New York—the Van Raalte plant—that is lagging unacceptably in sales and earnings. (*The New York Times*, May 25, 1975.)

— Royal Crown Cola Co., a soft drink marketer, long third in its industry behind Coca-Cola and Pepsi-Cola, finds itself shouldered aside by Seven-Up. A new president vows to rebuild RC into a "lean corporate organization." (*Business Week*, April 7, 1975, p. 24.)

— Recent scientific findings reveal that the gas propellant used in most aerosol products can conceivably cause harm to the earth's ozone layer and therefore can contribute to the gradual deterioration of living conditions on earth. The aerosol industry's sales have grown from one-half million cans per year in 1947 to over three billion cans in 1975. The suppliers of the gas fear a Congressional ban on sales of their product. (*New Yorker*, April 7, 1975, p. 47.)

— Gerald R. Armstrong, president of the Rocky Mountain Fuel Company, is the sole surviving employee of this once prosperous fuel company. His job is to effect an orderly liquidation of the firm, a process that began in 1947 and will continue for some time to come. (*The New York Times,* December 8, 1974, p. F9.)

— Since 1972, Litton Industries, a large conglomerate corporation, closed down, sold off, or cut back no fewer than fourteen subsidiaries, including its Stouffer hotel-restaurant operations, a Great Lakes shipyard and tugboat fleet, and a medical supplies manufacturer. (*Newsweek,* June 2, 1975, p. 56.)

Many times in any month, the daily papers and weekly news magazines carry stories such as these about companies whose managements believe they are in need of drastic pruning, resuscitation, or reorganization. In good times or bad, the necessity for reviving laggard business firms goes on, although the frequency and urgency do seem to peak during economic recessions.

WHAT ARE THE OBJECTIVES OF THE RETRENCHMENT PROGRAM?

A well-planned, well-executed retrenchment program may be the best, and perhaps the only, way for achieving one or more of the following objectives:

— In a national, worldwide, or industry-wide recession, to survive to live and fight another day.

— To undo an unwise or mistaken expansion, acquisition, or merger.

— To effect an orderly liquidation intended to preserve or rescue wasting assets.

— To reorganize the firm for a new purpose.

— To respond to market changes and to new economic or technological developments.

— To shift assets from a lagging operation to another with good growth and profit potential.

— To restore former profitability now lagging unacceptably.

— To revitalize a senescent organization.

— To restore liquidity to a financially overextended company.

— To convert a portion of the firm's fixed costs into variable costs.

— To bring the organization down to a more manageable size.

— To transform a highly centralized, massive firm into a decentralized collection of smaller units.

— To conform to a government order to restructure the firm.

— To revert to a single-industry firm from a multi-industry orientation.

— To reduce the vulnerability of the firm to rough economic weather, by becoming more fiscally prudent.

— To restore the confidence of the financial community in the credit-worthiness and viability of the firm.

— To run a tight ship; to recapture the lean, hard, and hungry attitudes of earlier, more vital years.

— To enhance the firm's attractiveness as a candidate for a takeover by another corporation.

— To prepare the firm for a merger with another firm that has overlapping product lines or market penetration, and thereby to avoid an antitrust action against the combined entity.

These foregoing objectives are not necessarily mutually exclusive. A specific retrenchment program always has multiple objectives that include one or more of the foregoing, and, perhaps, others not included in the listing.

IS THE CONTRACTION TO BE TEMPORARY OR PERMANENT?

Some firms undertake temporary contractions. Just as a well-skippered sailing vessel heaves to in a gale, so do firms adopt negative growth as the means for riding out financial or economic storms. Growth resumes when better weather returns.

Others must contract permanently because all hope is gone that the companies can ever be restored to their former grandeur. A few, intended to be of short duration, prove to be permanent because the tactics employed by their managements throw the firms into ever-descending spirals from which they cannot be rescued.

Be they temporary or permanent, retrenchments are forced upon the firms' managers by circumstances they perceive as beyond their control. Instead of taking prompt and decisive action, they procrastinate until retrenchment becomes unavoidable, and then, in their weakened condition and in a state of glassy-eyed panic, they try to cope.

It is far better to look ahead with clear-headed realism. If it appears that a program of negative growth is the best available option, then it should be started as soon as possible. The courageous, far-sighted manager can be likened to the patient with an inflamed appendix who accepts his surgeon's recommendation for immediate surgery rather than to wait until his bursting appendix causes life-threatening complications. To procrastinate unduly is to multiply immeasurably the difficulties of restoring the firm to good health.

WHICH SIZE-RELATED VARIABLES FOR MONITORING SIZE CHANGES?

When the sponsors of the retrenchment program reach a consensus on objectives, the next step is to devise concrete, quantifiable criteria for monitoring size changes. Such criteria are used both to follow progress and to construct models of the retrenchment's final phase. At any time during the negative growth of the entity, progress can be measured if the proper size-related variables are chosen. If examination of the variables reveals that progress toward the end goal is not as good as wanted, as Fig. 1-3 shows, timely and appropriate corrective action can be started.

Examples of size-related variables are shown in Table 1-1. Vari-

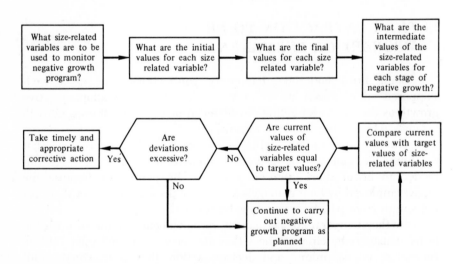

FIGURE 1-3.   Use of a set of size-related variables to monitor changes in accordance with a predetermined program.

TABLE 1-1
PARTIAL LIST OF SIZE-RELATED
VARIABLES *

Generally (but not always) as the firm grows in size, these increase:

1. Total assets
2. Annual sales
3. Number of employees
4. Investment in plant
5. Number of shares
6. Number of shareholders
7. Working capital
8. Long-term debt
9. Number and size of customers
10. Dividends paid
11. Resources used
12. Impact on community
13. Market power
14. Specialization of employees
15. Organizational complexity
16. Planning time horizon
17. Number of staff positions
18. Size of orders
19. Payments to suppliers
20. Formality of procedures
21. Stability
22. Fixed costs proportion
23. Overhead component of cost
24. Job security for all employees
25. Fringe benefits to employees
26. Proportion of risk insured
27. Vulnerability to legal harassment
28. Before and after-tax earnings
29. Value added
30. Public hostility

Generally (but not always) as the firm grows in size, these decrease:

1. Unit cost of product
2. Speed of response to external stimulus
3. Flexibility in response to sudden change
4. Communication effectiveness
5. Vulnerability to economic downturn
6. Dependence on few key individuals
7. Growth propensity (harder to double size)
8. Versatility of work force and staff personnel

* Some of these variables are dependent and some independent; i.e., some are causes and some, effects.

ables such as these, plus as many others as are needed, are used to prepare detailed schedules and pro-forma financial statements for selected milestones along the chosen negative-growth trajectory. Whatever means are chosen to monitor changes, it is important not to depend on vague, nonoperational, nonquantifiable goal statements, but to use quantifiable criteria for following progress toward the final goals.

The first impulse to use a single, global variable (such as profitability or sales volume) as the principal measure of size changes should be resisted. Although historical variables have a place, they fail because they provide after-the-fact information. What is much better is a set of variables that provide both past-performance indicators and early-warning pointers for quick detection of off-target size changes. Anticipation of deviations from plan can help keep down the financial and human cost of departures from the planned direction.

ALTERNATIVE MODES OF CONTRACTION

REDUCTION IN SCALE. Conceptually, if not in actual practice, the simplest form of contraction is the reduction in scale of operation. The character and basic structure of the entity is unchanged, but the outputs and inputs along with the magnitudes of the relevant size-related variables are reduced. For example, Arabesque Semiconductor Corp. undergoes a dimunition in scale. It experiences a drop in sales volume; it has fewer accounts on its books; it has a smaller backlog of unfilled orders; it carries less inventory; it buys fewer materials; it has less cash on deposit; it employs fewer people. Arabesque's product lines and mix remain unchanged as do its technology, method of sale, and the kinds of jobs its people do.

SUBSTITUTION OF CAPITAL FOR LABOR INTENSITY. A common form of change involves the substitution of labor-saving machinery for people. The result is many more sales dollars per employee, a higher ratio of fixed to variable costs, and a much smaller work force. In some instances, a small plant can produce the same quantity of output as did the formerly large, labor-intensive operation. Although the actual level of output may remain unchanged, this mode involves a large *qualitative* change in the nature of the operation.

REDUCTION IN HORIZONTAL INTEGRATION. This form of change involves a reduction in the number of autonomous units in a multidivisional corporation, or a reduction in the number of functions performed for one market level (or one stage of production). For example, *The New York Times* of June 18, 1975 carried a story about the Great Atlantic and Pacific Tea Company (A & P). Under new management, the firm cancelled its regular dividend payout and mounted a recovery plan that involves a massive closing of A & P stores considered either out-

dated or inefficient. There is to be a radical face-lifting of the remaining
outlets. By June of 1975, 600 stores were closed and 350 others were to
be closed later in the year. Thirty-five new supermarkets were opened
and fourteen existing stores enlarged and remodeled. In other instances,
a large bank closes one or more of its neighborhood branches; a number
of products in a multiproduct line are dropped; fewer customers are
called on by the field sales force.

Reduction in Vertical Integration.   If we think of the production system as consisting of a number of stages beginning with the mine,
sea, or farm and terminating at the retail sales level, then the extent of
vertical integration is measured by the number of stages encompassed
by the firm's operations. Reduction of the degree of vertical integration
involves a reduction in the number of stages in the production system
that the firm covers.

An example of a firm that reduces its vertical integration is the
(fictional) Widget Corp. This firm (data in Table 1-2) originally owns

Table 1-2
DATA FOR WIDGET CORP.
(1965, 1970, and 1975)*

Attribute	1975	1970	1965
Annual sales ($000)	$250,000	$200,000	$150,000
Market share	25%	20%	15%
Number of employees	600	1800	6,000
Number of shares outstanding	4,000,000	6,000,000	10,000,000
Market price per share (av.)	$30	$60	$10
Market value of shares ($000)	$120,000	$360,000	$100,000
Organizational state	Sales agency	Assembler and product marketer	Vertically integrated manufacturer, marketer

* Fictional data and firm.

mines, mills, and sources of raw materials. It uses these materials to fabricate its own semi-finished parts, supplies, and component parts. It assembles these intermediate goods into finished widgets that it stores in regional warehouses and sells to industrial firms throughout the nation through its own network of sales offices and captive distributors.

As time goes on, Widget Corp. disposes of its primary materials operations, then component fabrication facilities, then assembly plants. In the final stage of reduction in the extent of vertical integration, there remain only warehouses, the administrative apparatus, and the direct sales organization.

Reduction in the extent of vertical integration is primarily a qualitative change. Value added per dollar of sales is less; investment in plant and equipment is smaller; fewer people are employed. The ruling policy is "Buy, if possible, rather than make."

DISCONGLOMERATION.   Many conglomerate corporations combine both horizontal and vertical integration, but, in addition, have the non-integration property; that is, they consist of a collection of firms or divisions with unrelated markets and technology. Reductions in conglomeration are accomplished by divestment of one or more of the constituent firms.

THE EVER-DESCENDING SPIRAL (EDS).   Steps are taken to reduce the size of the organization, but each successive step further weakens the entity. As it shrinks in size, its losses grow apace, until there is no alternative but insolvency or dissolution. The EDS mode is characterized by positive feedback that reinforces the weakness of the company and saps its strengths.

TOTAL OR PARTIAL DISSOLUTION.   The inevitable result of an uninterrupted contraction is the demise of the entity—gradual or sudden. Personnel are discharged and dispersed; assets are distributed among its claimants. As a legal or operational entity, the organization ceases to exist. A study of the failure data in Table 1-3 reveals that this dire fate has overtaken many insolvent or bankrupt business firms.

Dissolution is the fate of the company or organization whose funding is withdrawn because its mission has been completed (the collapsible corporation in the business sector) or as was the case of the Manhattan Project, set up during World War II to manufacture atom bombs, but later disbanded and its scientific personnel dispersed.

Somewhat short of total dissolution is the case of the firm that discharges all but a few of its employees, sells off operating assets, and discontinues all regular activity. However, the funds realized from the

Table 1-3

INDUSTRIAL AND COMMERCIAL
FAILURE RATES 1946–1972

Yearly Average or Year	Failure Rate per 10,000 Firms	Year	Failure Rate per 10,000 Firms
1946–1950	21	1962	61
1951–1955	35	1963	56
1956–1960	53	1964	53
1961–1965	57	1965	53
1966–1970	44	1966	52
1950	34	1967	49
1955	42	1968	39
1958	56	1970	44
1959	52	1971	42
1960	57	1972	38
1961	64		

Source: U.S. Bureau of the Census, *Statistical Abstracts of the United States.* Washington, D.C.: Government Printing Office, various years.

liquidation are retained and reinvested until a suitable opportunity for reactivating the inactive shell in another promising field of endeavor can be found. Or there may be a partial distribution of assets with enough cash retained to keep the corporate shell in a stand-by state, ready to spring back to life at another time in another line of business.

Combination of Modes.   The actual retrenchment plan may combine any of the foregoing modes in either the positive or negative sense. There may be reductions in scale by chopping off a number of divisions, functions, or levels. There may be increases or decreases in labor intensity, depending on how this mode fits into the overall negative-growth strategy. One company may decide to shrink in size by converting its multiple-industry, horizontal integration into a single-industry, vertical integration. Still another company may decide to disconglomerate, using any one of a number of divestment alternatives for its nonintegrated, vertically or horizontally integrated subsidiaries.

ALTERNATIVE FUTURES

All change programs involve actions that take place in the future. Consequently, no one can seriously contemplate a program of negative growth without giving consideration to the state of the world in which the plan will unfold. A program, beautifully designed for one projected state of the national economy, fails miserably because a very different state prevails when the plan is carried out.

The uncertainty about the future presents the planners with a number of difficult choices. Ought there be a set of retrenchment strategies, one for each conceivable alternative state of the world? Should the planner assume that he can accurately forecast the future state and then design a program best suited for that forecast? Or should he design a compromise plan that is hardly optimal for any one of the predicted states of the world, but one that would be workable, come what may?

The main trouble with compromise programs is that they always seem poor in retrospect. If only the planner had known what the environment would be like, he would have adopted a plan much superior to the one he actually used. Critics, having the benefit of 20/20 hindsight, are always able to find fault by pointing out how much better everything would be if this or that course of action had been taken instead.

Another option is not to have any plan at all, but to begin with small steps and react to events as they happen, a variety of *muddling through*. This strategy is based upon the assumption that the planner really has not the faintest notion of what the future will be like, so he moves cautiously, step by step.

Below is a checklist of factors that should be considered in making estimates about the future or for creating scenarios about the most likely state of the world in which the planned negative growth will take place.

These factors should be examined:

— Health and medical developments.
— Educational trends.
— Demographic changes.
— Economic trends—regional, national and world-wide.
— The current business ethos.
— Legal and legislative actions.
— Contemporary social attitudes.
— Religious attitudes and public morality.
— War and peace developments.
— Scientific and technological developments.
— The political climate.

— Foreign affairs.
— Developments in the financial and commodity markets.
— Worldwide and local climatic conditions.
— Personal income, taxes, transfer payment programs.

TIME PATTERNS FOR CONTRACTIONS

Figure 1-4 contains sketches showing three common, negative-growth, time patterns—from an initial size S_i to a final size S_f. Diagram (a) shows a gradual decline; (b), a sudden contraction; (c), a staircase pattern.

The gradual forms, (a) and (c), have the advantage of allowing time to reexamine the results of each action and make necessary readjustments as one goes along. Also, the gradual approaches to retrenchment allow the affected parties to make their psychological adjustments to the change and to make plans for protecting themselves against any

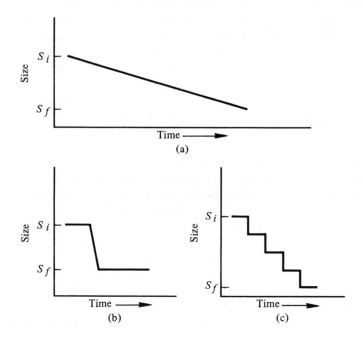

FIGURE 1-4. Three patterns of contraction: (a) a gradual decline, (b) a sudden, one-step contraction, and (c) a staircase pattern. S_i is initial size; S_f, final size.

adverse economic effects. It allows the firm to deal more considerately with any harmful impact the change has on suppliers and customers.

On the other hand, the sudden-change option, (b), has the advantage that there is less time for the development of overt resistance to change from interest groups that see themselves adversely affected by the retrenchment. If effective opposition can be presented, the retrenchment process becomes entangled with oppressive and costly delays and, perhaps, outright sabotage. To avoid conflict, many executives prefer to make swift, surgically precise cuts. In that way they get the pain and grief out of the way in as short a time as possible.

OPEN- AND CLOSED-LOOP CHANGE MODELS

When an artillery officer gives the order, "Fire," he is setting into free flight a projectile that, from that time on, is out of his control. If he wants to raise the likelihood of the shell's hitting the target, he manipulates the size of the powder charge, the angle of elevation of the barrel of the gun, and the azimuth angle, all in accordance with his prior training and the instructions in his artillery manual. If he has made the proper adjustments to take into account the range of the target, the wind velocity, the curvature of the earth, the variations in wind resistance at different altitudes, et cetera, he may hit the target. Shooting an artillery piece is an example of an open-loop process. All the preparation, planning, thought, aiming, et cetera, are done before the time of firing. Once the trigger is pulled, the projectile is in free flight.

Translated to the organizational change process, an open-loop method is used when there are no later opportunities to make corrections or alterations, or when making later changes is much too costly. For example, a company that is looking for a new plant location must examine the alternative sites with care until it finds one that is just right. It cannot build on one site as a trial, decide that that site is not exactly right, and move on to build again on another. Such trial-and-error procedures are much too costly for plant location decisions. The planning and study are done before the site choice is made. Just as the artillery officer takes great care in setting up his gun before giving the order to fire, so the officer in charge of the site location project does all of his preparatory work before he chooses a site.

Open-loop procedures are used when the planner operates in a climate of certainty, when making after-the-fact changes is prohibitively expensive, or when the change process is irreversible. One important advantage of the open-loop model is that all alternatives are evaluated on paper. There is a cost for staff time and some delay while the analysis is going on that may prevent stopping the "flow of blood." But with an open-loop procedure, the planner is not experimenting with real resources and human lives. Open-loop procedures are popular with staff people of contemplative, analytical frame of mind.

In contrast to the simple artillery shell, consider the more sophisticated radar-guided missile. When this weapon is fired, its position and speed are continuously monitored by radar. If the computer tells the control device that the missile is off target, in-flight corrections are made virtually instantaneously. This is an example of a closed-loop process in which periodic in-flight corrections are made to bring the system back on its intended path.

Closed-loop procedures are used in the presence of uncertainty or when sufficient time for advanced planning is unavailable. An example of closed-loop procedure is the typical trial-and-error decision sequence. If a step works well, it is adopted; if not, changes are made. For example, an office manager may want to buy new typewriters. There is nothing wrong with trying different brands and styles until he discovers which is best for his application.

Closed-loop procedures make less intellectual demands on the change manager, because if something he does works poorly, it can always be changed. There is, however, the disadvantage that he is operating with real resources and real people—not the paper models that can be used with open-loop procedures. Closed-loop procedures are preferred by action-oriented types, who fret if action is delayed, who are driven by inner voices that say, "Don't just stand there, do something."

SELECTED REFERENCES

BROOKS, JOHN, *The Fate of the Edsel and Other Business Adventures.* New York: Harper and Row, Publisher, 1959.

BUCHELE, ROBERT B., *Business Policy in Growing Firms.* Scranton, Pa.: Chandler Publishing Co., 1967.

EASTON, ALLAN, *Managing Organization Change: Selected Case Studies.* Hempstead, New York: Hofstra Yearbook of Business, Series 6, No. 4, 1969.

EISENBERG, JOSEPH, *Turnaround Management.* New York: McGraw-Hill Book Co., 1972.

JACKSON, HENRY M.: "To Forge a Strategy For Survival," *Public Administration Review*, Vol. XIX (Summer 1959).

WITTNEBERT, FRED R., "Bigness Vs. Profitability," *Harvard Business Review*, Vol. XLVIII (Jan.–Feb. 1970), pp. 158–166.

Chapter 2

The Anatomy of
Negative Growth

THE EVER-DESCENDING SPIRAL

In Chapter 1, the ever-descending spiral (abbreviated EDS) is defined as follows:

Steps are taken to reduce the size of the organization, but each successive step further weakens the entity. As it shrinks in size, its losses grow apace, until there is no alternative but insolvency or dissolution. The EDS mode is characterized by positive feedback that reinforces the weakness of the company and saps its strengths.

Examples of the EDS can be found in many areas of human activity. Consider these examples:

— A private, tuition-supported college is having budgetary difficulties. To help balance income and expense, it reduces the number of faculty, increases class size, and raises annual tuition. The result is a reduction in the quality of education and an increase in the cost of a four-year diploma. Enrollment drops and revenue follows. To cope, the college cuts faculty, raises class size, and raises tuition. Again enrollment declines. It repeats this behavior until the reduced enrollment level threatens the survival of the institution.

— A large northeastern city has expenses that exceed income from taxation and grants. But its leadership is convinced that the city must continue to offer the most generous social welfare programs in the country. It raises welfare payments, limits rents in nonpublic housing, provides free education on all levels, provides free hospital services, and many other benefits for the poor. As the tax burden necessary to pay for all of these services increases, the well-to-do and the middle-class segments of the population flee the city, and the city loses their contribution to taxes. To stem the decline in tax revenues, the city raises taxes on those who remain, thereby encouraging even more to move away. The places vacated by the middle-class residents are taken by welfare clients. Revenue continues to fall and outlays for social services continue to rise until the day comes when the city can no longer balance its budget and faces the unpleasant prospect of default on its bonded indebtedness, the municipal equivalent to bankruptcy.

— The XYZ Corporation sells its products in a highly competitive market where small price changes can cause large shifts in market share. XYZ's costs rise and require a price increase to sustain the expected return on investment. As its price rises, its sale revenue declines. This loss must be made up by further price increases, and so on until XYZ is forced to leave the market.

— Alpha Corporation under its new Vice President for Marketing adopts a modified policy on setting the size of the advertising budget. Henceforth, it allocates 10 percent of sales for advertising, with adjustments to be made monthly. In Alpha's market, sales are highly responsive to advertising. All goes well until, for no apparent reason, there is a sudden drop in sales for the month of May. Policy requires a cutback in advertising for June. In June sales have less advertising support, and they drop 15 percent, calling for further reduction in July's advertising budget. Each cut in advertising produces a corresponding cut in sales, and so on, until Alpha is out of business.

— Johnny Peterson transfers to a new elementary school that relies very heavily on achievement and I.Q. tests. He is a sensitive child who responds quickly to his teacher's expectations. If the teacher thinks Johnny will do well, he does. If she expects him to do poorly, he does. One day, Johnpny is feeling out of sorts and he is given an I.Q. test on which he scores as dull-normal. Thereafter his teacher treats him as dull-normal and reveals her expectations in her treatment of him. On the next achievement test, Johnny's scores drop again.

In the arcane parlance of general systems theory, the foregoing cases are examples of systems operating with positive feedback. Positive feedback tends to destabilize the system and to drive it to an extreme. In the case of the firm undergoing an EDS, positive feedback drives it through a sequence of damaging steps that results ultimately in extinction. (Negative feedback tends to stabilize a system.) Actions which tend to exacerbate an already bad condition, which are counter-productive, which cause progressive deterioration, which reward bad behavior and punish good behavior, are all examples of positive feedback that can throw the system into an EDS.

Of course, positive feedback does not always have harmful results. If it does not get out of control, it can work to the benefit of the system, too. If Alpha's sales had gone up in May instead of down, each step would have called for increasing advertising outlays, and these would have progressively pushed sales up and up. If Johnny Peterson had done exceptionally well on his first I.Q. test, his teacher would have expected superior performance and Johnny would have responded accordingly.

The trouble with positive feedback is that it can make the system go to either extreme once it becomes destabilized. A much better way is to employ negative feedback to stabilize the system, and then to use a control mechanism to guide the system along a predetermined path.

Figure 2-1 illustrates a multiple-indicator control system that can be subjected to either positive or negative feedback. It consists of a system, the output of which is monitored for several size-related variables. The magnitudes of the variables are compared with those established by the negative growth planner, and deviations are measured. If the deviations from planned magnitudes are not excessive, no corrective action is called for, and passive monitoring of the output continues. If, however, one or more deviations are excessive, some corrective action is called for. Now there is a choice between timely and appropriate action (negative feedback) that will restore the system to the desired state, or untimely, inappropriate action (positive feedback) that, if unabated, drives the system to harmful extremes.

Of course, no one who wishes the firm well *knowingly* takes untimely and inappropriate action that will damage the firm, but such

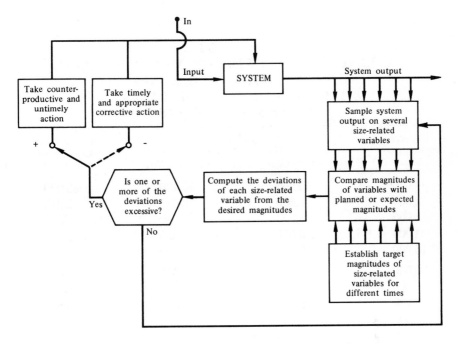

FIGURE 2-1. Schematic diagram of a multiple-indicator control system showing the possibilities of using either positive or negative feedback.

unfortunate actions can be the result of carelessness or ignorance of the workings of the system. As any careful study of the workings of our political and economic systems reveals, inappropriate action is more common than it should be, given the intelligence, training, and good will of the political and business leadership of the world.

THE ANATOMY OF AN IRREVERSIBLE SALES DECLINE

The Old Town branch of Widget Corporation manufactures the Model 7950 widgets sold to original equipment manufacturer (O.E.M.) accounts in the United States. The cost department has prepared a cost-versus volume chart, which is contained in Table 2-1 and graphed in Fig. 2-2. (Note that the average unit cost is the sum of fixed and variable unit costs.) Costs are high ($3.92 each) for a rate of 1000 units per hour and lower as the production rate increases, bottoming out at about 11,000 units an hour, and rising again above that most efficient rate.

TABLE 2-1
AVERAGE UNIT COSTS FOR MANUFACTURING WIDGETS (IN A PLANT DESIGNED FOR 10–15,000 PER HOUR) FOR RATES OF 1000 TO 20,000 PER HOUR *

HOURLY PRODUCTION RATE	AVERAGE UNIT FIXED COST	AVERAGE UNIT VARIABLE COST	AVERAGE UNIT COST (FIXED + VARIABLE)
1,000	$3.200	$0.720	$3.920
2,000	1.600	0.645	2.245
3,000	1.067	0.580	1.647
4,000	0.800	0.525	1.325
5,000	0.640	0.480	1.120
6,000	0.533	0.445	0.978
7,000	0.457	0.420	0.877
8,000	0.400	0.405	0.805
9,000	0.355	0.400	0.755
10,000	0.320	0.405	0.725
11,000	0.291	0.420	0.711 ←
12,000	0.267	0.445	0.712
13,000	0.246	0.480	0.726
14,000	0.228	0.525	0.753
15,000	0.213	0.580	0.793
16,000	0.200	0.645	0.845
17,000	0.188	0.720	0.908
18,000	0.178	0.805	0.983
19,000	0.168	0.900	1.068
20,000	0.160	1.005	1.165

* Fictional data, adapted from Marshall R. Colberg, et al., *Business Economics*, 3rd ed. Homewood, Illinois: Richard D. Irwin, Inc., 1964, p. 141.

The graph in Fig. 2-2 is an example of a short-run, steady state, cost curve. It should be interpreted as follows: given the present technology, sources of materials, labor force, union contract, and manufacturing organization and facilities, this is what it would cost to produce at the rate of x units per hour. The costs shown in the figure and table are *not* the costs that would be incurred if production rates were changed from one level to another. Making changes in the short-short run in-

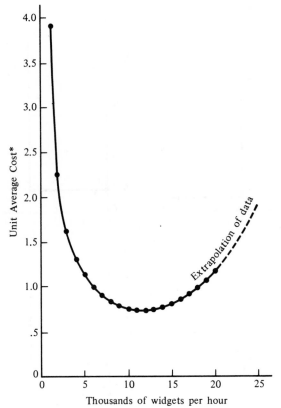

FIGURE 2-2. In a plant designed for 10-15,000 units per hour, unit average cost of widgets for hourly production rates of 1000 to 20,000 (short-run, steady state). (**Source:** Table 2-1)

volve additional transitional costs, as shown in Fig. 2-3. The short-run cost curve of Fig. 2-2 depicts a steady-state condition that would prevail after a full transition from one rate to another is fully accomplished.

Figure 2-4 shows a break-even chart for the data in Table 2-1 for two selling prices: $1.00 and $1.50 each. At the $1.00 price, break-even occurs at about 6000 and 17,000 pieces per hour. For the $1.50 price, break-even occurs at about 3500 units per hour.

Unfortunately for the widget industry, a major O.E.M. account designs widgets out of its end equipment and the industry experiences

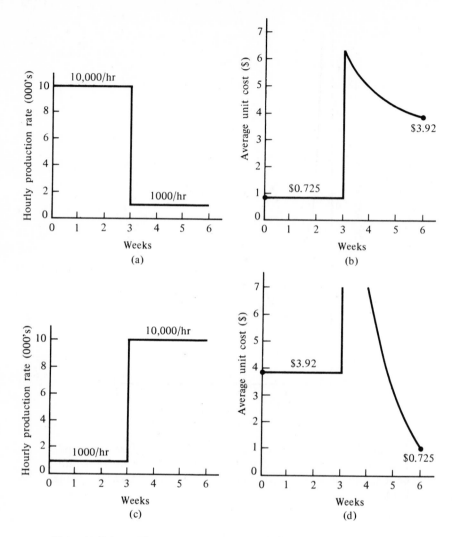

FIGURE 2-3.   The way average unit cost changes as the production rate is lowered abruptly [curves (a) and (b)] and the way it changes as the production rate is raised abruptly [curves (c) and (d)]. For both increases and decreases in the hourly production rate, it is assumed that it takes three weeks to return to a steady state condition with costs as in Table 2-1.

diminished demand and declining prices. The results for four quarters of 1976 are shown in Table 2-2.

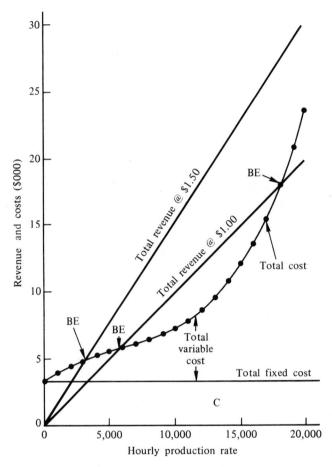

FIGURE 2-4. Break-even chart based upon data from Table 2-1.

TABLE 2-2

QUARTER OF 1976	PRICE	VOLUME PER HR.	TOTAL REVENUE PER HR.	TOTAL COST PER HR.	PROFIT OR (LOSS) PER HR.
First	$1.50	10,000	$15,000	$7250	$7750
Second	1.30	7,000	9,100	6139	2961
Third	1.20	5,000	6,000	5600	400
Fourth	1.00	4,000	4,000	5300	(1300)

Shutting down the plant altogether is no solution because, in the short run at least, the fixed charges of $3200 per hour will remain. The loss of $1300 per hour incurred by selling 4000 units at $1.00 each is smaller than the loss of $3200 per hour for selling none at all. (Widget loses $1900 *less* per hour by selling widgets at $1.00 each, because it still obtains some contribution to recovery of fixed costs.)

After a detailed survey of the market for the Model 7950 widget, the management realizes that something drastic has to be done to cut its losses. A decision is made to restructure the operation so that its most efficient output level will change from 11,000 to 5000 widgets per hour. This reorganization will involve a drastic cut in fixed costs (e.g., rent, executive payroll, machinery costs, etc.) with some increase in variable costs because of the necessity of retaining higher-paid, high-seniority workers and because more hand operations are substituted for machine operations. On the basis of these changes, revised cost data are prepared as shown in Table 2-3. Widget's management reasons that if its competitors also cut back operations permanently, prices will recover. In fact, by 1977, prices do rise. The financial results for 1977 are shown in Table 2-4.

TABLE 2-3
COST DATA FOR REDUCED SCALE OF OPERATION
1000 TO 10,000 UNITS PER HOUR

HOURLY PRODUCTION RATE	AVERAGE UNIT FIXED COST	AVERAGE UNIT VARIABLE COST	AVERAGE UNIT TOTAL COST (FIXED + VARIABLE)
1,000	$1.200	$0.712	$1.912
2,000	0.600	0.710	1.310
3,000	0.400	0.700	1.100
4,000	0.300	0.650	0.950
5,000	0.240	0.600	0.840 ←
6,000	0.200	0.690	0.890
7,000	0.171	0.750	0.921
8,000	0.150	0.850	1.000
9,000	0.133	0.900	1.033
10,000	0.120	1.000	1.120

Once again, Widget's management faces the questions: "Should we shut down and liquidate the plant? Should we cut back further so

TABLE 2-4

OPERATING QUARTER OF 1977–78	PRICE PER UNIT	VOLUME PER HR.	TOTAL REVENUE	TOTAL COST	PROFIT OR (LOSS) PER HR.
First	$1.00	4000	$4000	$3850	$ 150
Second	1.20	5000	6000	4200	1800
Third	1.25	6000	7500	5340	2160
Fourth	1.10	3000	3300	3300	0
First 1978	1.00	3000	3000	3300	(300)

that we can operate most efficiently at 3000 units per hour? Or should we go along as we are for a while, hoping that things will get better?"

CONVERTING FIXED COSTS INTO VARIABLE COSTS

The analysis in the preceding section and a close study of the accompanying cost and break-even curves clearly indicate that as sales and production decline, unit costs rise and profits shrink, because, in the short run at least, fixed costs must be spread over fewer units. Reasoning from the data, we see that a successful contraction requires that fixed costs *must* be reduced along the way if there is to be any real hope for survival of the entity. It may be that in cutting fixed costs, variable costs will rise, but a trade-off between fixed and variable costs is absolutely necessary.

There are many ways for transforming fixed costs into variable costs. Items:

— Change salesman's compensation from salary to commission only.

— Replace staff or service departments with purchased services.

— Replace company-owned retail and wholesale outlets with independently owned firms.

— Sell through exporters or commissioned agents instead of company-owned offices.

— Use manufacturers' representatives in less lucrative territories in place of factory-employed salesmen.

— Use outside contractors to do cleaning, alterations, drafting, land-scape maintenance, etc.

— For fabricated parts that require extensive fixed asset investment buy instead of making in-house.

— Use short-term rentals in place of long-term leases or outright pur-chases of fixed assets.

— Use public warehouses instead of company-owned warehouses.

— Use common carriers instead of company-owned and -operated transportation.

As one frustrated executive said, "When I buy a service from the outside, I know what it costs me. When I have it done in-house, I have no idea of the cost."

It is very much easier to stop buying a service or a component part from an outside contractor than it is to stop making it in-house. Many trade unions try to place impediments in the paths of firms that attempt to discontinue in-house operations in preference to purchased services. Layoffs, firings, and consolidations of staff and service departments can cause major disturbances within an organization, whereas change of a supplier of a purchased service causes hardly a ripple. Thus, before deciding to perform a service or function in-house that can also be purchased outside, the executives in charge should ask themselves if there will ever be any serious impediments to discontinuing the in-house service should a retrenchment be necessary.

The reasoning used in a contraction is directly opposite to that used in an expanding situation. In growth conditions, return-on-invest-ment computations invariably indicate that it is more profitable to invest in highly efficient fixed assets and to do many functions in-house. Rising fixed costs can be tolerated in growth situations, especially if in raising fixed costs there is a compensating reduction in variable costs. But when a contraction occurs, as a study of Fig. 2-4 shows, earnings can disap-pear very rapidly as fixed costs, spread over fewer units of output, gob-ble up profits.

AN EXAMPLE OF WHY PAYROLL COSTS CAN JUMP AS EMPLOYMENT DECLINES

Alpha Corporation has a large manufacturing plant in a suburb of Schenectady, New York. The plant is twenty-two years old and has a good employment record. There is a militant union in the plant that represents all hourly workers except for the skilled trades, who have their own unions. The plant union has been successful in obtaining yearly across-the-board increases for its members and recently obtained a provision for plantwide seniority to govern order of layoff, if any.

It has been the custom, over the years, for the union to agree that any wage increases negotiated for its members would apply only to those persons on the payroll at the time of the agreement. Except as required by the minimum wage laws of the state, the starting rates for newly hired people would not be adjusted upward. The normal hourly rate for new employees with up to two years' seniority is as follows:

1 day to 90 days (probationary period)	$2.50 per hour
3 months to 6 months	2.60 per hour
6 months to 9 months	2.65 per hour
9 months to 12 months	2.70 per hour
12 months to 18 months	2.80 per hour
18 months to 24 months	2.90 per hour

However, only those persons hired in the last 24 months earn these hourly rates. There was an across-the-board increment negotiated in the last contract that gave all employees then on the payroll a substantial increase. The numbers of persons on the payroll, their seniority, and their average hourly wage rates are tabulated in Fig. 2-5 along with a plot of the cumulative average rates based on the number remaining on the payroll after a mass layoff. Note that the average wage rate for full employment is about $4.66 per hour. The average hourly rate rises until it hits over $7.00 per hour when the force is reduced to about 1500 people.

If the staff curtailment is permanent, there will also be substantial severance pay obligations to be met by Alpha Corp. Thus, it can be seen that for Alpha Corp. the negative-growth process is not a simple reversal of the positive growth they experienced earlier in their history. When they started in business, wage rates were low and were allowed to grow slowly. As the company grew, it had a larger proportion of newly hired workers and its average hourly wage rates were relatively low. Now, if it wishes to contract and lay off its employees and return to an earlier size, it finds itself saddled with a very high average hourly wage rate and a high-seniority work force. Perhaps the only way to recapture the past low average wage rate is to shut down completely

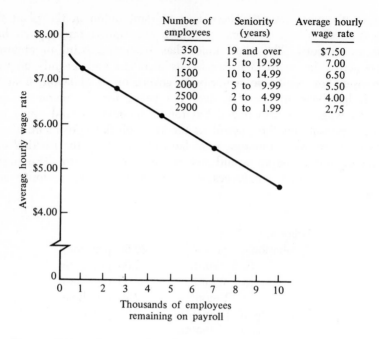

Number of employees	Seniority (years)	Average hourly wage rate
350	19 and over	$7.50
750	15 to 19.99	7.00
1500	10 to 14.99	6.50
2000	5 to 9.99	5.50
2500	2 to 4.99	4.00
2900	0 to 1.99	2.75

FIGURE 2-5. Average hourly wage rate versus number of employees remaining after layoff by seniority at Alpha Corp.

in the twenty-year old plant and relocate elsewhere, so that all employees will be starting at the entrance rates.

WHICH COMPETITOR WILL BE THE FIRST TO QUIT THE MARKET?

Alpha Corporation, Beta Corporation, Gamma Corporation, and Delta Corporation all produce and market the same highly sophisticated microelectronics components, and each competes vigorously with the others. Each firm has about a 25 percent market share, and each fights bitterly to hold its share. For five years since the product line was first developed and marketed, each firm has sold all of its output at satisfactory prices and each has earned a reasonable return on investment.

For the first time, however, the overall demand for the product is shrinking, prices are falling, and costs are rising. All four firms barely break even on the microelectronics product line. Moreover, technological developments in their customers' markets indicate that in future years the slow erosion of demand will continue unabated. It dawns on the industry's executives that with the excessive productive capacity, no one firm stands much chance to reap a profit. All four firms debate the wisdom of dropping the microelectronics component line and shifting their attention and resources elsewhere.

At Alpha Corp.'s board meeting, the president makes this statement:

"Our specialty components business is poor this year and I see no near-term prospect for improvement. It's my opinion that we ought seriously to consider going out of that business."

Alpha's board chairman asks, "If we do that and take our productive capacity out of the market, our three competitors will be given a new lease on life. Isn't that right?"

"Yes, you're absolutely correct. They should do very well for at least three more years until the reduced demand catches up with them."

"Hell, man," the chairman complained. "Why should we help those bastards? Why don't we wait them out? Then *we'll* have the three goods years instead of them."

"Maybe—if one of them quits. But how can anyone tell who will be willing to go first and make it better for the three surviving companies?" the president replies.

"I say we stay. I'll be damned if I'll go first and leave the cream for them."

"How long do we wait?"

"I don't know. Let's wait another six months. Maybe one of them is weaker than we think."

The foregoing example depicts a situation familiar to many executives whose companies have been caught unprepared in a declining market. If only one or more of their competitors would leave the market for the survivors! No one wants to be the first to leave; still everyone realizes that there is no longer room for all. Who will make the sacrifice and will thereby benefit the survivors?

There is no completely reliable way of telling which competitor is wavering and most likely to quit the market and which is certain to hang on doggedly. There are a number of clues that may help one to infer which will go and which will stay. There is a greater likelihood that a firm will leave first if:

— It is known to be looking for a merger partner, and a losing product diminishes its attractiveness.

— It is known to use return on investment (R.O.I.) reasoning in evaluating on-going and proposed new investments.

— The firm is suggesting to its customers that they develop alternative sources.

— The firm is proudly announcing an entirely new product line.

— The firm is advertising for engineers and scientists for a completely different product line.

— The firm is cutting back on the size of distributors' inventories.

— The firm's salesmen and process engineers are looking around for new jobs and answer your blind box, help-wanted ads.

— The firm is known to be cutting back on purchases of raw materials, or prices of raw materials drop without reason.

— The firm is desperately searching for new financing and would like to clear its decks of losing products.

— In a similar situation once before, the firm jumped out of the market first.

There is a likelihood that a firm will *not* be the first to leave the market if:

— The president or head man is known to be a stubborn, bulldog type.

— The firm is privately owned and known to be in highly liquid condition.

— The firm is known to be making large long-term forward purchase commitments.

— The firm is known to be reassuring its customers, suppliers, and distributors that it will remain in the market.

— The firm is advertising for salesmen and process engineers for this product line.

— The firm is increasing its advertising and promotion outlays for this product line.

SIZE: AN AMBIGUOUS CONSTRUCT

Although it is common knowledge that business firms come in many sizes—small, medium, large, and giant—what do we really mean when we use that word, *size?* When we assert that Firm A is larger than Firm B, what attributes are we comparing? Are we thinking of the numbers of persons employed by each? The number and aggregate floor space of their physical plants? The total assets used by the firms? The amounts of invested capital? The number of shareholders? The market value of the firm's outstanding securities? The impact of the firm on its community? Or is it some unspecified combination of some or all of these factors?

When General Motors is compared with American Motors, there is little confusion about which is the larger; G.M. is clearly bigger by all measures. But what if Firm A is larger in some attributes than Firm B, but smaller in others? For example, in 1975, International Business Machines ranked sixth in total assets and ninth in annual sales volume. By these measures, I.B.M. is clearly smaller than both G.M. and Exxon Corporation. But I.B.M. ranked first of all industrials in the market values of its securities and in market power. Was I.B.M. larger than G.M. or Exxon? A study of the rankings of the five hundred largest industrials conducted annually by *Fortune* magazine demonstrates this ambiguity. Firms higher on some size measures are smaller on other measures.

There is only one sure test for ascertaining if one firm is really larger than another, and that requires a precise attribute-by-attribute comparison. Only if Firm A's scores on every size measure exceeds the corresponding scores for Firm B, can we say without ambiguity that Firm A is larger in size than Firm B. If Firm A has larger scores on some size-related attributes, and smaller scores than Firm B on others, we cannot really say with conviction whether Firm A is larger than, smaller than, or equivalent in size to Firm B. In such ambiguous cases, all we can say with precision is that for some size-related measures, Firm A is larger than Firm B; but for other measures of size, Firm B is larger than Firm A.

The construct, size, is even fuzzier when we attempt to compare two very dissimilar firms. For example, although it does make sense to compare the sizes of two branches of a multibranch savings bank, it makes very little sense to compare the sizes of a branch bank and a taxicab company. As a rule, size comparisons are meaningful only when made between two very similar entities (e.g., two branch banks or two taxicab fleets). They are not meaningful when the two firms being compared differ substantially in function, organization, and technology.

Quantitative size comparisons on a measure-by-measure basis are most meaningful when made on a single firm at different points in time. However, even then, some ambiguity creeps in if the firm undergoes significant qualitative changes that cause the size-related attributes used for comparison purposes to become incomparable. This ambiguity is illustrated in Table 1-2.

In 1965, Widget Corp. is a vertically integrated producer of a full line of widgets, which it sells to industrial accounts. In addition to its national sales organization, the company has several large factories which either manufacture all the component parts, or assemble the parts into finished product. In 1965, Widget Corp.'s sales are $150,000,000 per annum, which represents about a 15 percent share of the total widget market.

By 1970, the management of Widget Corp. has sold off its components fabricating plants and buys component parts from outside suppliers. It still continues to assemble these purchased parts into finished product in a centralized assembly operation. The company's annual sales grow to $200,000,000, which is about 20 percent of the total market for widgets.

During 1975, the company completes it divestiture of all manufacturing facilities. It now imports its product from Japan. All Widget Corp. has left of its original organization is the national sales force, its central and regional warehouses, and a small administrative staff. Its sales have reached $250 million, which is about 25 percent of the total market for widgets in the United States.

As a study of Table 1-2 shows, Widget Corp. grew in some attributes (sales volume and market share) but shrank in other ways (value added, number of employees). Its market value of outstanding shares peaked in 1970, as did its price per share of common stock. Can anyone say with any assurance when in its history Widget Corp. was largest in size?

The situation is much clearer in the case of Columbia Gas System, one of the largest natural gas suppliers in the United States. As a study of Table 2-5 shows, from 1956 to 1973, the five principal size-related variables:

1 / Operating income (in millions of dollars).

2 / Investment in plant (in millions of dollars).

3 / Number of customers served (thousands).

4 / Total long-term debt and common stock equity (in millions of dollars).

5 / Total product delivered (billions of cubic feet),

all show steady year-by-year increases (except number 5 in recent years). Leaving aside, temporarily, the effects of inflation, we can say with confidence that Columbia Gas System did exhibit significant increases in size over the time interval 1956–73.

TABLE 2-5
MAGNITUDES OF FIVE SIZE-RELATED
VARIABLES FOR COLUMBIA GAS SYSTEM,
1956–1973 *

Year	Sales Income [a]	Investment in Plant [b]	Number of Customers [c]	Total L.T. Debt and Common Stock Equity [d]	Total Product Delivered [e]
1956	340	844	1345	662	605
1957	369	1085	1382	884	646
1958	412	1204	1410	1003	699
1959	447	1286	1439	1027	735
1960	501	1355	1459	1064	792
1961	524	1407	1478	1083	809
1962	555	1494	1505	1135	861
1963	579	1571	1531	1135	904
1964	593	1691	1568	1223	939
1965	633	1797	1597	1283	1025
1966	669	1899	1625	1324	1103
1967	683	1962	1654	1353	1118
1968	706	2117	1688	1490	1173
1969	773	2312	1772	1554	1262
1970	822	2485	1798	1693	1301
1971	927	2664	1830	1778	1362
1972	1016	2799	1857	1990	1423
1973	1049	2992	1860	2086	1350

* **Source:** Columbia Gas System Annual Reports.
[a] Millions of dollars, rounded.
[b] Millions of dollars, rounded.
[c] Thousands of firms and residential customers combined, rounded.
[d] Millions of dollars, rounded.
[e] Billions of cubic feet.

SIZE: A MULTI-DIMENSIONAL CONSTRUCT

Often, in the literature of business, economics, or sociology, when an author uses the concept of size he tries to find a single variable to serve as a valid surrogate for size. Some authors use total investment; others use total assets, value added, sales volume, number of employees, or market power. The actual choice of the variable used to represent size depends upon the particular research objectives and the availability of numerical data. Since the New York Stock Exchange and the Securities and Exchange Commission both insist that firms publish certain limited financial and market information for the enlightenment of investors and stockholders, it is hardly an accident that such financial data are widely used in business and industry studies.

But one variable is hardly enough to support important size-change decisions for the firm. As the data for Widget Corp. (Table 1-2) show, a selected variable may indicate movement in one direction, when, in fact, the firm is drifting in quite a different direction (e.g., sales move up but total employment drops, or vice versa).

Some size-related variables move together because they really are measures of the same underlying variable. For example, total assets and stockholders' equity usually move together. There are, however, exceptions to this rule. It is quite conceivable that in one particular firm, stockholders' equity may drop substantially without affecting total assets. This can happen in instances when equity is exchanged for long-term debt, as is shown in Table 2-6.

Thus, to monitor changes in size more effectively, it is usually wiser to use many variables rather than to try to rely on a few intended to serve as surrogates. Although many size-related variables may seem to be highly correlated and, therefore, to move together, the correlations

TABLE 2–6
EXAMPLE OF CHANGE IN STOCKHOLDERS' EQUITY THAT LEAVES TOTAL ASSETS UNCHANGED *

BALANCE SHEET ITEM	BEFORE EXCHANGE	AFTER EXCHANGE †
Current liabilities	$ 20,000,000	$ 20,000,000
Long-term debt	20,000,000	40,000,000
Common Stock and retained earnings	60,000,000	40,000,000
Total liabilities and capital = total assets	$100,000,000	$100,000,000

* Fictional data for Kivet Manufacturing Corp.
† The $20,000,000 book value of capital stock is exchanged for $20,000,000 principal amount of 20-year subordinated debentures which are added to previous long-term debt.

are rarely perfect, and special circumstances can cause the interrelationships to be far from one-to-one.

METHODS FOR DISPLAYING
SIZE CHANGES

Because of the ambiguity, complexity, and multidimensional nature of size changes of a firm, the executive in charge of overseeing the change process will not be satisfied with simplistic verbalizations or vaguely impressionistic statements. Helpful to him is an inventory of size-monitoring techniques that he can use for thinking about, writing about, reporting on, and discussing size changes. Then he has good communication tools allowing him to deal with the complex issues he encounters without semantic or conceptual confusion.

COMPUTATION OF SIZE-CHANGE INDICES.   Although using a single number to represent a number sequence can cause losses in information, it is sometimes convenient to use some form of univariate or multivariate index as a means for compressing numerical sequences. The following two formulas ought to take care of most cases the executive will encounter. If more complex formulas are needed, a professional statistician can be consulted.

A simple application of the familiar compound interest formula can be used to compute the net size-change percentages over any specified interval of time:

$$P_n = A_o \, (1 + r)^n$$

where P_n is the final value of the variable,
             A_o is the initial value of the variable,
             r is the annual rate of simple interest,
             n is the number of years.

Adapting this formula to the computation of size changes of a variable gives two forms:

Form (1a) (used when the magnitude of the variable increases over the interval in question):

$$\underset{(\%)}{r} = \left[-1 + \left(\frac{\text{magnitude of variable at end of time}}{\text{magnitude of variable at start of time}} \right)^{1/n} \right] \times 100 \tag{1a}$$

and Form (1b) (used when the magnitude of the size-related variable decreases over the time interval):

$$\underset{(\%)}{r} = \left[-1 + \left(\frac{\text{magnitude of variable at start of time}}{\text{magnitude of variable at end of time}} \right)^{1/n} \right] \times 100 \qquad (1b)$$

Formulas (1a) and (1b) are used to compute size changes on a variable-by-variable basis. Another form of size-change index gives a composite. The formula for the geometric mean for a series of m numbers can be adapted to construct this composite size-change index:

$$\text{Composite size-change index} = \left[\prod_{j=1}^{m} (i_j) \right]^{1/m} \qquad (2)$$

where m = the number of variables being combined,
$\quad\quad\quad i_j$ = the ratio of the jth variable's magnitude for the particular year to the value for the base year,
$\quad\quad\; \prod$ = the symbol of successive multiplication.

For any year in which a size change has occurred, the index will be larger than one, if size has increased; smaller than one, if the size has decreased. This formula is only a very rough indicator of size change when some variables increase and some decrease, but it works fairly well when all changes are in the same direction. Table 2-7 contains indices computed from Formulas (1a), (1b), and (2) for the Widget Corp. data of Table 1-2.

Columns (1), (2), and (3) of Table 2-7 contain the size-change growth rates found by using Formulas (1a) and (1b). At the bottom of this table are three composite change indices. If we accept the six variables as indicative of the size of Widget Corp., then we can see that the composite index indicates an aggregate increase in size from 1965 to 1970, a decrease from 1970 to 1975, and a decrease from 1965 to 1975. These results indicate the ambiguity when some size-related variables increase and others decrease.

Table 2-8 contains size-change indices computed from index construction Formulas (1a) and (2) [(1b) is not needed because all values are increasing], for the Columbia Gas System data of Table 2-5. The base year used is 1956, and size change indices are computed for each of the five variables for the intervals 1956–1960, 1956–1965, 1956–1970,

TABLE 2-7
SIZE-CHANGE RATES VARIABLE-BY-VARIABLE AND COMPOSITE BASED ON WIDGET CORP. DATA, 1965, 1970, 1975 *

NAMES OF SIZE-RELATED VARIABLES	VARIABLE-BY-VARIABLE SIZE CHANGE RATES [a]		
	1965–1970 (1)	1970–1975 (2)	1965–1975 (3)
Annual sales	+15.3%	+11.8%	+18.6%
Market share	+15.3%	+11.8%	+18.6%
Number of employees	−82.6%	−73.2%	−115.0%
Number of shares outstanding	−29.2%	−22.5%	−35.7%
Market price per share	+144.9%	−41.4%	+44.2%
Market value of all outstanding shares	+89.7%	−73.2%	+6.3%
Composite size index [b]	1.38	0.622	0.859

* Based on data from Table 1-2.
[a] Using Formulas (1a) and (1b).
[b] Using Formula (2).

and 1956–1973. Composite size-change indices for the four intervals are also shown at the bottom of Table 2-8.

In the case of Columbia Gas systems, there appears to be steady year-by-year growth in all five variables and in the composite indices. (However, the size-related variables based on dollar amounts may need adjustment to take into account the effects of inflation.)

A NOTE ABOUT THE IMPACT OF INFLATION

When assessing relative growth performance with size-related variables expressed in money terms, it may be desirable to adjust current dollars to reflect the erosion of purchasing power of United States currency. Firms with sales income that rises from year to year at a rate smaller than the rate of decline of the value of the dollar, may, in reality, be exhibiting negative growth. For example, as the data in Table

TABLE 2-8

SIZE-CHANGE RATES, VARIABLE-BY-VARIABLE (COMPOUND RATES) AND COMPOSITE SIZE-CHANGE INDICES FOR COLUMBIA GAS SYSTEM, 1956–1973 * (CURRENT AND CONSTANT $)

NAMES OF SIZE-RELATED VARIABLES	VARIABLE-BY-VARIABLE COMPOUND CHANGE RATES †			
	1956–1960	1956–1965	1956–1970	1956–1973
Operating income	8.06%	6.40%	5.21%	6.46% [a]
	6.34%	4.84%	3.57%	3.60% [b]
Investment in plant	9.93%	7.85%	7.46%	7.28% [a]
	7.16%	6.25%	4.94%	4.41% [b]
Total number of customers served	1.64%	1.73%	1.96%	1.82%
Total long-term debt and common stock equity	9.96%	6.84%	6.46%	6.58% [a]
	8.08%	5.26%	3.96%	2.72% [b]
Total quantity of product delivered	5.53%	5.44%	5.24%	4.56%
Composite size change index ‡	1.40	1.73	2.15	2.54 [a]
	1.32	1.58	1.78	1.90 [b]

* Based on data from Table 2-5.
† Computed from Formula (1a).
‡ Computed from Formula (2).
[a] Current dollars line.
[b] Constant dollars (current deflated by C.P.I.), Table 2-9.

2-9 imply, a 1947 dollar would be worth 66.9¢ in 1967 and 50.4¢ in 1973. A 1967 dollar would be worth only 75¢ in 1973 and even less in 1975.

Thus, using current dollars which have a different purchasing power each year can give grossly misleading indications of growth. As Table 2-8 reveals, the size-related growth indices for Columbia Gas System indicate larger growth for current dollars than for constant dollars (operating income 6.46% as compared with 3.60%; investment in plant, 7.28% as compared with 4.41%; total long-term debt and common stock equity, 6.58% compared with 2.72%).

TABLE 2-9
CONSUMERS' PRICE INDEX FOR THE
UNITED STATES 1947 TO 1975 *

YEAR	C.P.I.	YEAR	C.P.I.	YEAR	C.P.I.
1947	66.9	1956	81.4	1966	97.2
1948	72.1	1957	84.3	1967	100.0
1949	71.4	1958	86.6	1968	104.2
1950	72.1	1959	87.3	1969	109.8
		1960	88.7	1970	116.3
1951	77.8	1961	89.6	1971	121.3
1952	79.5	1962	90.6	1972	125.3
1953	80.1	1963	91.7	1973	133.1
1954	80.5	1964	92.9	1974	147.7
1955	80.2	1965	94.5	1975	Not Available

* Source: U.S. Council of Economic Advisors, *Economic Report to the President,* January 1975, p. 302.

The need for such adjustments is less when comparative size change data are examined. In any year the erosion of the value of the United States currency affects all current-dollar variables for all entities being compared in the same way. Variables expressed in units other than dollars (or other currency denominations) need not be adjusted for inflation. For example, an employee or a cubic foot of gas are the same in one year or another for purposes for monitoring organizational size changes.

The data shown in Table 2-9 are for consumer prices, usually at the retail level. Some economic analysts prefer to use the Wholesale Price Index; others, the Gross National Product deflation series. All three are heavily weighted with the steady downward drift in the buying power of the American dollar; any one of the three can be used to transform current dollar into constant dollar statistics. Table 2-10 contains data for the Wholesale Price Index and the G.N.P. deflator for the years 1947–1974.

VARIETIES OF GROWTH

An entity exhibits *zero* growth when none of the size-related vari-

TABLE 2-10
WHOLESALE PRICE INDEX AND G.N.P.
DEFLATOR FOR 1947–1974

YEAR	WHOLESALE PRICE INDEX [a]	G.N.P. DEFLATOR [b]
1947	74.0	74.64
1948	79.9	79.57
1949	77.6	79.12
1950	79.0	80.16
1951	86.5	85.64
1952	86.0	87.45
1953	85.1	88.33
1954	85.3	89.63
1955	85.5	90.86
1956	87.9	93.99
1957	91.1	97.49
1958	93.2	100.00
1959	93.0	101.66
1960	93.7	103.29
1961	93.7	104.62
1962	94.0	105.78
1963	93.7	107.17
1964	94.1	108.85
1965	95.7	110.86
1966	98.8	113.94
1967	100.0	117.59
1968	102.9	122.30
1969	106.6	128.20
1970	110.4	135.24
1971	113.5	141.35
1972	117.2	146.12
1973	127.9	154.31
1974	147.5	170.11

Source: U.S. Council of Economic Advisors, *Economic Report to the President,* February 1975, pp. 252, 308.
[a] 1967 = 100, all finished goods.
[b] 1958 = 100, total G.N.P.

ables show significant changes in magnitude over time. As a special case, we also characterize as zero growth the situation in which size-related variables do change, but act to cancel out. (E.g., sales rise in one sector but fall in another; assets used rise, but the number of employees declines, etc.)

Overall growth implies significant changes in *all* or *many* important size-related variables. Such growth is *positive* when the increases in magnitudes of the underlying variables are consistent and is *negative* when the size-related variables show consistent reductions in magnitudes.

Overall growth is *proportional* (synonym: *balanced*) when all size-related variables exhibit comparable increases. There are changes in scale, not in kind. Growth is *unbalanced* when important size-related variables show nonproportionate changes, or when the nonproportionate changes overwhelm the changes in scale. Balanced growth (positive or negative) usually occurs when the firm undergoes no significant changes in organization, function, or technology. Unbalanced growth usually involves substantial changes in these three factors.

We use the notion of *relative* growth to refer to comparisons in size of the single entity over time, and the notion of *comparative* growth to refer to increases or decreases in corresponding measurements between two different firms over time. Evidence of comparative growth would be a widening or narrowing over time of the size of the gap between two firms (or major subdivisions of a large firm).

Overall growth is a multivariate construct. Univariate growth refers to changes in the magnitude of a single size-related variable. From time to time, in common speech or in the business literature, we find references to growth as measured by a single variable. Whether the author means overall growth or univariate growth can only be determined from study of the context. Some authors do use a single variable as a surrogate indicator for overall growth.

When some important size-related variables exhibit increased magnitudes and others decreased magnitudes, we cannot tell with certainty whether the growth is zero, positive, or negative. We can use Formula (2) to help form a judgment, but we have to be careful that we include the correct size-related variables in forming the composite index. In such ambiguous cases, it is safer to list those variables that are larger and those that are unchanged or smaller without making any positive statements about the entity's being larger or smaller than before. Fortunately, as the case of Columbia Gas data showed, in some situations, it is easy to tell if overall positive or negative growth occurred.

SPECIFYING THE UNITS AND LEVELS
OF GROWTH ANALYSIS

The executive charged with steering his organization through a period of negative growth does not deal with a vague or abstract entity. He operates with responsibility for a definite segment of the firm. If he is the chief executive of his company, he may be dealing with either a part or the whole.

A conglomerate corporation with a family consisting of fifty large subsidiaries may wish to divest itself of one or more of its component firms. A simple corporation may be having trouble with a single division or department. If the national economy of the United Kingdom is depressed or the labor force becomes impossibly strike-happy, the multinational corporation may wish to shrink or even terminate operations there. A large parent organization may, on the whole, be showing fine growth, but it may have a few sick subsidiaries, divisions, or departments that require surgical intervention.

A horizontally integrated firm may wish to drop or add a few branches. A vertically integrated company may wish to increase or diminish the number of levels of vertical reach back from the market to the source of raw materials.

Thus, the complexity of most firms makes it virtually meaningless to speak about positive, zero, or negative growth in a vague nonspecific manner. The units under examination must be identified and specified with clarity. Which particular corporate groups, subsidiaries, divisions, departments, or satellites are failing to meet expectations? Which links of the corporate chain or which of the satellites are to be lopped off or are to be put on the operating table for reductive surgery? Any program for negative growth, therefore, must identify the organizational units and must specify which components of the firm are to be dealt with.

GRAPHIC DISPLAY TECHNIQUES

Figures 2-6 through 2-10 show a number of different graphic display techniques that negative-growth managers should find useful in presenting growth data for verbal or written reports.

Figures 2-6(a) and 2-6(b) contain two representations of Widget Corp. sales data. The top curve shows sales performance relative to a base year (1970). The bottom curve shows the sales in millions of dollars.

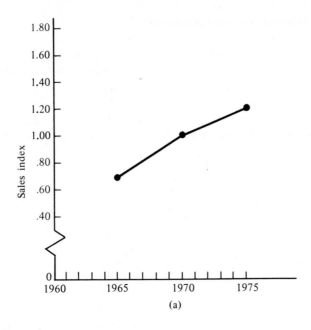

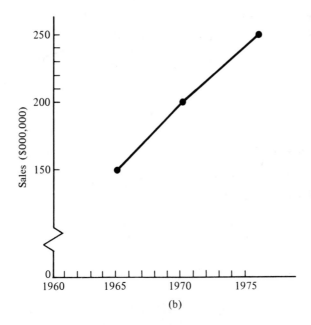

FIGURE 2-6. (a) Relative sales performance indices for Widget Corp., 1966, 1970, 1975 (1970 = 1.00). (b) Three-year sales for Widget Corp. (Computed from data in Table 1-2.)

Figure 2-7 shows Widget Corp. data in profile form. Data for six size-related variables for each of three years are plotted as profiles. The fact that the profiles intersect shows that there is some question about whether Widget grew over the time interval.

Figure 2-8 shows variable-by-variable time-series data for Widget Corp. This form of display helps show how each variable changes over time.

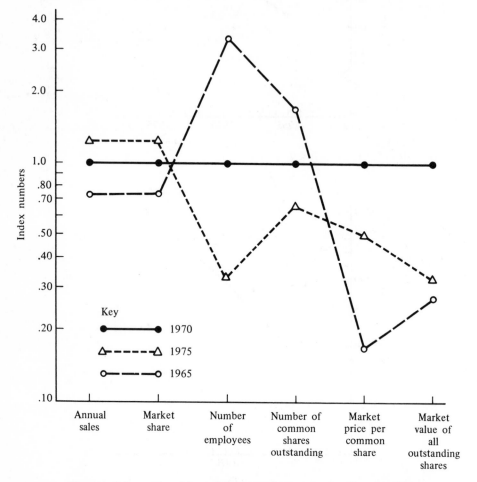

FIGURE 2-7.   Graphic, relative, multivariate profile of indices relative to a base year (1970 = 1.00). Note that both 1965 and 1975 size profiles cross the 1970 baseline, making it difficult to say with any degree of certainty in which of the three years Widget Corp. was the largest. (Data computed from Table 1-2. Widget Corp., 1965, 1970, 1975.)

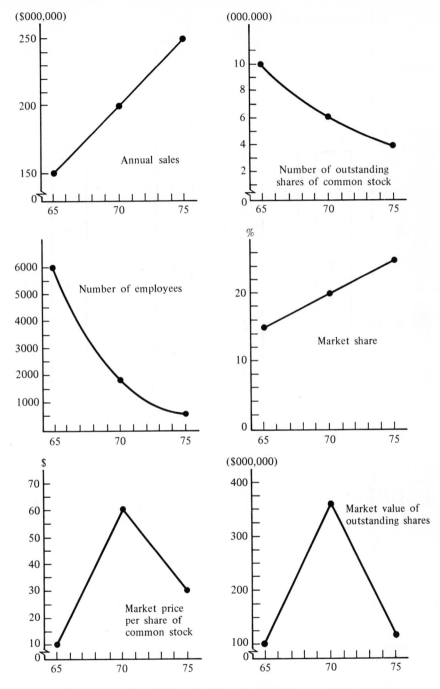

FIGURE 2-8. Graphic, relative, variable-by-variable display of size-related variables for Widget Corp., 1965, 1970, 1975. (Data computed from Table 1-2.)

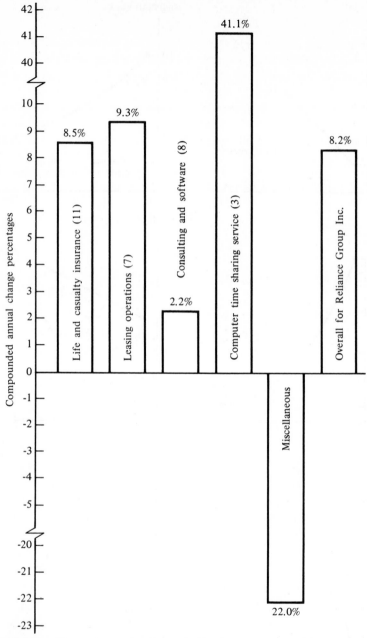

Figure 2-9. A comparison of the changes in total revenues of five major sectors of the Reliance Group Incorporated from 1970 to 1974. Percentages are compound rates computed from Formulas (1a) and (1b). Items in parentheses refer to the number of companies in the sector. (**Source of primary data:** Reliance Group Incorporated Annual Report for 1974)

Figure 2-9 shows the changes in revenues for five major sectors of the Reliance Group Incorporated, a large conglomerate. Displays such as this enable the analyst to compare the performance of various sectors of a multidivisional firm.

Figures 2-10(a) through 2-10(d) show comparative data for several firms in the oil industry. Figure 2-10(a) contains time-series data for seven firms and enables the analyst to make firm-by-firm, growth-in-sales comparisons. Figure 2-10(b) shows comparative data for changes in refinery capacity. Figure 2-10(c) shows comparative time series data for changes in net income. Figure 2-10(d) shows the market shares of several categories of gasoline marketers over time.

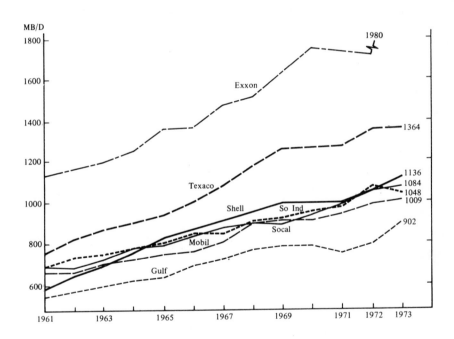

FIGURE 2-10(a).   Seven-company comparison, total petroleum product sales in the United States. (**Source:** *Competition in the Petroleum Industry,* Public Affairs Dept., Exxon Company, U.S.A., January 1975)

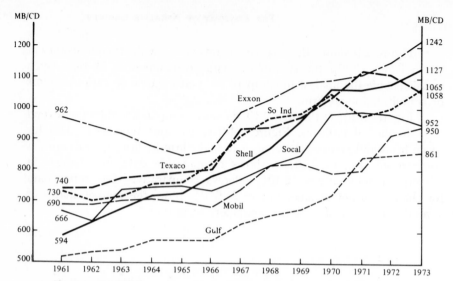

FIGURE 2-10(b). Seven-company comparison, crude refining capacity. (**Source:** *Competition in the Petroleum Industry,* Public Affairs Dept., Exxon Company, U.S.A., January 1975)

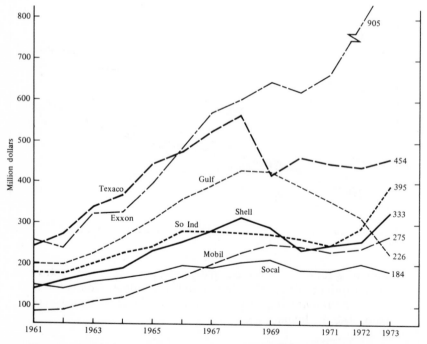

FIGURE 2-10(c). Seven-company comparison, U.S. net income. (**Source:** *Competition in the Petroleum Industry,* Public Affairs Dept., Exxon Company, U.S.A., January 1975)

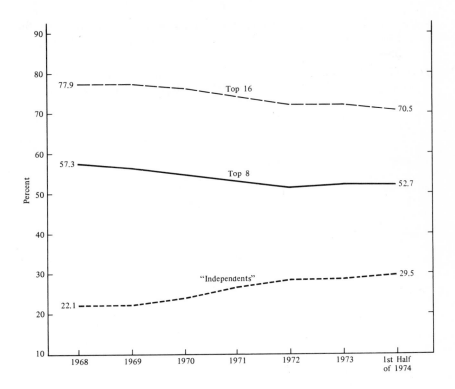

FIGURE 2-10(d). Share of U.S. retail gasoline sales. (**Source:** *Competition in the Petroleum Industry,* Public Affairs Dept., Exxon Company, U.S.A., January 1975)

SELECTED REFERENCES

GLEIM, GEORGE A., *Program Flowcharting.* New York: Holt, Rinehart and Winston, Inc., 1970.

GROSS, HARRY, *Make or Buy.* Englewood Cliffs, N.J.: Prentice-Hall, Inc., 1966.

HOAD, W. M. and P. ROSKO, *Management Factors Contributing to Success or Failure of New Small Manufacturers.* Ann Arbor, Mich.: University of Michigan Business Research Bureau, 1964.

MILSUM, JOHN H., ed., *Positive Feedback: A General Systems Approach to Feedback and Mutual Causality.* London: Pergamon Press, 1968.

SILVER, MORRIS, and RICHARD AUSTIN, "Entrepreneurship, Profit and Limits to Firm Size," *The Journal of Business,* Vol. XLII (July 1969), pp. 277–281.

STIEGLITZ, HAROLD, "The Chief Executive's Job and the Size of the Firm," *The Conference Board Review*, Vol. VII (Sept. 1970), pp. 38–40.

TOSI, H. and H. PRATT, "Administrative Ratios and Organizational Size," *Academy of Management Journal*, Vol. 10 (1967), pp. 160–168.

PART II

SELECTED PROBLEMS IN THE FUNCTIONAL AREAS

Chapter 3

Negative Growth Within the Marketing Function

THE PRODUCT DELETION DECISION

The professional gardener knows that from time to time he must prune his trees, plants, and shrubs to keep them vigorously alive. So it is with a company's products, product lines, and service offerings. They, too, grow old and no longer make their proper contribution to the well-being of the firm. Perhaps a ruthless pruning, bordering on euthanasia, is unthinkable when one is dealing with human beings, but it is a necessary fact of life when one is dealing with moribund products. (The term *product* as used here also means product-line and service offering.)

Clues to the Loss of Vitality

SALES DECLINE.   The first clue to recognition of a dying product is a declining sales trend. Customers order less or stop ordering altogether. Salesmen complain that the product is harder to sell. At one time the product contributed a major share of the firm's overall sales revenue; now its contribution is waning.

The vigilant sales manager tries to discover if it is only his firm's sales of the product that are suffering, or if the trend is industry- or worldwide. If industry- or worldwide sales are holding up well, or even growing, he knows that there is something wrong with *his* firm's marketing effort (perhaps that defect is readily corrected). But if industry sales, too, are showing the steady downward drift (or plunge) and careful investigation reveals that, economically feasible means being used, the decay is irreversible, he knows that the death watch has begun.

PRICE DECLINES.   Another early-warning symptom of a sick or dying product is a sustained price decline. Sometimes price declines are temporary, brought about by external factors, and there is the reasonable expectation that the price level will right itself in time. On the other hand, the price decline may be permanent and not reversible because of shrinking demand, excessive productive capacity, low-cost foreign competition, or other long-run factors.

However, price declines alone are not sufficient indicators of product morbidity. Before it is decided that the price decline is permanent and caused by uncontrollable, external factors, it is wise to conduct a careful study of within-industry pricing behavior. Downward pressure of price levels can be self-induced by reckless bidding by overstimulated commissioned salesmen who are exhorted and pressured to sell, sell, sell, no matter what. In one instance, a price decline was caused by an overzealous newcomer to the market trying to establish a sales record for the purpose of an upcoming stock market flotation. Only if research indicates that the causes of the decline are intractable should it be treated as evidence that the product is near extinction.

DIMINISHED PROFITABILITY.   Suggestive but not conclusive, lowered profitability calls for a searching examination of causes. Is the lowered profit caused by uncontrollable, rising costs of labor and materials that cannot be offset in other ways? Is it a result of overspending on advertising and promotion? Is demand dropping? Are prices falling? Or is it a combination of these adverse factors?

True profitability can be badly distorted by arbitrary overhead allocations to the various elements of a multiple product line. A much better indicator of performance is the contribution margin test. (The contribution margin is the excess of sales revenue over variable costs.) Do the contribution margins closely parallel the profitability trend? If not, only limited confidence ought to be given to profitability computations in evaluating the health of elements of a product line. As is demonstrated in Table 3-1, it is quite possible to make a good product look

TABLE 3-1

NUMERICAL EXAMPLE OF HOW ARBITRARY ALLOCATION OF OVERHEAD COSTS CAN DISTORT PROFITABILITY

	Product A	Product B	Product C
Annual sales volume ($)	20,000,000	10,000,000	15,000,000
Cost of goods sold ($)	9,000,000	4,500,000	10,000,000
Allocated overhead ($)	12,000,000	4,000,000	3,500,000
Book profit (Loss) ($)	(1,000,000)	500,000	1,500,000
Book profit as a % of sales	(5%)	5%	15%
Contribution margin ($)	$11,000,000	6,500,000	5,000,000

sick, and a bad one look healthy by deliberate manipulation of overhead allocations. In Table 3-1, Product A, which shows a book loss of $1 million, seems inferior to Product C with a book profit of $1.5 million. The contribution margin test, however, shows that Product A makes a much greater contribution to recovery of fixed costs than Product C. To drop Product A because of its apparent but spurious book loss would be a disastrous error for this company.

AVAILABILITY OF SUBSTITUTES. A product, at one time perceived by customers as worthwhile and satisfying, although unchanged, may suffer in comparison with competitive offerings of either similar but improved versions, or actual substitutes. For example, the high-priced, console, home radio receiver, a prime source of home entertainment from 1927 to 1944, was displaced by the black-and-white television receiver. That improvement in home entertainment is, in its turn, being supplanted by color television. When black-and-white television became popular, the motion picture industry suffered shattering declines in box office receipts.

Technological changes cause products to lose their markets. The pharmaceutical industry is a good example of how products have short life cycles because of the availability of a never-ending stream of new, improved substitutes. New pain killers compete with the humble aspirin tablet; new broad-spectrum antibiotics replace older, less effective sulfas and other bacteriocidal preparations.

MORE ATTRACTIVE ALTERNATIVES.   A product seems to be worth-while; its sales are steady, its profitability up to expectations, yet it may be a candidate for deletion because more attractive ways are uncovered for the use of scarce resources. Discovered are more profitable ways to invest the firm's limited capital, more fruitful uses of limited plant capacity, better ways to deploy scarce managerial or scientific talent, better ways to spend advertising money, and more advantageous avenues to channel the creative energies of the firm's staff.

The astute executive keeps foremost in his mind that his firm incurs both outlay costs *and* opportunity costs. He knows that in addition to the costs that can be found in the records and income statements, there is the cost of income foregone by overlooking more profitable ways of utilizing scarce resources. Thus, if an economic, financial, and marketing study indicates that a highly desirable opportunity must be foregone if the existing product line is to remain intact, he finds it wise to examine the possibility of deleting the least attractive component of the product line, even if that candidate for deletion still exhibits reasonable profitability and market potential.

Obstacles to Product Deletion

ENTRENCHED INTERESTS.   Dropping a product line means loss of jobs, reductions in rank, loss of prestige and organizational status, loss of influence. To avoid such losses, persons and groups with a stake in the continuation of a product try to influence the decision-making process in their favor. They use pressure tactics, obstruction, falsification of cost data, alibis, self-serving advice, bitter arguments over the "unfairness" of overhead allocations, slowdowns, wildcat strikes, sabotage, etc. Their anguished cry is, "Why us? Why not the other departments?"

JOINT PRODUCTS.   If the nature of the manufacturing technology is such that joint products are produced, one successful and the other not, it is not usually possible to drop the unsuccessful product. For example, a sawmill cuts logs in grade 1, 2, and 3 lumber (plus sawdust). Grade 1 is used for exterior finishing carpentry; grade 2, for internal construction members; grade 3 cannot be used for construction but may be used for fences or concrete forms. The market demand for the three grades is rarely proportional to the supply. Grade 1 may be in great demand, but its supply is severely limited. Grade 3 is not in much demand, but its supply is vast. It would be nice if the yield of grade 1 could be raised and the yield of grade 3 reduced, but all grades are produced, like it or not. The dairy, meat packing, and chemical processing industries are other examples of joint product producers.

COMPLEMENTARITY.   Two products are complementary if they tend to be used together (e.g., toothpaste and tooth brushes; razors, blades, and shaving cream), if one product's prestige rubs off on others (the Cadillac and the Chevrolet), or if the sales of one affects the sales of another. Complementarity is an important factor in selling and distribution when offering a full line gives a supplier a comparative advantage over his competitors. For example, many customers like to do one-stop shopping. Dropping one component of an assortment can cause the customer to go elsewhere. Distributors like to carry some prestigious products because it helps them to sell other things to their customers on the same sales call. Loss of that leading item hurts other sales.

Complementarity can exist in manufacturing as well as in sales. The existence of one product reduces the cost of production of others.

If complementarity is a significant factor in product strategy, discontinuance of one or more key elements of a full line causes disproportionally large losses in the value of the surviving elements of the line.

RESTRICTIVE LABOR AGREEMENTS.   Seemingly obscure provisions in collective bargaining agreements make dropping a product line impossibly costly. For example, the plant that makes the product to be discontinued employs all high-seniority people who earn above-average hourly wage rates. The union contract calls for company-wide seniority in the event of staff reductions. The low-wage people must be terminated and the high-wage employees retained and transferred to other work. A product, formerly profitable because it employed recently hired people, now is saddled with high-wage earners, and its profitability vanishes.

Examples such as this show that arbitrary assignment of low-wage earners to one product and high-wage earners to another can distort profitability calculations. Indeed, such arbitrary employee assignments can make one product seem unprofitable when, in fact, it is not. This result is shown in Table 3-2. The old Product A employs the same number of people as the new Product B. But because the A people were hired earlier, they have higher wage rates. The wage bill for A is $4 million, whereas for B it is only $2.4 million. The result is that Product A *seems* to be producing a loss of $1 million and Product B, a profit of $600 thousand. Actually, as the data in the table show, if nothing else but the work assignments of the employees were changed, the profit picture for the two products would be quite different.

Many labor agreements require high severance pay for discharged employees. This adds to the cost of discontinuing a line. Some contracts have clauses forbidding the practice of "contracting out"; that is, having work performed by outside suppliers as long as there are union members available for employment. Thus, the alternative of discontinuing the

TABLE 3-2

COMPARATIVE PROFITABILITY OF TWO
PRODUCTS WITH IDENTICAL SALES VOLUME
AND COSTS, OTHER THAN FOR DIRECT
LABOR, BUT HAVING THE SAME NUMBER
OF EMPLOYEES *

	OLD (A)	NEW (B)
Sales income (annual)	$10,000,000	$10,000,000
Direct labor †	4,000,000	2,400,000
Direct materials	2,000,000	2,000,000
Other costs	5,000,000	5,000,000
Profit (Loss)	($1,000,000)	$ 600,000

* Fictional data.

† Products A and B employ the same number of people. However, the people employed on Product A have from ten to twenty years seniority, and the average hourly wage is $7.00 per hour. The people engaged in making Product B have an average of two years' seniority and earn an average hourly wage of $4.20. If Product A is discontinued, because of the plantwide seniority provision in the union contract, all people on Product B would have to be dropped from the payroll and replaced with Product A's employees. Is Product A more or less profitable than Product B?

manufacture of a product in-house and having it made elsewhere is blocked by a restrictive labor contract.

STRENGTHENING A COMPETITOR.   In an industry that is suffering from excess supply, all competitors suffer from low or nonexistent profit margins. If one of the competitors leaves the market and takes his capacity out of production, the surviving firms are left stronger than before. Thus, dropping a product may cause a strengthening of one or more direct competitors who may also be competitors on other products. This relative gain in financial and market strength of the competitor will reduce or eliminate the comparative advantage expected by the firm dropping the product.

REDUCTION IN SALES FORCE EARNINGS.   Unless the discontinued product can be replaced by another with approximately the same (or more) sales potential, the sales force will experience a drop in earnings. This drop may mean that the firm must employ fewer salesmen to call on customers. The smaller sales force must either make fewer calls per customer or overlook some accounts. In either case, competitors gain, and the firm with the weaker sales force loses market penetration.

WRITE-OFF OF INVENTORIES.   Many firms who sell through industrial distributors are required to offer their distributors inventory price protection in order to induce them to carry a full line rather than stocking only the fast-selling numbers. Thus, companies guarantee to protect the distributors against price reductions, obsolescence, and other events that could cause the distributors to suffer inventory losses. Some distributor contracts require the selling firm to take back merchandise for credit if items are discontinued or stop selling. Agreements may require issuance of credit memoranda to compensate the distributor if prices are reduced by the manufacturer. Thus, the decision to drop a product may make it necessary to take back for full credit all the inventory in distributor stocks. If these stocks are large, the reversal of sales income in the year in which the returns are made can prove very painful to the people back at headquarters who earn commissions, overrides, and incentive payments on distributor sales.

Product Deletion Strategies

When a product deletion is decided upon, one or more of the following alternatives should be considered.

GO OUT WITH GUNS BLAZING AND FLAGS FLYING.   Outright discontinuance with public announcement, auction sale of assets, bargain sale of raw materials, work in process, and finished goods inventories, and publicized help in relocation of displaced employees.

FOLD YOUR TENT AND SNEAK AWAY IN THE NIGHT.   Outright discontinuance but with no public announcement. Bid high on quotation requests to avoid getting new orders. Sell off inventory in secret deals. Mothball idle equipment for discreet sale later. Switch personnel to other jobs.

BECOME SALES AGENCY.   Discontinue manufacture and buy product for resale from foreign supplier or former competitor. Keep present line intact and keep all customers.

BECOME CONTRACT MANUFACTURER.   Close down the sales effort for this product, but retain the facilities and become a contract supplier for private label sales to mass marketers or others who do not want to manufacture the product.

DIVESTMENT.   Combine all operations related to this product into a self-contained subsidiary. Sell subsidiary to employees under favorable conditions; sell to interested parties for cash or other noncash consideration; spin off subsidiary to shareholders as stock dividend.

SELL KNOWHOW.   Sell machinery, jigs, tools, parts, etc. and key employees along with knowhow to foreign firm for cash or cash plus royalty. Swap facilities for foreign firm's knowhow and license to produce its product here.

RELOCATE.   Find a place in the world more conducive to economical manufacture of product. For example, try Hong Kong, Puerto Rico, Taiwan, Korea, Mexico, etc. if low labor cost can save the product from extinction.

CHARITABLE CONTRIBUTION.   Donate the entire operation to a charity. Give it to an organization that will employ the handicapped. Give it to a community development corporation that can use it to train the disadvantaged. Continue to buy product from new owners until they can get the operation running and self-sufficient.

A Checklist of Affected Parties

Just to be certain that no one with a legitimate interest in the product deletion decision is overlooked, below is a checklist of persons, groups, or organizations whose interests might be affected favorably or adversely:

— Shareholders of all classes
— Creditors of all classes
— Dismissed employees and their families
— Retained employees and their families
— Top-, middle-, and lower-management people and their families
— Would-be employees, high school graduates
— Cognizant labor unions
— Local community and business people
— Suppliers of materials and services
— The credit reporting agencies
— Customers, past and present
— Salesmen, manufacturer's representatives

— Distributors and their staffs
— Dealers and their staffs
— Providers of warranty service and spare parts
— Advertising agencies and the media
— Common carriers
— Governmental agencies, statistical reporters
— Professionals (lawyers, accountants, consultants)
— The Internal Revenue Service, Sales and Use Tax Bureaus
— State labor department
— Competitors, domestic and foreign
— Licensees

An Important Caveat

The complexity of a product deletion decision should not be underestimated. Because of the presence of such factors as product complementarity, jointness, arbitrary overhead allocations, differential wage rates, and obligations to all affected parties, the decision *cannot* be made on the basis of product analysis alone. The elimination of a *seemingly* unprofitable product or line can actually throw the firm into an ever-descending spiral from which it may never emerge.

There is only one safe and sure way to perform the analysis of a product deletion decision of any consequence, and that is by using a point-to-point, variable-by-variable, quality-by-quality, *before and after* analysis. The important question that must be asked and answered completely is:

What does the company look like with the subject product(s) in its line, *and* what will it be like with the products(s) deleted?

Any other form of analysis is fraught with confusion and potential for disastrous error.

ALTERNATIVE FORMS FOR OVERSEAS SALES

There are more than 140 member states in the United Nations, and each presents the American marketer with a unique set of marketing problems. Each nation has its own peculiar import and currency restrictions; each imposes special limitations of foreign-owned enterprises within their borders; each has its own systems of tariffs and export taxes; each has its own special cultural, religious, social, and political institutions.

By using identical forms of marketing organization, no single American firm can hope to realize sales income from every nation that can use its products. However, there are several organizational arrangements in use that enable the firm to obtain revenue from overseas sales with whatever degree of direct financial involvement it cares to make. A company already engaged in overseas marketing can reduce its involvement by adopting a form that requires less fixed investment.

The main forms in use today are listed below in the order of the financial commitment required.

UNSOLICITED SALES TO EXPORTERS DOMICILED IN THE UNITED STATES. A number of distributors have export departments that specialize in sales to specific foreign countries. These firms buy from American companies, pay with dollars, and take care of all details of exporting, shipping, insurance, and financing orders to their customers. This type of export distributor requires no more financial involvement by the seller than does any domestic customer. The export distributor requires a regular trade discount and usually tries to keep the names of his customers secret.

UNSOLICITED SALES TO BUYING OFFICES OR TRADING COMPANIES. Large foreign buyers obtain the services of buying offices in various supplying countries. These firms or persons represent their foreign principals, handle the price negotiations, arrange for all the technical detail of exporting goods, and arrange for suitable financing. As in the case of the export distributors, the selling firm needs no extra investment or personnel to handle this type of business.

SOLICITED SALES MADE THROUGH COMMISSIONED SALES AGENTS. These sales agents, domiciled in their home countries, are the equivalent of the American manufacturer's representative. They carry no inventory but solicit orders from companies in their home territory, and will work for commissions only. They usually agree to carry no competing lines, but in return they ask for exclusive representation in their country. The seller has the responsibility for taking care of the financing, transportation, insurance, export licenses, etc.

Usually, a small export department headed by an export sales manager and a small staff can handle a reasonable volume of sales generated by resident agents. An occasional trip abroad is necessary to meet with the agents and to visit some of the more active accounts.

SALES THROUGH INDIGENOUS DISTRIBUTORS OR TRADING COMPANIES. If the volume of business in a country justifies, an indigenous distributor or trading company will request exclusive representation of the products in the home country. Such firms buy for their own account, expect trade discounts, and try to keep the names of their customers confidential. The seller must handle all the technical detail of exporting goods to the destination unless the trading company has a buying office in the United States.

LICENSING AGREEMENTS. This kind of arrangement involves a transfer of technical knowledge to a foreign-owned firm in exchange for cash or cash plus a royalty. Occasionally, the licensee will request that his personnel be trained in the United States by the licensor firm. Also, the licensee may wish to purchase machinery, tools, jigs, fixtures, testing equipment, and component parts in the United States until such things can be acquired in its own country. Some agreements require that the licensor agree to update the technology continuously and that the licensee be granted rights to sell in countries other than its own. Therefore, the licensing agreement should carefully specify the geographical boundaries of the licensor's marketing rights. When he adopts this form, the United States firm surrenders whatever market potential it might have had to its licensees in the assigned territories in exchange for fees and royalties.

SOLICITED SALES FROM COMPANY-OWNED SALES OFFICES. When the marketing potential justifies the fixed expenses and investment involved in this form, the marketer may prefer to set up factory-owned and staffed offices in selected foreign countries. By this means, the firm can obtain the full-time attention from the sales force, certainly more than can be expected from a commissioned agent who must also sell other lines. The sales manager can be either an American or a foreign national known and trusted by the home office. In addition to all the technicalities of exporting merchandise, the home office must become involved in the financing and absentee management of a remote office in a strange land.

JOINT VENTURES WITH FOREIGN NATIONALS. When it is not practical to manufacture the goods in the United States (for example, when the country has high protective tariffs) and ship them to the foreign market, some firms prefer to set up manufacturing facilities abroad. However, in order to limit the size of the financial and managerial involvement, and because many countries will not allow wholly-owned subsidiaries to be established in their lands, a joint venture with indigenous businessmen becomes attractive.

DIRECT INVESTMENT IN FOREIGN-BASED OPERATION.   This is the form widely adopted by the giant multinational firms that views the entire world as its base of operations, although it may have its headquarters in the United States.

Which of the foregoing organizational forms is used depends upon many factors including:

— Taste and desire to engage in foreign ventures.
— The availability of funds to support foreign operations.
— The possibility of reciprocity between domestic and foreign-based entities.
— The availability of good managerial personnel that can be trusted to run a remote operation.
— The ability to tolerate the size of the fixed costs of operations for foreign-based subdivisions.
— The size and profit potential for particular foreign markets.

TRANSFORMING FIXED SALES COSTS INTO VARIABLE COSTS

Lead-Acid Corporation (LAC) is a large manufacturer and marketer of lead-acid storage batteries that are used in automobiles, trucks, motor buses, railroad passenger cars, tractors, and other kinds of vehicles.* LAC sells directly to large users through its O.E.M. division; to the foreign market through its Export Division; to the private brand resellers through its Private Label Sales Division; and to thousands and thousands of small resellers through its four regional sales offices (northeastern, southeastern, southwestern and northwestern regions). All these sales divisional managers report to the Vice President and General Sales Manager, Mr. Martin Faraday.

* Fictional case.

Mr. Faraday is very pleased with the performance of his nation-wide sales organization. He boasts particularly of the close and friendly relationships formed between the company, through its sales people, and its customers. According to Faraday, LAC owns every customer on its books. What he means by that is that there is a bond of loyalty between each account and the company that no departing salesman can undo.

The only dark cloud on Mr. Faraday's horizon is the deep depression in the automobile industry and the fact that LAC's fixed cost of selling is so high that even a small dip in sales volume causes the company to run at a loss. Smaller cars, foreign competition, and possible competition from alkaline storage batteries are factors that may prove damaging unless Faraday can reduce the level of fixed costs in the sales organization.

All salesmen work on straight salary plus an annual profit-sharing bonus. The regional and district offices, too, are staffed with salaried personnel. When, in 1960, LAC proudly announced that henceforth all employees in the sales organization would be shifted from the hourly, weekly, and commission-only pay status to annual salary, Mr. Faraday was awarded the "Sales Executive of the Year" award from his professional association. In his acceptance speech, he said, "We are introducing a new era of stability and tranquility into the storage battery industry." Things went very well from 1960 until 1973. The company's sales continued to grow, and the sophistication of the sales effort grew apace. Every modern management technique was first tested at LAC. Sales reporting was computerized first by Faraday's team.

Beginning with 1973, a gradual erosion in sales and profit margins is detected. Labor costs, costs of basic ingredients, all are affected by the rapid inflation in the national economy. Japanese and German competition grows keener. For three consecutive quarters of 1974, LAC shows lower and lower earnings per share. In the first quarter of 1975, a loss is reported for the first time in the company's history.

LAC's economic planning staff undertakes a long-range forecast of the outlook for the storage battery industry and for LAC in particular. What they predict is a slow average growth in usage of lead-acid batteries, but a reduction in LAC's market share and a ten- to twenty-year interval of ups and downs in the national economy. Thus, they predict, if LAC does not adjust its organizational structure and cost relationships, it can look forward to years of minimal prosperity interspersed with years of outright losses. The only solution, the group advises, is to restructure the organization to provide a higher degree of flexibility and responsiveness to year-to-year fluctuations in overall demand for the company's products.

Translated into Faraday's portion of the operation, this means a change in the salary-only policy for the sales department. Faraday calls in a prominent management consulting firm and asks them to prepare alternative sales organizational arrangements based on a number of sales-fluctuation scenarios he gives them.

FARADAY'S ALTERNATIVES.   The consultants identify a number of alternative sales organizational arrangements for consideration. Some of them are so extreme that there is not much likelihood of their being adopted, but they are included in the list for the sake of completeness. The list includes the following alternatives:

1 / Salaried sales people on all levels.
2 / Commission-only salesmen on all but managerial levels.
3 / Manufacturer's representatives in several territories.
4 / Appoint exclusive distributors in selected territories.
5 / Set up independent sales agencies owned and operated by re-leased LAC salespersons in several districts.
6 / Set up an independent national sales organization and assign it all sales except O.E.M., private label, and export sales.
7 / Any of the foregoing in combinations.

FARADAY'S EVALUATION CRITERIA.   In his attempt to arrive at an evaluation of the alternative sales arrangements, Faraday consults his staff and collectively they arrive at these evaluation criteria (order not significant):

1 / Continued close relationships with customers.
2 / Ease of implementation and transition.
3 / Lowest overall sales cost (including trade discounts).
4 / Ease of introduction of new products.
5 / Most flexibility in event of wide fluctuations in sales.
6 / Least loss of market share.

On the basis of these criteria, Faraday and his staff rank each of the first six alternatives by desirability. Their rankings are as shown in Table 3-3 (1 = highest ranking):

TABLE 3-3

ALTERNATIVE	CRITERION NUMBER					
	1	2	3	4	5	6
1	1	1	5	1	6	1
2	2	3	4	3	3	2
3	3	2	1	2	1	5
4	6	5	2	6	2	6
5	4	4	3	4	4	4
6	5	6	6	5	5	3

However, alternative 7, which is an unspecified combination of the other six alternatives, may yet contain the best arrangement, because it allows the sales organization to be tailored to the specific local conditions and to the availability of top-quality personnel to carry out the chosen arrangement. (See Chapter 9 for methods for ranking alternatives on multiple criteria and other evaluation techniques.)

SELECTED REFERENCES

ATWOOD, CHARLES, *The Sales Representative's Handbook.* New York: Beekman Publishing, Inc., 1969.

BERG, THOMAS L., *Mismarketing: Case Histories of Marketing Misfires.* New York: Doubleday and Company, 1971.

FAYERWEATHER, JOHN, *Management of International Operations.* New York: McGraw Hill Book Co., 1960.

The Financing of Exports and Imports: A Guide to Procedures. New York: Morgan Guarantee Trust Co. of N.Y., 1973.

FREY, ALBERT W., ed., *Marketing Handbook*, 2nd. ed. New York: Ronald Press, 1965.

"Manufacturers' Representatives vs. Company Sales Force," *Industrial Marketing* (Feb. 1962), pp. 85–86.

RISLEY, GEORGE, *Modern Industrial Marketing.* New York: McGraw Hill Book Co., 1972.

SEMLOW, WALTER J., "How Many Salesmen Do You Need?" *Harvard Business Review*, Vol. XXXVII (May-June 1959), pp. 126–132.

Chapter 4

Negative Growth
in the
Personnel Area

INVOLUNTARY SEPARATION
OF EXECUTIVES

A Painful Experience

At a business luncheon, a well-known executive was reminiscing to his companion about his wartime experiences.

"You know, Charlie," the executive said with a far-away look in his eyes. "When I was piloting a high-altitude bomber over Germany and we dropped our load of bombs, all we could see on the ground was flashes and lots of black smoke. None of us in the plane's crew could really picture what was really happening on the ground when the bombs exploded. . . . I may have been responsible for hundreds of civilian casualties on each mission, for all I know. . . . But if I had to

kill an enemy soldier face to face, I couldn't bring myself to do it. . . .
I couldn't, I know it. . . . I couldn't bring myself to do it."

He stopped speaking for a moment, took a deep drink from his
highball glass, then added:

"Do you know why I'm reminded of the war? . . . No? . . . I
just dictated a memo to the head of personnel ordering him to send layoff notices to over five hundred of our people. . . . Imagine that? . . .
Five hundred jobs up in smoke for who knows how long. . . . But you
know, I didn't feel a thing in here. . . . It was just like the time I
dropped the bombs. . . . But when I get back to the office, I have to tell
my P.R. man, Howie Mason, that he's fired. . . . Damn it, I can't bring
myself to do it. . . . That's why I'm dawdling here with you when I
should be back at the shop chopping off heads. . . . Howie and I are
fraternity brothers. We were roommates at college. Our wives and kids
are friends. We play golf together every Saturday. Why, he even got
me this job." He let out a deep sigh of despair. "I guess I'm just a soft-
hearted coward. . . . I'm here drinking my lunch when I should be
working. . . . What a life. . . . I hate that part of my job more than
anything I can imagine."

The executive's companion, the man named Charlie, smiled, shook
his head in sympathy and said:

"Too bad, Harry. I guess that's why they pay you all that dough.
You don't think you get it just for boozing it up with space salesmen
and slaving away in nightspots with the visiting hicks from Peoria and
River Rouge."

"No, I guess not," Harry said. "Hey, let me tell you what happened
to me when I was with the company for just a year. I was working for
old Cappy who was V.P. for Marketing when I came. Well, I kept trying
to have him and his wife at my house for dinner. We invited him several
times but he always said no and gave some dumb excuse. . . . One day,
at a sales meeting, we were drinking together. I saw he had loosened
up a bit, so I asked him, 'Hey Cappy, how the hell is it that whenever
I ask you and your frau to dinner at my house you always refuse, and
with such phony excuses?'"

"Yeah? What did he say?" Charlie asked.

"Cappy was pretty soused, but he put a stern look on his face
and said, 'My boy, one of these fine days I may have to fire you. It'll be
one hell of a lot easier on my goddamned ulcers if I'm not emotionally
involved with you or your lovely family.' Cappy thought about it some
more and continued. 'And I recommend that you conduct yourself the
same way with your subordinates. It's too damned painful when you
have to chop a bright young man with a houseful of kids. If you're a
decent man, it hurts too much. It takes too much out of you. If you're

a louse, and it doesn't hurt you at all, or you even enjoy the experience, we don't want you working for us.' How about that? Boy, I wish now that I'd taken his advice with Howie Mason."

Executives firing other executives, the analogue of fratricide, is such a stressful experience for the people who have to do it that all kinds of evasions and face-saving, ego-saving stratagems have been devised to make the task less unpleasant for all concerned.

Objectives of the Firing Process

No one but an outright sadist or bitter enemy wants to cause the discharged person any unnecessary injury or to shatter his self-esteem. The principal objective, of course, remains to remove him neatly and painlessly as possible from the payroll.

If the man is going to continue working in the same or allied fields, it is important that he remain friendly to the company. All executives have access to highly confidential information that can be used to harm the firm's interests. Data such as costs of production (usually a highly guarded secret), lists of customers, prices charged customers, new products in development and not yet announced, and other trade secrets are in jeopardy if the discharged executive bears a grudge against the firm because he was treated unfairly or with unnecessary harshness.

When the discharged person finds a new position, it may very well be with one of the firm's best customers. It will not be at all helpful to the company if, because of his hostility, he is instrumental in the firm's losing a large share of its sales. Perhaps the discharged executive may find himself working for a governmental agency, for example, the Internal Revenue Service or as Contracting Officer for the Department of Defense. As an avowed enemy of his former employer, he could cause considerable harm if he were motivated to do so by an urge for revenge.

A discharged executive may have some specialized knowledge that could be of continuing use to the firm if it were available at reasonable cost. A good post-termination relationship makes it more possible that this useful knowledge may be available if required.

One piece of executive wisdom is worth passing on from generation to generation. *"Be nice to everyone: Someday he may be your boss."*

Specific Reasons for Discharging Executives

Although there are as many reasons for wanting to discharge a particular executive as there are men and positions, a culling of the literature and the results of countless interviews allows these generalizations. An executive may be fired because:

1 / He is actually incompetent and it took a long time to find out.

2 / Although once considered competent, he has lost his powers, energy, or good judgment.

3 / He no longer fits in with the way the company is doing things; he cannot make adjustments to new conditions.

4 / He has been found to be dishonest or unethical.

5 / He is of bad character; he drinks excessively, gambles excessively, is known to consort with criminals, or has been convicted of a criminal offense.

6 / His job no longer exists either through reorganization or discontinuance of a part of the operation.

7 / He is earning too much money. He can be replaced for much less money than he is earning.

8 / He is less competent than his subordinates and is blocking their pathways to promotion. They will be lost to the company unless the blockage can be removed.

9 / He is known to be disloyal to the company's interests.

10 / He is about to be vested with a large pension contributed solely by the company. If he is discharged before he is fully vested a large sum of money will revert to the company.

11 / He is a source of conflict and irritation to his fellow executives and his subordinates.

12 / He is an insecure person and cannot tolerate any highly competent people around him. As a result, there is excessive turnover of people with high potential.

13 / He has been found accepting bribes from the company's suppliers, and offering bribes to I.R.S. examiners.

14 / He has caused the company's image to suffer by his actions and behavior.

15 / He has taken such extreme positions in the recent labor-management negotiations that one of the union's demands for settlement is that this man be discharged immediately.

16 / He has made bad errors in judgment that have caused the company to suffer large losses.

17 / Whenever he makes errors, he engages in elaborate attempts to cover up or shift blame.

18 / He can no longer accept responsibility. He avoids hard assignments, refuses to make difficult decisions, takes too much time off from work.

19 / He has an irreconcilable difference with the other executives over company policy and refuses to back down no matter how many times he is voted down in the company councils.

20 / He has antagonized a controlling stockholder or an influential member of the board of directors.

Commonly Used Separation Stratagems

ABRUPT DISMISSAL.   Although abrupt dismissal is the least subtle of the firing techniques, it has the virtue of openness and finality. Both the ax-wielder and the subject know where each stands. The abrupt dismissal technique has many variations.

1 / Send the subject a telegram on Saturday morning notifying him that he has been discharged and that his final check (containing a severance cushion) will be hand-delivered to his home within twenty-four hours. By appointment, if suitably escorted, he may visit the plant to pick up his personal effects any time during the upcoming week.

2 / The company places a blind box ad in the help-wanted section of the local newspaper exactly describing the subject's qualifications. To be sure he does not miss it, another executive points it out to the subject. When the subject sends in a resume, he is called into the boss's office and finds his boss in a towering rage. The subject is berated for his patent disloyalty and fired on the spot. Before the stunned victim can come back to his senses, the boss calls the security office and tells them that the subject has been fired. The security men place locks on all the files in the victim's office. As a subvariation, the subject is confronted with one or more errors he has committed (and who has not made an error from time to time?), and the boss works himself up into a frenzy and fires the man.

3 / Lacking the courage or stamina to do the nasty job himself, the boss takes a short business trip and has a management consultant do it for him while the boss is away. The victim is called on the telephone by the hatchet man, and when he comes to the victim's premises, he breaks the bad news in as friendly and gentle a manner as his considerable experience allows. As part of the task, the consultant may give on-the-spot employment counselling or offer to assist the subject find a new job. If the victim calls his boss for an explanation, he is told that the boss is away for a week or so and cannot be reached.

4 / The executive's employment agreement with the firm has a fixed term. Both parties have the obligation to notify the other of their intention to seek a renewal of the agreement at least six months before the expiration date. The company allows the deadline to pass without renewing. When the subject asks their intention, he is advised that the company does not intend to renew.

5 / A press release is placed with a friendly newspaper editor containing the announcement that _____ has joined the company as _____, as of the following Monday. As it happens, the position filled by the fortunate fellow mentioned in the news item is the position currently held by the subject. If there is any chance that the subject may fail to see the item, someone is assigned the task of pointing it out to him.

6 / While the subject is away on his annual vacation, he is sent a telegram telling him that a recent reorganization of the firm has eliminated his job and that he is not expected to return to his office at the end of his vacation.

7 / Relatively rare is the case where the dismissal takes place in two stages: first an abrupt notice, then a request for the subject to continue work until a replacement is found.

8 / As one condition of employment, the executive is required to sign several copies of an undated letter of resignation. One day he receives one of the letters with the current date filled in.

9 / The executive is informed that through the working of intracompany politics, the son of one of the directors (or one of the top executives) has been selected to fill his position. Everyone is sorry, but they are helpless to stop it. No, there is not any other place in the firm just now, so it is the end of the road for him with that company.

10 / It is very mysterious, but a telephone call from corporate headquarters contains the firm order that this man be terminated forthwith. No one has any idea what could have happened to provoke such action. Perhaps at one time or another, the subject may have done something to annoy the top man. Sorry, but there is nothing we can do; orders are orders.

THE FREEZE-OUT.   The purpose of the freeze-out technique is to force the unwanted executive to submit his resignation. He may be isolated, humiliated, transferred, or otherwise indirectly, with varying degrees of subtlety, notified that the company would like him to leave. Some variations of the freeze-out technique are

1 / The victim is relieved of his regular duties and given a fancy-sounding staff title, but his assistants and secretaries are taken away from him. His new quarters are somewhere in a backwater or inaccessible location. If he has any correspondence, he uses the typing pool. Meanwhile, it becomes common knowledge throughout the organization that anyone consorting with the pariah will be deemed disloyal to the company. Sharing rides, lunch, or coffee breaks with him are all taboo.

2 / The company causes a notice to appear in the press that contains an announcement that the subject is retiring, or moving to another company (plans withheld at his request). The date and location of the farewell party is announced. The victim, of course, discovers that he is leaving the company by reading about it in the press.

3 / The subject is offered a transfer to a new location in the company equivalent of Siberia, with full knowledge that he cannot possibly accept because of personal or family commitments. He is told that the alternative to accepting the transfer is to resign.

4 / Although the new position carries a lofty-sounding title, it is known throughout the company and the industry that by accepting the new job, the subject is actually being demoted in rank and stature. To accept transfer to this "doghouse" job is tacit acceptance that his career is in eclipse. Rather than accept the demotion, the subject resigns.

HELPING STRATAGEMS.   Because the company has no desire to harm the redundant executive and it wishes to retain his good will, it may try to find him a satisfactory substitute to his present position, but, of course, outside of the company.

1 / An executive placement firm is retained, without the subject's knowledge, to find him a new job. The consultant finds a willing employer and contacts the subject to persuade him to accept the new position.

2 / The company has decided to change its sales operation from salaried salesmen to manufacturer's representatives. It offers several of its displaced sales executives first call on exclusive territories.

3 / The company has some small sidelines or peripheral operations that could be profitable if properly managed, but which are not receiving enough attention. The redundant executive is offered the presidency of a spun-off subsidiary organized to further the promotion of the hitherto neglected items.

4 / The redundant executive is offered company help in setting himself up in his own business, perhaps in partnership with other managers about to be discharged. The business may involve some type of purchased service or supplies. The company may wish to participate in the new venture(s) by contributing equipment, placing guaranteed orders, or by making a financial investment.

5 / A large supplier of the company treats it as a house account or uses a salaried or commissioned salesman to service the account. The company requests that the supplier take on the discharged executive as their new account executive.

6 / The company has a considerable influence with its industry trade association and persuades the association's governing board to appoint the discharged executive as its operating head.

7 / Because it is a regular and generous contributor to the development fund of the local, private university's business school, the firm persuades the dean of the business school to offer the discharged executive a two-year appointment as adjunct professor of business administration.

8 / The company helps the subject set himself up in a management consulting practice. It agrees to retain his services for an extended term.

9 / The company commissions the discharged executive to write a definitive history of the firm and agrees to purchase a substantial number of copies of the book, for which the author receives generous royalty income.

10 / The company retains a firm that specializes in out-placement services. They provide pre-termination counseling including: confidence rebuilding, vocational analysis, aid in setting up workable marketing strategies, aid in resumé preparation, videotaped rehearsals of employment interviews, and periodic reassurance.

An Important Caveat

Not only must the company think of the effect on the persons being discharged, but it must also be concerned with the morale of the surviving executives. When a firing takes place, each executive watches the event with mixed feelings because he knows that someday it may happen to him. If the company treats the redundant executive with cruelty, humiliates him, or needlessly damages his career potential, this callousness will be noted and remembered. The survivors can be expected to develop defensive strategies intended to protect themselves from similar actions by the company, should their time come. If the situation is bad enough, a large part of an executive's time can be spent in action nonproductive for the company, but protective to the careers of the executive employees. Thus, a schism develops between the long-run goals of the firm and the personal goals of its executives, a fragmentation of interests that can prove very damaging to both.

No matter how shocking or distressing it may be at the time it happens to him, every executive knows that being fired from his job is always possible and often justified from the company's viewpoint. Therefore, it is not the *fact* of the firing that leaves festering sores on both the discharged and surviving executives, but the manner in which it is done. If the unpleasant task is performed with professional skill and aplomb, the manner in which the act itself is carried out will cause no lasting damage. But if the act is done with cruelty, malice, unnecessary stealth, or gross clumsiness, these characteristics will be impressed upon the minds of the discharged persons and the survivors, and the company's image and reputation can be tainted for years to come. The almost universal mistrust that many Americans feel toward big business originates, in part, from callous treatment individuals receive from thoughtless business leaders.

A NONUNION STAFF CURTAILMENT PROCEDURE

Who Goes? Who Stays?

When a major staff curtailment must be carried out (e.g., from 1000 down to 400 employees), the number of employees who remain on the payroll (400) and the number who are severed from the payroll (600) is the same whether or not the employees are represented by a trade union. The presence of a labor-management agreement, in such cases, influences *only* the basis for selecting the persons to be let go or retained and not the numbers in each category.

Virtually every union contract mandates seniority, either companywide, plantwide, or by classification, as the sole and overriding criterion for establishing who leaves and who remains. Management's judgments of the relative worths of each retained or discharged employee's services are totally irrelevant. What counts above all is the hiring order.

Thus, the decision problem for management in the layoff or permanent separation of union personnel is simple. Place the employees names in rank order of hiring date and cut from the bottom of the list. Of course, there will usually be a few disputes about the rankings, because there is always some ambiguity even in so simple a ranking scale. But the unions have rules for resolving such disputes and once resolved, the cutting procedure is trivially simple. Not so with nonunion staff. Here a rational procedure that reflects management's valuation judgments is called for.

A Staff Curtailment Procedure

The following procedure, shown in flow-chart form in Fig. 4-1 can be used for classifying employees into two categories: *retain* and *terminate*. There are two assumptions: (1) There are more people than jobs, and (2) there are no new jobs and, therefore, for every job there is now a person on the payroll who can fill it competently.

1 / Establish the number of jobs that will remain after the staff curtailment is finished and prepare a list of those jobs.

2 / On paper, assign every employee now on the payroll to one or more of the jobs. Some jobs will have only one name; others will have several. Some names will be matched to only one job; some to several jobs. There should be no unassigned jobs or names.

3 / Examine the assignments to see if there is any job with only one name assigned to it. If so, place that person's name on the *retain* list. Repeat until there are no jobs with only one name. Remove those jobs and names from the lists.

4 / For each remaining job, rank the names according to the multiple-criteria evaluation procedure described below.

5 / For any two or more jobs, is the same name at the top of the ranking? If so give that person his first choice of job. Put his name on the *retain* list. Remove the name and the job from the list and the rankings. Repeat for other multijob firsts.

6 / Assign the top-ranking name to the job and place the name on the retain list. Repeat until there are no unassigned jobs.

7 / Place the names not assigned by the foregoing procedure on the TO BE TERMINATED list.

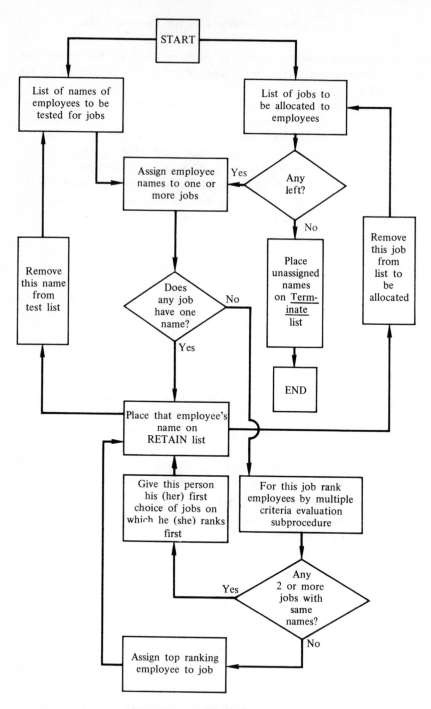

FIGURE 4-1. Flow chart of a staff curtailment procedure.

In a large staff curtailment, it is possible that new jobs are created by combining old ones. If such be the case, and none of the employees currently on the payroll are qualified to fill those jobs, then the jobs should be removed from the list and the procedure carried out to fill the unchanged jobs. The new jobs can be filled later by conventional personnel search procedures.

Multiple Criteria Evaluation Subprocedure

When there are two or more qualified candidates for a particular job, it is necessary to devise a procedure that can identify the best candidate from the firm's point of view. Any single criterion can be used, but a better method is to use a form of multiple criteria reasoning, because such a method will give a choice more responsive to the needs of the firm. Also, a formal procedure will help remove the effects of bias, hatreds, prejudices, and other irrelevant influences:

A list of criteria suited for this purpose follows:

1 / Level of competence and experience in job.

2 / Payroll cost (salary, fringes, severance pay, if terminated).

3 / Employment record (absenteeism, merit ratings, etc.).

4 / Debt of loyalty owed to employee by firm.

5 / Value of employee to direct competitors.

6 / Effect on morale of retained employees if this person is terminated.

7 / Estimate of future value of this employee to firm.

8 / Effect on external community if this employee is dropped.

9 / Place of employee on age, sex, and racial make-up of employees retained and about to be terminated.

10 / Hardship to employee if terminated.

11 / Promises made by firm to employee.

12 / Veteran's status of employee.

13 / Legal considerations, Fair Employment Act, etc.

14 / Special considerations, physically handicapped, etc.

Some of the foregoing criteria can be used for doing a course screening and others for a quality-point computation. Although it may seem to be a lot of work to perform a multiple criteria test on hundreds or thousands of employees, the task can be assigned to a computer and done in a matter of hours. Details of a procedure for performing the rankings are shown in Chapter 9.

STAFF CURTAILMENT IN A UNIONIZED FIRM

Union and Management Attitudes

In spite of a long history of trade unionism in the United States, many executives still harbor unrealistic notions about the attitudes of unionized employees and their union leaderships. Management's personnel logic aims at promoting the efficiency and productivity of the firm by motivation of individuals. Appeals, incentives, rewards, and punishments are all geared to those two ends.

Trade union logic, in contrast, is aimed at advancing the welfare of the workers as a group and toward minimizing the human cost of management's policies. Unions are concerned with economic gains, job security, industrial democracy, reduction of management's dictatorial power over the workers, and not with profits for the stockholders.

Management views the unions' aims and actions as counterproductive and impractical, and as a deliberate attempt to erode management's right to manage.

Trade unions hold that management treats the workers as interchangeable parts to be cast off when worn out or no longer needed. The unions believe that they must be vigilant in protecting their members against management's predilection toward deception and double-dealing.

No doubt, in theory, the union can be viewed as a third party in the employee-union-company triangle, but the executives of the firm will never reap any benefits from trying to provoke or exploit divisions between the union and its members, or between factions within the union. Here and there may be an isolated, maverick employee who places his loyalty to the company above his loyalty to his union, but the manager who misinterprets these rare instances as being representative is deceiving himself.

The commonest result of instability within a union or of an insecure union leadership is an escalation of the demands on the company. Factions and contenders for leadership positions vie with each other in their promises of economic benefits for their members that only the company can redeem at high cost.

Somehow the conflicting aims of unions and management must be reconciled. Compromise is more easily achieved in the euphoric atmosphere of positive growth, but negative growth presents unparalled difficulties in the path of peaceful collaboration as all parties scramble for shares in a decreasing pool of benefits.

Rather than use the shock of negative growth as a union-busting opportunity, the astute management will cast aside this temptation and will try to enlist the union's cooperation in effecting an orderly contraction. If this means taking actions that appear to strengthen the union, so be it, because a secure union leadership will usually be easier to work with. A hostile, uncompromising relationship can cause the firm to enter the ever-descending spiral from which it may never emerge.

The Seniority Provision

The cornerstone of the trade union movement's drive for job security and equity for its members is the seniority provision of the collective bargaining agreement. This concept is held in such high regard that for many persons it stands with the Ten Commandments. As a matter of general principle, the order of layoff or permanent separation is determined by order of seniority. But the principle standing by itself is not precise enough, because there are many different ways for assigning seniority to employees.

SENIORITY BY CLASSIFICATION: OCCUPATIONAL.   Persons in a skill category, usually a hard-to-learn craft or semi-profession (i.e., plumber, electrician, tool and die maker, carpenter, etc.) are granted seniority rank in order of their date of hire by the firm. This kind of seniority is not transferable across craft boundaries. A plumber cannot be asked to do the work of a carpenter. In the event of a contraction, it is quite possible for a carpenter hired January 15, 1965 to be laid off while a plumber hired on January 15, 1972 is retained.

SENIORITY BY CLASSIFICATION: LABOR GRADE.   Persons in skill categories that are accretions of skills learned in lower-level jobs are granted two types of seniority: within the skill category and across a set of skill categories. For example, a small office has these job classes: clerk, typist, stenographer, secretary, administrative assistant. The higher-level person can always be expected to be able to do the work of the lower-level job, but not vice versa.

When a person joins the office staff as a novice clerk, his seniority clock begins to run; one hand for office employment and a second hand for clerking. As he gains skill and experience, he moves up to typist. The office hand continues running, but he starts from the bottom of the typist seniority ranking. This process continues as the employee is promoted up the hierarchy. Each position involves a new, in-step seniority along with the place on the office employee seniority list.

If it becomes necessary to reduce the number of persons in a high-level position, the lowest seniority incumbents are reduced in rank. They displace (bump) lower-seniority individuals in the next lower rank, until the required number of persons remain. The largest number of terminations take place in the lowest ranks among the employees with the least office seniority.

DIVISIONAL, DEPARTMENT, OR PLANTWIDE SENIORITY. This form of seniority applies to all members of the designated unit regardless of skills or type of work. Implicit in the arrangement is the notion that employees are interchangeable parts and that every person can do everyone else's job. In the event of a layoff, people are cut in reverse order of seniority.

In some companies, plantwide seniority is combined with seniority by classification: labor grade, so that a layoff requires demotions in rank and bumping.

SYSTEM- OR COMPANYWIDE SENIORITY. If the company has a single location, company- or systemwide seniority is equivalent to plantwide seniority. But if the firm has multiple locations, companywide applies across *all* locations. Thus a staff curtailment involves extensive bumping and intercity employee relocations.

SPECIAL CONDITIONS FOR TEMPORARY LAYOFFS. If it is known that the reduction in the work force is of short duration, many agreements allow for relaxation of seniority rules to reduce the immense costs and dislocations caused by bumping, relearning rusty skills, changing places of work, long travel to places of work, etc. But if the cutback is known to be permanent, stringent application of seniority rules is required.

SEVERANCE PAY. Employees who are to be permanently separated are usually granted severance pay in proportion to their length of service. An employee who is displaced from his job by bumping and does not wish to accept the new position has the option of accepting severance pay in exchange for surrendering his job and the seniority rights it entails.

OTHER CONDITIONS AFFECTING SENIORITY RIGHTS.   If there are any differential benefits not equally available to all employees in the bargaining unit, such benefits are allocated in accordance with seniority. For example, if limited overtime is offered, high-seniority employees have first call. If one job is better in one respect than another similar job, the higher-seniority employee may bid for the better job.

If an employee surrenders his union membership to become a foreman (or other nonunion job), and he is discharged from that position, many agreements require that his full seniority and former job rights be restored. This is to prevent the company from promoting a troublesome employee out of the bargaining unit and then firing him.

Shop stewards, as long as they hold that position, are assigned super-seniority as protection. If they leave the stewardship, in many contracts, they return to their former seniority rank, except for the additional seniority accrued during the stewardship.

Periods of nonemployment (e.g., leaves, military service, maternity leaves, long illnesses, layoffs, etc.) may or may not be included in computing seniority, depending on the conditions in the specific agreement.

WAYS AN EMPLOYEE CAN LOSE SENIORITY.   As defined and limited by the terms of the collective bargaining agreement, employees may lose their seniority rights:

1 / By voluntary resignation.

2 / By discharge for just cause.

3 / By failure to come to work without adequate notice.

4 / By failure to report for work after an authorized leave.

5 / By failure to report for work after recall from layoff.

6 / After accepting severance pay.

7 / If the length of the layoff interval exceeds the employee's accumulated seniority before the date of layoff.

An example of provisions dealing with seniority, severance pay is shown in Exhibits A and B (adapted from materials created by Prof. Lawrence Stessin).

SENIORITY PROVISIONS OF A COLLECTIVE BARGAINING AGREEMENT

Seniority

Section 1.   Stewards, members of the Shop Committee and the officers of the Union shall head the seniority list while functioning as representatives of the employees.

Section 2.   Plantwide seniority shall prevail. The seniority rights of employees shall be determined from the last date of hire (time of ringing in and going to work).

Section 3.   In all layoffs and recalls, the seniority and ability of the employee to perform the work shall be the determining factors.

Section 4.   When the capability of the senior employee is disputed, a reasonable probationary period not to exceed fifteen (15) days will be granted when so requested by the Shop Committee for the sole purpose of demonstrating capability and knowledge of the job, provided that nothing in this paragraph shall be construed to indicate that a learning period will be granted.

Section 5.   New employees shall be on probation for a period of thirty (30) days and shall have no seniority rights for that period. The Union shall, however, represent such employees in grievance in matters. At the end of the thirty (30) days' probationary period the seniority of such new employees shall accrue retroactively from the first day of going to work.

Section 6.   When in the opinion of the Company, a decrease in business requires a reduction in the working force, probationary employees shall be laid off first. Thereafter, employees with least plantwide seniority will be laid off first.

Section 7.   Whenever possible, the Company shall furnish the Chairman of the Shop Committee at least two (2) days before all layoffs and recalls with a list of the employees affected. Whenever possible, any employee shall be given at least two (2) days notice before layoff.

Section 8.   All recalls will be made by first calling the oldest employees in point of seniority with the ability to perform the work available.

Section 9.   Employees being recalled to work after a layoff shall be notified by the Company by a registered letter or telegram (telegram to be followed by a confirming registered letter) sent to such employee's last known address on the Company's records. If such letter is not returned, and the employee fails to report to work within five (5) working days thereafter, such employee shall be considered to have quit his job and his name shall be removed from the seniority list, and such employee shall forfeit his seniority unless a valid excuse is given for his failure to report for work. Employees shall notify the Company of any change of address either by registered mail or in person and if in person, they shall be given a written acknowledgement by the Company.

Section 10.   When new jobs are created within the bargaining unit, promotions made, or vacancies occur, the employee with the greatest seniority shall be given the opportunity to fill such new job, promotion, or vacancy, if he so desires, providing he has the ability to perform the work. The Company shall post all new jobs, promotions, or vacancies on the Company bulletin boards. The employees who desire the job shall notify the Company and the Union of their willingness to do the work. The employee selected shall be the one with the greatest seniority where ability among candidates is approximately equal.

Section 11. The Company will provide the Chairman of the Shop Committee with a copy of the seniority list and keep him advised of all changes. A permanent seniority list of all employees, including those sick, on leave and laid off, will also be maintained.

Section 12.   Any employee promoted to a position outside of the bargaining unit, who is later deprived of his position and returned to regular work within the bargaining unit, shall have his name immediately restored to the plant seniority list with all accumulated seniority credited and he shall forthwith become and remain a member of the Union in good standing.

Section 13.   An employee shall lose his seniority if:

a.   He voluntarily quits.

b.   He is discharged for just cause.

c.   He fails to report for work for three (3) working days, without notifying the Company and without a valid excuse.

d.   He fails to report for work within three (3) days after his leave of absence expires, without a valid cause.

e.   He fails to return to work after a recall following a layoff within five (5) working days, without a valid excuse.

f.   He is laid off for a continuous period equal to the seniority he has acquired at the time of such layoff period.

EXHIBIT B
SEVERANCE PAY PROVISIONS OF A COLLECTIVE BARGAINING AGREEMENT

Severance Pay

Section 1.   Any employee who is laid off or whose employment with the Company is severed through no fault of his own shall receive a severance allowance. "No fault of his own" shall be construed to include:

a.   Technological changes (changes in layout, equipment, or processes) which cause a job to be permanently abolished.

b.   Merger, consolidation, or permanent shutdown of a department or plant.

c.   Layoff arising from the employee's being deemed incapable of meeting job requirements.

Section 2.   Any employee who has completed five (5) or more years of service with the Company who involuntarily resigns for personal reasons and who leaves the service of the Company in good standing shall be eligible for severance pay.

Section 3.   For an employee to be eligible for severance pay he shall have accumulated a minimum of one (1) year of continuous Company service. In lieu of serverance pay, the Company may offer an eligible employee a job, in at least the same pay class, in the same general locality. The employee shall have the option of either accepting such new employment or requesting his severance pay. If the employee returns at a later time to his original job classification, seniority accumulated in the interim job shall be credited to his overall seniority in his job classification.

Section 4.   Severance pay shall be computed as follows:

COMPANY SERVICE	WEEKS OF SEVERANCE ALLOWANCE
1 year but less than 2 years	2
2 years but less than 3 years	3
3 years but less than 4 years	4
4 years but less than 5 years	5
5 years but less than 6 years	6
6 years but less than 7 years	7
7 years but less than 8 years	8
8 years but less than 9 years	9

9 years but less than 10 years	10
10 years but less than 11 years	11
11 years but less than 12 years	12
12 years but less than 13 years	13
13 years but less than 14 years	14
14 years but less than 15 years	15
15 years or over	16

a. A week's severance allowance shall be equal to the employee's base wage for a forty-(40)-hour week less the maximum weekly state unemployment payment to which he is entitled.

b. Payments will be made weekly rather than in a lump sum. Weekly payments will be computed on basis specified above, regardless of any other employment in which the employee may engage.

c. The Company will mail to the employee at his last known address all payments due him in accordance with the above schedule.

Section 5. An employee who would otherwise have been terminated in accordance with the applicable provisions of this Agreement and under the circumstances specified in this article may, at such time, elect to be placed upon layoff status for eighty (80) days. At the end of such eighty (80) days' period he may elect to continue on layoff status for a period not to exceed eighty (80) days, or be terminated and receive severance allowances. The severance allowance will amount to full pay based on the base wage for a forty- (40) -hour week, less the maximum state unemployment compensation the employee was entitled to at the time of layoff.

Section 6. In the event of termination due to death of the employee, severance pay as specified above will be paid to the employee's next-of-kin or legal heir.

Section 7. The payment of all severance pay due an employee in accordance with the above provisions shall constitute termination of his status as an employee of the Company.

Section 8. The Company shall assist employees laid off for nondisciplinary reasons to obtain employment elsewhere by providing a current list of known appropriate available jobs.

Seniority in Mergers or Consolidations

When two plants or divisions that each have plantwide seniority are merged, the seniority rankings for the combined entity is decided upon by some form of treaty. Five alternative arrangements are

1 / Merge seniority lists by date of hire. For layoffs cut from the bottom of the merged list.

2 / Decide upon the number of employees to be retained, select half the number from each plant in order of their seniority in their plants.

3 / Decide upon the number of employees to be retained, and select equal percentages from each plant in order of their plantwide seniority to make up the desired number.

4 / Merge the two lists by rank; e.g., first from A, then first from B; second from A, second from B until the desired number is selected.

5 / Award one plant's workers superseniority. At the bottom of A's list, begin B's part of list in order of seniority (e.g., A has 500 names; B's first name is 501 on the combined list, B's second highest seniority, 502, etc.)

Management's Options

In the typical negative growth situation, management is faced with existing collective bargaining agreements that must be honored. These agreements were negotiated at a time when the company was prospering, when it was on the steep upward slope of its growth curve, when employment was rising. It is easy to make seemingly minor concessions to the union to keep peace, to avoid interruptions in production, and to agree to seniority provisions in the contract with the unions that cost the company very little but make the union happy.

Plantwide seniority and its extreme counterpart, system- or companywide seniority can be advantageous to management when the company is growing rapidly. On the average, plantwide seniority results in lower wage costs than other more rigid seniority systems. However, when it becomes necessary to make permanent staff reduction, plantwide, systemwide, or companywide seniority can have horrendous consequences. The disadvantages of this form of seniority are

1 / Rising average wage costs as work force shrinks in size.

2 / Extensive job transfers because of interminable bumping sequences.

3 / Transitional losses because frequent job changes require relearning. Waste and spoiled work are widespread.

4 / Substantial costs for relocation of staff and travel-time reimbursement.

Obviously, while the collective bargaining agreement is in force, its provisions must be honored. However, if before or during the implementation of a program of negative growth, the seniority provisions of the agreement can be renegotiated or the enforcement of the more restrictive and costly provisions can be compromised, worthwhile savings can be achieved. Companies who have a good working relationship with the unions in their plants, who have the reputation for fair dealing, and who do not take every opportunity to undermine the union leadership and the members' faith in their unions have a better chance of persuading the union leadership that the changes sought do not threaten their survival.

SELECTED REFERENCES

BEACH, DALE S., *Personnel: The Management of People at Work*, 2nd. ed. New York: The Macmillan Company, 1970.

CHRONBACK, LEE J. and GOLDINE C. GLESER, *Psychological Tests and Personnel Decisions*. Urbana, Ill.: University of Illinois Press, 1957.

The editors of *Fortune, The Executive Life*. New York: Doubleday and Company, 1956.

FINE, SIDNEY A., *An Introduction to Functional Job Analysis*. Kalamazoo, Mich.: W. E. Upjon Institute for Employment Research, 1971.

GINZBERG, ELI, et al., *The Unemployed*. New York: Harper and Row, 1943.

LISTON, ROBERT A., *The American Poor: A Report on Poverty in the United States*. New York: Delacorte Press, 1970.

SCHEER, WILBERT, *Personnel Director's Handbook*. New York: Dartnell Publications, 1970.

SEIDMAN, JOEL, et al., *The Worker Views His Union*. Chicago: The University of Chicago Press, 1958.

STRYKER, PERRIN, *The Men From The Boys*. New York: Harper and Brothers, 1960.

"The Unemployment Problem," *Factory* (July 1961), pp. 85–90.

Chapter 5

Selected
Managerial
Aspects

TERMINATING RESEARCH AND
DEVELOPMENT PROJECTS

The decision to discontinue one or more promising research and development (R & D) projects is devilishly difficult and painful because such projects carry the hopes for ultimate recovery and resumption of growth. An outstanding success is much like winning a multimillion-dollar lottery. It alters the outlook of the faltering firm and assures its early revitalization. Yet these projects are voracious consumers of scarce current resources so crucial to the immediate survival needs of the firm.

The termination decision is complicated by the perennial, well-intended, but self-serving hopefulness of the research and development people. Optimists at heart, they see success around every corner. They warn that cutting off a promising project at this late or critical stage, when success is so close at hand, is foolish and utterly wasteful. They say they are still ahead of groups in other companies, and any slowing of effort or reduction on support will cause them to fall behind in the race. Everything spent up to that time will be wasted if the competitors finish first.

But days stretch into weeks; weeks, into months; months, into years. The hoped-for successes and technological breakthroughs continue to elude the scientists. Just one more expensive item of equipment; just one more new avenue of exploration; just one more infusion of funds; just one more month. . . . How long can it be allowed to continue?

For nonscientist executives and corporate directors, the mysterious goings-on in the firm's R & D laboratories can be likened to gambling at a roulette table. Just one more spin of the wheel and the firm can recoup all of its losses. The stakes are continually raised so that a winning number can erase all former losses. But before long, the funds available for both gambling and essential life needs are depleted.

ACCOUNTING TREATMENT OF R & D OUTLAYS. The accounting treatment of R & D expenditures in financial statements and annual reports to shareholders can be a major factor in the project discontinuance decision process. Some firms capitalize research outlays that will pay off in future years. Such treatment makes good sense, because it is unreasonable to burden current operations with items that have a much delayed payoff. Others treat R & D outlays as current expenses, because they represent a systematic and continual renewal of wasting technology.

Depending upon the accounting treatment, project termination can have quite different balance-sheet and income-statement consequences. If R & D outlays have been and continue to be recorded as current expense, cutting those outlays have a salutory effect on reported earnings, in the short run at least. If R & D has been capitalized, cancellation and abandonment of a project requires that all accumulated charges be written off in a short time. The result is lower reported earnings at a time when bad financial news can cause maximum harm to the prospects of the firm.

PAST R & D OUTLAYS ARE SUNK COSTS. The two choices, continuation or abandonment of questionable projects, involve future events and, consequently, the decision should be forward-, not backward-looking. Past R & D outlays are best treated as sunk costs, irrelevant for decision-making purposes. What counts is simply this:

1 / What will the company be like if the projects are continued as before?

2 / What will the company be like (in the short, intermediate, and long term) if support is stopped?

If analysis reveals that the company will be better off if support of the borderline projects is discontinued, then prompt termination or cutting back is obligatory.

CHECKLIST.   The following checklist of questions ought to be helpful in arriving at answers to the foregoing questions:

1 / If the project is ever successful, what would be its contribution to the company's goals as they are now formulated?

2 / Are the goals of the project feasible, considering the constraints of time, funding, manpower, and state-of-the-art?

3 / Are present manpower resources spread too thin?

4 / Will termination release badly needed funds or other resources better applied elsewhere?

5 / Has the leading figure in the project been lost to it?

6 / Are fresh ideas running out and the project personnel merely marking time, making work for each other, and shifting their attention to job security?

7 / Are the project personnel spending a substantial part of their working day on personal projects, outside consulting, or other noncompany activities?

8 / Have the main objectives been achieved in outside laboratories? Are they soon likely to be achieved elsewhere?

9 / If the goals of the project continue to be worthwhile, would it be better to farm out the work, or somehow transfer, sell, or exchange the current knowhow to an outside organization (e.g., a university facility, a nonprofit research organization, etc.)?

10 / What would be the effect on the morale of the remaining R & D personnel? On stockholders and security analysts of the effects of discontinuing specific projects?

CLOSING THE INEFFICIENT PLANT

From time to time newspapers and the television news report the closing of a neighborhood factory and the hardship caused to terminated employees and the local, small, retail firms. The company's action in shutting down seems inexplicable and heartless. Readers and viewers are left with the impressions that the decision to discontinue the plant's operation was capricious, totally selfish, without any compelling rationale, unjustified, and wholly unexpected. When questioned about their firm's motives, official spokesmen give the standard answer that the plant is inefficient and no longer competitive. Actually, of course, the decision to close comes as the climax of a long sequence of events, surprising to no one with adequate knowledge of the true causes, and probably inevitable if the parent firm is to survive as a viable entity. Why do firms close plants and shift operations to other locations? What makes one plant inefficient and another not inefficient?

A Plant Out of Control

The overall productivity of this plant is much lower than other comparable operations. Employees have bad work habits and hostile attitudes toward the company. They slough off during regular hours so that they will be required to work overtime at premium pay. Restrictive work rules require two to three men on a job where one would be enough. (For example, to repair one inoperative air conditioner, a plumber, an electrician, a laborer and two helpers stand around waiting for each man to do his fraction of the job when it could be done by one man in a half day.) Rules require that a full-time electrician be on the payroll to turn the power on in the morning and off at night. If the plant works Saturdays and Sundays or extra shifts, the underutilized electricians must be paid double time.

Work limitation is the rule. Any attempt to increase the rate of output is resisted as a "dehumanizing speedup." Quality of output is poor. The inspectors belong to the same union as the operatives and are reluctant to report bad work. In-process troubleshooters and repairmen earn premium wages and have a vested interest in a steady flow of rejections to keep their ranks swelling.

Absenteeism and lateness are very high. Employees punch in each other's time cards so that their fellow workers will not be docked for being absent or late. Workers gather behind piles of cartons in the storage area to play cards, gamble, place bets on horse races, engage in sexual liaisons, drink liquor, sell narcotics, engage in horseplay. Attempts to enforce discipline on errant employees are met with slowdowns, damaged work, sabotage, misdirected shipments, and other dilatory tactics.

Supervisors who try to be strict in applying the work rules and in issuing warnings to employees who violate company regulations are threatened with physical violence. Several foremen have been waylaid on their way home and beaten up unmercifully. Foremen are afraid to say a harsh word to any worker for fear of reprisals against themselves or their families.

The management is convinced that this plant is totally out of control and that the only solution is to shut it down as soon as possible and to transfer operations to another location far away from this one.

Large-Scale Dishonesty and Pilferage

The general manager of this plant is discharged for flagrant dishonesty. He is found using company employees and company-owned materials for building a large addition to his personal residence. Furthermore, he is found to be soliciting and accepting bribes from suppliers and contractors in the form of cash, merchandise, and services.

The general manager's offenses are well-known throughout the plant and offices. In fact, he is the subject of both envy and jokes. There is a tacit understanding that every salaried and hourly employee is entitled to his little racket so long as he does not get too greedy, obvious, or careless.

Secretaries take home stationery and supplies. Employees deliberately damage merchandise so that it can be sold to them as "seconds" at drastically reduced prices. Salable items are regularly pilfered from stock rooms and show rooms. Bribes are solicited and received from suppliers. Salesmen receive kickbacks from customers for unrecorded overshipments, free samples, and falsified credit allowances. Stock clerks ship merchandise to their own homes for later resale. Shipping clerks enter into collusion with truckers and place extra items into shipments which the driver resells; he then splits the proceeds with the shipping clerk.

Maintenance department employees steal hand tools and expensive maintenance supplies, including such items as copper wire, plumbing fittings, solder, building insulation, electrical fittings, etc. Porters run a little sideline selling company's paper towels and toilet paper at cut prices. Middle-level executives use company-owned automobiles for personal vacation and weekend travel and charge the gasoline, oil, and repair costs to their company credit cards. Foremen and truck drivers fill their gas tanks (and those of their friends and neighbors, too, at a big discount) from company gasoline supplies.

Middle managers and salesmen submit falsified and inflated expense vouchers substantiated by forged receipts. Everyone has his little extra-income source. Employees who are too honest or fearful to engage in these practices are either forced to keep silent or are driven out of the company.

As time goes by, each employee becomes acclimated to whatever level of extra, nontaxable income he has been able to extract from the company. Since every person likes to improve himself (and maybe save a little), he seeks systematically to expand his scope and increase the size of his take.

Meanwhile, back at corporate headquarters, the controller fumes helplessly at the outrageous costs in this plant. Hiring a new general manager has a temporarily beneficial effect as the employees and supervisory personnel size up the new man. If he, too, can be corrupted, they will try every way they can think of to do so. If he is not corruptable, they will attempt to intimidate him into looking the other way as they resume their not-so-little "fiddles" and sidelines. If they are unsuccessful in taming the new general manager and he cracks down by either arresting or dismissing the culprits, the employees must find another way to maintain their standards of living. At the next collective bargaining negotiation, they present the management with unexpectedly large demands for wage increases, restrictive work rules, and more generous fringe benefits. No matter which way the situation evolves, the division has earned the sobriquet, "inefficient plant."

Noncompetitive Wage Rates

This plant has operated in a northeastern city for over twenty-five years, and many of its employees have spent their entire working lives there. At peak, factory employment exceeded 2000 men and women, but at present the roster contains only 1000 names. When employment was at its highest, the average hourly wage rate for factory people was about $3.75. Now, because only high-seniority people are left (average seniority is 15 years) the rate has risen to $6.00 per hour plus fringes of 30 percent of payroll costs.

Thus, the average wage bill (including cost of fringe benefits) for this plant is

$$\underset{\text{employees}}{1000} \times \underset{\text{per hour}}{\$6.00} \times \underset{\text{fringes}}{1.30} \times \underset{\text{hr/wk}}{40} \times \underset{\text{wk/yr}}{50} = \underset{\text{per year}}{\$15,600,000}$$

A wage-cost survey of other cities in which the firm has manufacturing facilities indicates that an equivalent operation could be set up in a southeastern city with an average hourly wage rate of about $3.00 with a fringe benefit cost of 20 percent of payroll cost.

To relocate the plant would cost an estimated $2,600,000 for moving, hiring, training, and startup costs. Since the union contract calls for one week severance pay for every year of employment, the severance pay bill would amount to

$$\frac{1{,}000}{\text{employees}} \times \frac{15}{\text{yr}} \times \frac{\$6.00}{\text{per hr}} \times \frac{40}{\text{hr/wk}} = \$3{,}600{,}000$$

Recapitulating the costs and estimated savings, we have

Annual payroll costs in present location	$15,600,000
Est. annual payroll cost in new location	7,200,000
First-year saving in payroll costs	$ 8,400,000
Less severance pay	(3,600,000)
Less relocation costs	(2,600,000)
First-year saving from move	$ 2,200,000
Second-year savings	$ 8,400,000
(assuming that wage rates rise same percentages in each location)	

Clearly, if the indicated savings could be realized from a relocation of this 25-year-old plant, the existing plant is properly characterized as "inefficient."

Other Reasons Why Plants Lose Their Economic Viability

Each plant dies in its own way. Items:

— Because of a systematic and persistent migration of the working-age population, it becomes impossible to find enough skilled people to continue efficient operations.

— Because of an increasing average age of the population of the city in which the plant is located and the large number of parochial schools, budgets for public education are regularly defeated. The plant's executives cannot find adequate schools for their children. Rather than carry the burden of paying for private-school education, the executives agitate for relocation of the facility.

— The trade unions in the plant cannot control the workers. There are too many wildcat strikes, slowdowns, work limitation arrangements. Quality and output are unreliable. Orders are delayed and customers return a high percentage of the plant's products as defective.

— The layout of the plant, multiple floors, freight elevators, crowded and inadequate parking and off-street loading and unloading facilities make efficient operation impossible.

— The neighborhood in which the plant is located has become a dangerous slum. There are numerous burglaries; employees are attacked on their way to work; female employees refuse to work there any longer.

— Public utilities have been experiencing increased demand for water, gas, electricity, and live steam but have been unable to construct additional capacity because of the vociferous opposition of homeowners and environmentalists. The plant experiences more and more service interruptions.

— Business is booming, and a substantial expansion of the plant is required. No expansion space is available, and the city is unwilling to condemn the land adjacent to the factory because of opposition from local homeowners.

— Real estate taxes, fire and casualty insurance rates have risen to exorbitant levels. Because of a rash of fires, the fire insurance carrier has notified the plant management that it will not renew. A serious flood hazard exists because of a construction program that has permanently altered the grading of the surrounding land.

— Because of a year-by-year drop in the underlying water table, the land on which the plant is located is sinking. The walls are showing large cracks and the foundation seems to be deteriorating, requiring expensive shoring up and eventual rebuilding.

PROPOSITIONS ABOUT POSITIVE AND NEGATIVE GROWTH

Specialization and Despecialization

As the firm grows in size, more and more of its functions are fractionated and specialized. For example, as the firm grows from a very small to a larger size, its one-girl bookkeeping department is replaced by a six-girl group consisting of: head bookkeeper, accounts receivable, accounts payable, cash sales, cash disbursements, and purchases clerks. As the firm's business grows, the one accounts receivable position is split into several alphabetic groups (accounts receivable, A–D; E–G;

H–K; etc.). When very small, that same firm had a one-man personnel department, too. Ultimately, along with the firm's growth, this department expands to contain such specialized job titles as: Employee Benefits Manager, Personnel Researcher, Labor Relations Manager, Manager of Personnel Records, Wage and Salary Administrator, etc.

As the firm shrinks in size, most of the functions performed when it was larger still remain to be done, but they are combined and recombined into fewer and fewer positions. Large size involves narrow but deep specialization; small size, broad versatility. *Reduction in the size of a firm inevitably demands despecialization of the work force.* Where employees have been hired or retrained for a narrow specialty, and they are to be retained throughout the contraction, either formal or on-the-job retraining is necessary to adjust to the lesser degree of specialization demanded by the combined functions.

Periodic Reexamination of Ongoing Functions

As the organization goes through stages in negative growth, it is wise to conduct periodic reexaminations of the worth of the contributions of each of the functions being performed. Perhaps that function can be dispensed with altogether. Or maybe it can be combined with another for savings. Is it possible that the services performed by the function can be purchased from outside vendors at lower cost for comparable quality?

The flow chart in Fig. 5-1 shows the underlying logic for a periodic reexamination of ongoing functions during a negative-growth program. The procedure starts with an identification of the specific function to be evaluated. The first question is, *Is it still needed?* If not, the function is discontinued. Although the question may seem overly obvious, it is quite possible that a function is being carried along, no longer needed, but no one ever bothers to ask why.

If still needed, we ask, *Can it be combined with another function?* If yes, it is combined and any savings that can be are realized. If not, we ask whether the service can profitably be procured from outside vendors. If so, arrangements are made for buying it, and the staff so released is either transferred or discharged. If not, we accept the fact that the function continues to be essential to the proper operation of the smaller-sized entity.

Services can often be purchased from outside vendors who specialize in rendering the particular service rapidly and efficiently at

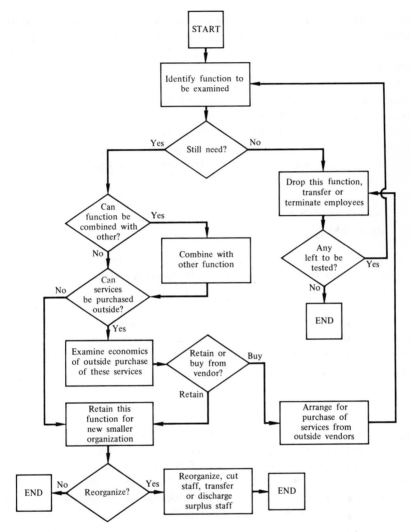

FIGURE 5-1.   The underlying logic of a procedure for periodic reexamination of existing functions.

reasonable cost. If the demand for the particular service fluctuates, there
is no cost to the company during the intervals when it is not required.
This is in contrast to the salaried, in-house service department that must
be retained on the payroll during slack periods and must either be transferred to other work for which they may not be fully qualified, or
assigned nonessential "make-work" projects. Many managers have dis-

covered that an underloaded department quickly develops the ability to look very busy in spite of the fact that there is very little to do.

When the services are not available from an outside vendor in the desired quantity and quality, an alternative to hiring permanent staff is to use a temporary staffing agency. These people provide temporary employees, often much more competent than is available in the labor market, as substitutes for vacationing or sick employees. They can supply skilled staff for short-term and intermediate-term projects. Temporary agencies are useful for filling peak demand without the need for additional hiring, and for operating nonrepeating activities.

Bringing Back Frugality as a Way of Life

The talent for self-deception is widely distributed throughout the population, and businessmen have their proportionate share. Applied to a negative-growth situation, self-deception and wishful thinking take the form of an almost blind faith that better days must soon return. All we need do is hunker down and wait. Like the overaged southern belle of fiction, ensconced in her crumbling mansion surrounded by reminders of her former splendor, the executive practicing self-deception waits for hard times to go away. Of course, it is not impossible that his firm's luck will change for the better with time. But, a wiser, more prudent, more reality-oriented course is to act on the assumption that hard times are here to stay and to adopt programs that will enable the firm to prosper with a reduced level of visible ostentation.

Accepting the contraction as permanent does not preclude a resumption of growth. Is it not a fact that the firm, once much smaller, did experience healthful and vigorous growth? But it did not grow overburdened with the remnants of former splendors. It probably grew in a hard, lean and hungry state. That is the condition that must be recaptured.

A number of steps, practical and strongly symbolic, can be taken to restore a forward-looking frugality.

1 / Eliminate frills and perquisites, even if it is more expensive to remove them than to keep them. Appearances count, and the appearance of self-indulgence can undermine efforts to return the firm's employees to the Spartan frame of mind so necessary for successful negative growth. The firm's top executives should set a good example of frugality.

2 / Simplify paperwork and administrative procedures. Reduce the numbers of copies made of memoranda and reports. Remember that every copy requires someone to read it, file it, and clutter his mind with its contents.

3 / Reduce the floor space so that everybody is close together again. There is nothing more depressing and backward-looking than large empty spaces and unoccupied desks. The temptation to put people back to work at the vacated desks is too hard to resist for long. Create obstacles to additional hiring; limited space is one kind of obstacle.

4 / Get surplus equipment out of sight. The work load can easily expand to fill the underutilized equipment without contributing anything worthwhile to the productivity of the enterprise.

5 / Work hard at the appearance and actuality of achieving the habit of frugality. It may come hard to the formerly affluent, but it is an easy habit to forget if it ever becomes necessary to return to ostentation as a way of life. Create conditions in which both the temptation and opportunity to do things the expensive way are reduced or eliminated altogether. Keep records of the savings made by increased frugality and give nonmonetary rewards (praise, recognition, etc.) for people who show progress in that direction.

Avoiding Loss of Customers
When Salesmen Leave the Firm

Who owns the customer, the company or the salesman? If the company owns the customer, losing a salesman is no more costly than losing any other competent employee. However, if the salesman owns the customer, the loss of a key man can prove very, very, expensive.

In some lines of business, the relationship between a salesman and his customers is so close that the customer follows the salesman to whatever company he works for. For example, in the stock-brokerage business, when a registered representative moves from one firm to another, most of his customers switch their accounts to the new firm. A similar situation exists in the job-printing industry. It is not unusual for a job-printing house to make substantial additions to their sales volume by hiring away a competitor's salesman who takes his accounts along with him when he moves. In fact, printing salesmen are known to trade their extensive customer followings for partnerships in job-printing firms badly in need of sales.

If the salesman can take his customers with him when he leaves his employing firm, in effect he owns those customers. If when he leaves a firm the customers remain loyal to that firm, then the firm owns the customer. When the company organizes its sales effort in a way that fails to cement customer loyalty to itself, it remains vulnerable to sudden loss of sales if one or more key salesmen are lured away by competitors or if the salesmen have the urge to go into business for themselves.

When customers are salesman-owned, the task of keeping them happy and loyal to their employers is likely to prove expensive. Such salesmen enjoy above average earnings and use their bargaining power to full advantage. The result for the firm is a relatively high cost for personal selling and a continuing vulnerability to a sudden loss of customers to competitors.

The situation can be quite different for the firm that directs its sales management effort toward earning and retaining customer loyalty for itself. To do so involves a much greater degree of involvement between the firm and all levels of purchasing influence in the buying firm's organization. Instead of using the salesman as the sole point of contact between the firm and its customer, the salesman's role is changed to that of an easily replaceable account executive who calls on the troops from the home office to support his sales effort.

The firm establishes friendly and regular contact with the customer on all levels of purchasing influence. For example, for a marketer of industrial goods, e.g., electronics components, these levels would be involved:

1 / The buyer whose name is on the purchase order.

2 / The director of purchasing.

3 / The specifying engineers.

4 / The quality control manager.

5 / The production manager.

6 / The general manager of the operation.

7 / The corporate controller.

8 / The customer service manager.

By establishing good relations on all these levels of influence, the selling company becomes much less vulnerable to the loss of any one employee, and the customer is much less likely to desert the selling firm as a source of supply just because one of the salesmen changes jobs.

SELECTED REFERENCES

CHINITZ, BENJAMIN and RAYMOND VERNON, "Changing Factors in Industrial Location," *Harvard Business Review,* Vol. XXXVIII (Jan–Feb 1960), pp. 126–136.

CLELAND, DAVID and WILLIAM R. KING, *Systems Analysis and Project Management,* 2nd ed. New York: McGraw Hill Book Co., 1970.

DALEY, ROBERT, ed., *How America's Employees are Stealing Their Companies Blind.* New York: Harper Magazine Press, 1970.

GREENHUT, MELVIN, *Plant Location in Theory and Practice.* Chapel Hill, N.C.: University of North Carolina Press, 1956.

HARRINGTON, ALAN, *Life in the Crystal Palace.* New York: Alfred A. Knopf, 1959.

HEMPHILL, CHARLES F., *Security for Business and Industry.* Homewood, Ill.: Dow Jones–Irwin, 1971.

MINTZBERG, HENRY, *The Nature of Managerial Work.* New York: Harper and Row, Publishers, 1973.

NOVICK, DAVID, "What Do We Mean By Research and Development?" *California Management Review,* Vol. 11 (Spring 1960).

STESSIN, LAWRENCE, *The Disloyal Employee.* New York: Man and Manager, Inc., 1967.

Chapter 6

Selected
Organizational
Aspects

DIVESTITURE STRATEGIES

A Jaundiced View
of the Soaring Sixties

In the decade of the 1960's the American business and financial community became possessed by a collective insanity that manifested itself in a wild, mindless wave of ill-conceived mergers and acquisitions. Executives of small, medium, and large firms found themselves captivated and stupefied by a "captain of industry" complex.

The collective madness was fueled by a congeries of factors including:

1 / Industrywide acceptance of employee stock options as a major part of the executive compensation package. The favored tax treatment

of profits realized with these generous option plans made it possible for a twenty-thousand-dollar-a-year man to become a millionaire in less than two years.

2 / The acceptance by the financial and investment community of "poolings of interests" accounting, which enabled a high price-to-earnings company to purchase a low price-to-earnings firm and to report higher earnings per share as a result of the consolidation. It was the financial equivalent of changing a sow's ear into a silk purse. By acquiring plain-Jane companies with undistinguished earnings prospects, the merged combination, through the flim-flam called synergism, was transformed into a higher price-to-earnings glamour girl.

3 / Favored treatment by Internal Revenue of interest on convertible debentures compared with cash dividends on common and preferred stock.

4 / The uncritical acceptance by the sophisticates in the investment community of the Steadman formula, which established price-to-earnings ratios for common stocks by capitalizing projected rates of growth in earnings per share. There resulted a phenomenon called *Supermoney* (so called by Adam Smith, pseudonym of Jerry Goodman of *Fortune* magazine) by which a dollar of earnings is magnified many times over in the market price of the company's shares.

5 / Questionable practices by mutual fund managers to give their funds the appearance of rapid growth in asset value per share. Examples were the purchase of "letter stock" at a large discount, but the stock being carried at market value in the prospectus; a sheeplike rushing to buy shares of a few favored companies which, in a self-fulfilling prophecy, soared to unheard-of heights. It was not without reason that these fund managers were called the "gunslingers of Wall Street."

6 / A general cynicism and lack of integrity among members of the financial community who were willing to play along with the unsound practices because to fail to go along would cause them to be branded as "old fashioned, fuddy-duddys." Many were goaded into ill-advised action by the then-current wisdom of the Street that "no one over thirty can make money in this market." Trading in grossly inflated equities was laughed off with the quip, "They're for buying and selling, not for eating."

During this decade there was a tremendous wave of mergers and acquisitions. Small companies gobbled up large ones, using highly questionable convertible debentures as coin. Large firms absorbed small ones; many well-established firms were swallowed up, either willingly or through successful raiding tactics. The conglomerate form of organization, a heterogeneous collection of unrelated corporations, became the model to be emulated.

Like all overinflated investment bubbles of the past, this, too, burst. From the end of the sixties until the mid-seventies a new wave swept over American industry, a wave of sober sanity, resulting in countless overt and covert divestitures and disacquisitions. As early as 1971, the *Wall Street Journal* (Oct. 26, 1971) noted that 80 percent of the companies responding to its survey questionnaire indicated that they were considering at least one divestiture.

Of course, not all divestitures are the result of ill-conceived mergers or acquisitions. Some come about because of changes in the economic outlook for a segment of the business. Others result from governmental action, from lagging profitability of a division, from the availability of a superior investment opportunity for limited resources, from the unwillingness of a controlling group to spread itself too thin over too many enterprises, or from an unwillingness to commit large amounts of money to an enterprise of unknown potential.

Why Potential Customers Are Interested in Acquiring the Entity

A divestiture will be most successful and will result in the smallest loss to the selling firm if a willing, eager, financially capable buyer can be found. A number of reasons why buyers might be interested in acquiring the about-to-be divested entity follow:

1 / Employees offer to buy the entity in an attempt to save their jobs.

2 / Divisional management personnel arrange a buyout so that they can be in their own business.

3 / Former owners would like to regain ownership of the entity they sold off earlier.

4 / A competitor would like to add products to his line; to add to his market penetration; to obtain the services of scarce, skilled personnel; to obtain secret knowhow; or to obtain additional productive capacity at bargain prices.

5 / A customer wants to assure a steady source of supply, which may be threatened if the entity goes out of business.

6 / A supplier wants to assure continued demand for his output, which may disappear if the entity ceases operations.

7 / A company with excess capacity in its factory or sales department would like to incorporate the entity's products with its own.

8 / An investment group wants to buy the entity with the intention of holding it until a more propitious time arrives for making a public offering, or it intends to combine this entity with others it owns for a subsequent public offering.

9 / A company with a narrow, specialized line of business wishes to diversify without the delay and expense of trying to penetrate an unknown market.

Methods of Accomplishing a Divestiture

The methods listed below are based on the assumption that the segment to be disposed of is an autonomous subsidiary corporation. If it is an unincorporated division, many of the methods will not be applicable. These are some of the better-known ways to effect a disacquisition of an unwanted segment of the firm:

1 / Liquidation: sell off inventories, and tangible and intangible assets; discharge or transfer employees; pay off all liabilities; distribute residual cash to shareholders; file notice of dissolution with proper authorities.

2 / Same as 1 above, except that residual cash is retained along with the intact corporate shell. Funds are reinvested in income-producing investments.

3 / Same as 1 or 2 above, but tangible and intangible assets are sold off as a going business to a buyer who intends to continue the operation. Employees transfer to the buying firm.

4 / Shares of the subsidiary are sold to a buyer for cash or other consideration. Buying group may consist of former employees or former managers.

5 / Shares are offered at a fair and attractive price to the parent firm's shareholders on a prorata basis. Unsold shares are sold in a public or private offering.

6 / Shares of the unwanted subsidiary are hypothecated as collateral for a loan from a bank, a lending institution, or to a private investment group. The loan is in default and the collateral forfeited in satisfaction of the unpaid loan amount.

7 / Shares are given to the parent firm's shareholders on a prorata basis as a stock dividend. Subsidiary becomes an independent, publicly owned entity.

8 / A part of the undesired subsidiary's common stock is sold in a public offering, and the parent retains either a majority or a minority interest.

9 / The subsidiary is merged with another company and an entirely new corporate entity formed. The selling firm receives a proportionate share of the common stock of the new corporation, which the parent can dispose of as it sees fit in time.

Methods of Payment for the Divested Entity

There are as many payment plans possible as there are people to dream them up. A few are listed below.

1 / Full cash payment upon closing of title to 100 percent of the shares of the entity.

2 / Partial cash on passing of title plus serial notes.

3 / Partial cash plus serial notes plus contingency adjustment (upward or downward) based upon sales and earnings of the divested entity.

4 / If the entity is merged into another, a combination of cash, notes, convertible debentures, and common or preferred stock in the new entity.

5 / Shares of the buying firm as full payment.

6 / An outright exchange with cash to boot (from either party) of another piece of property for the divested entity.

7 / Sale of shares with installment payments; voting rights to be retained by seller until a specified proportion of selling price is paid (e.g., 60 percent).

Because the tax treatment of the alternative methods of payment is so varied and so dependent on IRS interpretations, advice of a competent tax counsel must be obtained before any final sales agreement is made.

REVIEWING THE MANAGERIAL SPAN
OF CONTROL

The span of control (synonyms: span of management, span of supervision, span of responsibility) refers to the number of subordinates under the aegis of a given supervisor or manager. The so-called span of control problem is important because a wrong choice of span can harm the efficiency of an organization. With too few supervisors, productivity falls and smoothness of operation falters; with too many, supervisory costs are unnecessarily high.

The data in Table 6-1 illustrate the organizational consequences of various spans of control, applied uniformly to all supervisory levels. The

TABLE 6-1
SPANS OF CONTROL *

SPAN OF CONTROL	NUMBER OF SUPERVISORS IN THIS LEVEL †						TOTAL NUMBER
	1	2	3	4	5	6	
5	2000	400	80	16	3	1	2499
6	1667	278	46	8	1	0	2000
7	1429	204	29	4	1	0	1667
8	1250	156	20	3	1	0	1430
9	1111	124	14	2	1	0	1252
10	1000	100	10	1	0	0	1111
11	909	83	8	1	0	0	1001
12	833	69	6	1	0	0	909
13	769	59	5	1	0	0	834
14	714	51	4	1	0	0	770
15	667	45	3	1	0	0	716
16	625	39	3	1	0	0	668
17	588	35	2	1	0	0	626
18	556	31	2	1	0	0	590
19	526	28	2	1	0	0	556
20	500	25	1	0	0	0	526

* In a plant of 10,000 operatives, the number of supervisory jobs, the number of levels of supervision, and the numbers at each level for spans of control from 15 to 20 workers per foreman.
† Rounded.

table shows the number of supervisory positions and the number of levels in a supervisor hierarchy in an organization having 10,000 workers (not including supervisors and support personnel). In a plant of this size, a span of five employees per foreman requires 2000 first-level foremen, 400 second-level supervisors, 80 third-level managers, 16 fourth-level managers, 3 fifth-level managers and one sixth-level executive. In contrast to the foregoing vast army of supervisory and managerial personnel, a span of 20 requires only 500 first-level foremen, 25 second-level supervisors, and one top-level executive. Obviously, in view of the payroll costs of supervision only, the choice of a specific number for a span of control can have momentous financial consequences.

What Is the Right Number?

Trying to find the right number for the span of control is like trying to add a column of 10,000 six-digit numbers by hand. You know that there is one right answer, but every time you add the column you get a different answer. There undoubtedly is a right number for the span of control, but to this date no one has been able to figure out how to arrive at that magic number.

Some organizations use spans as large as 100; others use spans as small as five. The spans at the upper levels of management tend to be smaller than those found at lower levels. Moreover, the nature of the work is different at higher and lower levels, and it changes from day to day. At this stage in the development of the theory and practice of organization design, the best one can do is to develop a set of guidelines for managers to follow in trying to decide how many workers per supervisor. The table below contains field research results of a study of 100 companies (E. Dale, American Management Association).

NUMBER OF EXECUTIVES REPORTING TO THE PRESIDENT OF THE FIRM	NUMBER OF FIRMS REPORTING THIS NUMBER
1–4	10
5–8	35
9–12	31
13–16	18
17–20	2
21–24	4

Analysis of the Supervisor's Job

Any study of the typical supervisor's job reveals that a substantial portion of his working day is spent on nonsupervisory work. (By supervisory work is meant direct, face-to-face interaction with subordinates, although this may also include talking on the telephone and written correspondence.) For example, an hour-by-hour observation of a group of factory foremen reveals the following kinds of activities:

1 / Face-to-face interactions with subordinates.

2 / Report-writing, time-keeping, paper work, answering the telephone.

3 / Planning and scheduling upcoming work assignments.

4 / Attending committee meetings.

5 / Interaction with his superiors.

6 / Interaction with his fellow foremen.

7 / Handling grievances with union representatives.

8 / Coping with emergencies, repairs, stockouts, breakdowns, absenteeism, lateness, sickness, accidents, power failures, tool breakages, etc.

9 / Personal time, fatigue, men's room, personal calls, idle time.

Of these nine classes of activity, only the first, seventh, and eighth vary directly with the number of subordinates in the typical supervisor's span of control.

It should be noted that the supervisor, too, is a member of a work group. He and his peers interact among themselves and with their common superior, and these two items cause a drain of mental and physical energy.

To make a first stab in answering the "how many" question, it is necessary to discover what portion of the foreman's workday is available for direct supervision of subordinates. Is it 10 percent, 20 percent, 50 percent, 80 percent? If it should happen to be as little as 50 percent, whatever the theoretically correct span might be, clearly it would have to be adjusted downward to take into account the reduced time available for direct supervision of employees.

An important inference from the foregoing reasoning is: *A foreman can handle more subordinates if he can devote more of his working day to direct supervision, and less to nonsupervisory activities.* And a direct corrolary: *Whatever is the optimum span of control, it must be adjusted downward as the foreman is given more nonsupervisory work to do.*

As the size of the firm increases and there are more layers in the managerial hierarchy, the demands for adequate communication and control produce a growing proliferation of paperwork, conferences, committee meetings, etc. Thus, size, in itself, creates conditions conducive to a shrinking of the span of control and to further enlarging the number of layers of supervision. By similar reasoning, as the size of the organization decreases, the communication and control pathways grow shorter, and the need for extensive paperwork, meetings, and impersonal control procedures lessens. Consequently, the nonsupervisory load on the foremen can be reduced and his span of control enlarged.

Content of the Face-to-Face Activity

The direct supervisory activity of the typical foreman contains various mixtures of the following elements:

1 / Instructing and coaching.

2 / Mediating disputes between workers.

3 / Pacifying irate members of the work force.

4 / Conversing with workers.

5 / Listening to workers' grievances and complaints.

6 /   Disciplining workers for minor infractions.

7 / Inspecting work and work methods.

8 / Interviewing and orienting newcomers.

9 / Counselling workers.

Researchers who have made systematic observations of the behavior of work groups suggest that the interactions of the workers among themselves, between the individual worker and the foreman, and among subgroups, factions, and temporary coalitions vis-a-vis the supervisor, all combine to take up disproportionate segments of the foreman's time. A foreman who supervises ten workers all of whom interact hourly will be busier with the ten, than would be a sales manager who supervises 20 field salesmen who report in person once a week. Thus, the span of control must be reduced if there is a tightly packed work group, and it can be increased substantially, if the workers rarely ever interact among themselves.

Poor work habits, lateness, absenteeism, excessive turnover all make greater demands of the supervisor's time and mental energy. A firm with a poorer record on these factors must allow for a smaller span of control than would a firm with a better performance record. A high level of tension, petty squabbling, uneasiness, high noise levels, bad weather, etc., all of which tend to disturb the tranquility of the workplace, diminish the foreman's ability to cope with a larger span of control. With greater stability and tranquility, the span of control can be increased.

The Line-Staff Tradeoff

Relieving the supervisor of his nonsupervisory work load can be accomplished in two ways: (1) by redesigning the workflow and administrative procedures to lower the nonproductive work or (2) by providing the foreman with staff help. The latter, however, involves additions to the payroll for assistants to the foreman.

Increasing the number of staff aides to foremen, depending upon the nonsupervisory workload, of course, allows the span of control to be increased, and this increase allows the number of layers in the managerial hierarchy to be lowered. The higher payroll cost for assistants is offset by savings in the numbers of supervisors required and in greater overall efficiency brought about by the flatter organization form. For example, in Table 6-1, if the original span of control is seven, there is a total of 1667 supervisory positions, 238 of which are above the first level. If by giving each foreman a full-time assistant, the span of control is doubled, there is a total of 770 supervisory jobs, 56 of which are above the first level. Thus there would be 770 supervisors and 770 assistants for a total of 1540 positions, as compared with 1667 positions in the earlier condition, a net saving of 127 positions. Moreover, assistants earn less than the foremen, and lower-level supervisors, less than upper-level men; there, too, is a substantial saving in payroll costs. If it should happen that the foreman's span of control can be increased with the addition of a part-time assistant, then the savings could be even greater.

Firms that use the assistant-to-the-supervisor alternative may find that the arrangement has two additional benefits:

1 / The assistant-to position provides an excellent training place for the incumbent, either for the actual supervisor's position or for other administrative assignments in the firm. For firms that have a regular management-trainee program, the assistant-to rank can be a valuable adjunct.

2 / With the larger number of supervisory positions (but the smaller number of levels being retained) the firm is in a better position to continue some of its essential operations during a strike. This freedom is especially important for public service firms, sole-source

suppliers, and firms whose customers depend on them for uninterrupted supply. The reduced vulnerability to disastrous interruptions from a work stoppage is the equivalent to bringing an extra increment of bargaining power to the labor-management negotiation. In the long run, skillful management negotiators can translate the extra bargaining power into x cents a hour in savings either in the hourly rates or in fringe-benefit costs. Such savings, if indeed they are actually achieved, can help offset any additional cost of supervision brought about by the extra staff positions.

ALTERNATIVE ARRANGEMENTS
FOR SERVICE DEPARTMENTS

The RST Scientific Instrument Corporation is engaged in the design, development, manufacture, and marketing of a broad line of proprietary and custom-made scientific measuring and testing instruments that it sells to the full spectrum of American industry and to the Department of Defense. The largest part of the company is its engineering division, which consists of the following departments:

1 / Instrument and measurement, research and development.
2 / Product development, proprietary.
3 / Manufacturing methods, jigs, tools, and fixtures.
4 / Factory maintenence and repair.
5 / Customer service and repairs.
6 / Military products and testing equipments.
7 / Special products, custom designs.
8 / Short-order and sample-instrument department.
9 / Mechanical engineering, engineering physics.
10 / Trade-show displays, traveling exhibit design.

Each department is headed by a chief engineer, and each is organized, equipped, and operated, as much as possible, as an autonomous profit center. An elaborate system of intrafirm pricing allows each department to act as if it were in business for itself.

From the time it was first organized in 1940, RST has enjoyed continuous growth that has paralleled the growth of the various branches of the electronics industry. There have been intervals of expansion, especially before and during the World War II, the Korean War, and the war in Vietnam. In addition, the rapid development of the United States' space and missile programs has contributed to the further expansion of the company.

In the economic recession of 1973 to 1976, RST's sales slacken, and for the first time, it has five successive calendar quarters in which it reports declines in sales and large losses. As a result of the poor performance, the board of directors requests the resignation of its president. As a face-saving measure, he is appointed vice-chairman of the board, a sinecure with very little direct responsibility for day-to-day operations.

As a second step, the board requests the new chief executive to retain a prominent consulting firm for the purpose of reviewing the organization of the engineering division with the aim of raising its efficiency and reducing its bloated costs. The consultants begin a top-to-bottom review of the division and after three months of intensive study, put out their preliminary report on one phase of the operation.

The report contains the following observations:

1 / Every department maintains a large and well-equipped model and machine shop.

2 / Each machine shop is equipped to meet the peak demand expected by that department.

3 / Each shop employs skilled machinists and model-makers.

4 / The average machine utilization rate, on a year-round basis, is less than 10 percent.

Considering the tremendous investment in fixed assets, the amount of time the machines are idle, and the low utilization of the highly skilled and highly paid machinists and model-makers, the consultants express an opinion that here is a good place to start restructuring the organization. They note that similar conditions exist in the drafting service area. Here, too, there is underutilization of skilled drafting and mechanical design facilities, primarily because every department manager insists on being self-sufficient and the work load fluctuates widely over the year.

The consultants offer the following options on how the machine and model-shop functions should be restructured:

1 / Do nothing, leave things as they are.

2 / With the exception of a few hand-operated tools for simple jobs, remove all heavy, expensive equipment from the departments, sell it off at auction, and require that the departments buy parts from outside vendors. Each department will have its own engineering buyer, who will develop good outside vendors.

3 / With the exception of a few hand-operated tools for simple jobs, remove all heavy, expensive machinery from the departments and establish a new engineering machine and model shop as a centralized service department to serve all departments. Sell off surplus equipment.

4 / Same as (3), but set up the centralized department as a subsidiary and grant it the right to solicit business from other customers. Require the internal departments to use the new centralized facility.

5 / Same as (4), but grant the other departments the right either to go outside to vendors of their own choice or to use the new centralized facility.

Alternative 1 is unacceptable because of the tremendous waste and underutilization of expensive facilities.

Alternative 2 has the advantage of one's being able to know just what every part made on the outside costs, but has the disadvantage of introducing the rigidities of the procurement cycle and the delays associated with outside procurement.

Alternative 3 has the advantage of cutting out underutilization of machinery and highly paid manpower, but it leaves the departmental executives to the tender mercies of the new shop manager. He now has the power to favor one department over another, and this power is an anathema to the department heads.

Alternative 4 has the advantage of allowing the shop manager to improve his scheduling and of obtaining extra income for the company from outside sales during slack periods. It has the disadvantage of distracting the shop manager from his central mission, that is, servicing the departments. If he is given a profit incentive on the outside work, he may very well give his outside customers preference in delivery and service.

Alternative 5 has the advantage of redressing some of the power the shop manager has over the department managers. Since the latter are able to by-pass the company-owned centralized shop in favor of buying from outside vendors, an element of competition is introduced that the managers believe will make the shop manager less arrogant and more attentive to their complaints.

ORGANIZATIONAL CLIMATE

What Happens in a Layoff?

An organization that goes through a rapid retrenchment and a substantial staff curtailment moves through several easily recognized stages.

STAGE 1.   Things are bad and seem to be getting worse. Everyone knows or fears that something unpleasant is about to happen, but no one knows exactly what it will be. There is widespread fear, anxiety, and foreboding. Cassandras takes center stage and the Panglossians are subdued. Most employees, although worried, go about their routines. A few of the more highly mobile employees have thoughts about bringing their resumés up to date. They also look at the help-wanted ads with greater interest.

The grapevine is active, but no highly credible information flows through its labyrinthian pathways. The most popular game is trying to read the expressions on the faces of supervisors and middle and top managers. Many employees try to pump the executives' secretaries, but they, too, are still in the dark.

STAGE 2.   A decision for a major cutback is taken in executive session, but participants are cautioned to keep all plans secret until the entire plan is worked out. In a matter of hours, the grapevine carries the news and anxiety reaches new highs. People stand around in clusters speculating about what will happen and who will be affected. Managers are grim-faced and uncommunicative, but the frequency and accuracy of the leaks through the executives' secretaries grow apace. Very little work is being done and what is, is full of errors. People with psychosomatic ailments take sick leave and absenteeism rises. The more mobile employees mail out their updated resumés, call their friends in other companies, and visit employment agencies. Employees shout at their spouses and order them to curtail the family's discretionary spending.

Interdepartmental rivalries become much more intense as groups snipe at each other in an effort to have others bear the brunt of any curtailments. Managers become noticeably less cheerful and outgoing; they circulate throughout their domains less. They become less accessible to their subordinates.

STAGE 3.   The axe falls. Although everyone feared it would happen and the cut is not wholly unexpected, it is still a great shock. People walk around, faces pale, lips pressed tightly together, staring ahead, avoiding the eyes of their colleagues. Women sit at their desks crying quietly and slowly putting their personal belongings into shopping bags. A few people can be seen gesticulating wildly and heard shouting in sudden outbursts of emotion.

The survivors commiserate with the persons given notice, and the survivors look at each other with apparent guilt and relief, but visibly saddened by the imminent departure of their associates. No one at all is working. Managers are unavailable, locked up somewhere in conference. No one really knows which supervisor will go, too, and which will remain. Security guards stand around quietly, but quite visible, to step in if any one becomes hysterical or does anything violent to another employee or to company property. A few people arrange to meet outside the office for a farewell drink, but few want to join them.

STAGE 4.   Empty desks and offices are there for all to see. An air of funereal gloom permeates the office. Surviving supervisors circulate, trying to be cheerful and reassuring everyone that the worst is over. Pep meetings are held to reinforce the survivors' self-esteem and feelings of security. New work and space asignments are made and employees attack their new tasks with vigor. Gradually surplus furniture is removed and empty offices are closed or reassigned. New pictures are hung, and personal effects redistributed.

STAGE 5.   The interval of grief and depression is over. People go back to their old or new routines. The departed are nearly forgotten. The only mention of them is a more and more open discussion of their mistakes. Morale is high, and managers assure everyone that they are the chosen people, held in the highest esteem by the firm. If a former employee returns for a visit, he or she is greeted politely, but with barely concealed embarrassment. People excuse themselves and hurry away. *The change has been absorbed.*

Reduced Opportunities
for Advancement

Everyone knows that it is more prestigious to be a player on a pennant-winning baseball team than to hold the same position on a cellar club. In like manner, more prestige accrues to the employees in a more successful, rapidly growing firm, than in a firm with declining prospects.

This loss of prestige and the reduction in opportunity for advancement associated with the negative-growth climate mean that the more mobile employees, whose services are in greater demand outside the firm, contemplate leaving. A certain percentage of the employees with highly marketable skills find better-paying jobs and jobs with better opportunity for advancement. Left behind are the less venturesome, less secure people with less-marketable skills.

If this trend continues unabated, the company finds itself left with the lease venturesome, least skilled people, a portion of whom will be mere time-servers, on-the-job retirees, who wait patiently for their pensions, afraid to rock the boat for fear that they, too, will be singled out in the next staff reduction. Keeping a low profile is their strategy.

There is no doubt that such a change in the composition of the management and work force can have a profound effect on the behavior of the firm. Firms once vibrant, aggressive, forward-looking, quick to react, vigorous competitors lose these youthful qualities. In their place are such attributes as conservatism, excessive caution, risk aversion, slow response, backward looking, and other evidences of encroaching organizational senility.

The loss of vitality of the firm eventually, through a subtle self-selection process, produces a reinforcement of senile attributes. As a result, the firm finds itself enmeshed in an ever-descending spiral with slow, cumulative attrition, resulting ultimately in its demise.

Forewarned of such depressing possibilities, the managers of a negative-growth program will make a conscious effort to preserve favorable opportunities for the remaining staff, to retain the best people, and not to allow the organization to suffer deterioration because of neglect. Staff reduction by attrition, although less stressful for the executive in command, invariably causes the loss of the best people. That should not be allowed to happen if the organization is ever to recover and to be ready for resumption of growth after the period of retrenchment is over.

SELECTED REFERENCES

GELLERMAN, SAUL W., "The Corporate Personality," *The Management Review*, Vol. 48, part 1 (1959).

KITCHING, JOHN, "Why Do Mergers Miscarry?" *Harvard Business Review*, Vol. 45 (Nov.–Dec. 1967), pp. 84–101.

KOONTZ, HAROLD and CYRIL O'DONNELL, *Principles of Management*, 4th ed. New York: McGraw Hill Book Co., 1968.

LOVEJOY, FREDERICK A., *Divestment for Profit.* New York: Financial Executives Research Foundation, 1971.

MISHKIN, W. S., *Corporate Spin-offs, Shell Corporations and Selling and Divesting.* New York: Hawthorne Books, Inc. 1972.

NIERENBERG, G. I., *The Art of Negotiating.* New York: Cornerstone Library, 1971.

SARTAN, AARON Q. and WESLEY A. BAKER, *The Supervisor and His Job.* New York: McGraw Hill Book Co., 1965.

SCHARF, CHARLES A., *Asquisitions, Mergers, Sales and Takeovers: A Handbook With Forms.* Englewood Cliffs, N.J.: Prentice-Hall, Inc., 1971.

STRANGE, M., ed., *Acquisition and Merger Negotiating Strategy.* New York: Hawthorne Books, Inc. 1971.

Chapter 7

Liquidity and Financial Stringency *

LIQUIDITY DEFINED

The flow of funds that takes place in a going concern can be likened to the flow of liquid in a hydraulic system that consists of a central storage tank and pipes that conduct fluid to and from the tank. This hydraulic analogy is diagrammed in Fig. 7-1(a). The fluid (funds) runs out of the storage tank in a combination of steady and intermittent outflows. If the fluid is not replaced, the tank soon runs dry. There are also pipes that

---

* Several of the procedures and techniques mentioned in this chapter involve complex legal, tax, and accounting issues. Depending upon the specific set of facts and the laws of the jurisdiction in which the firm operates, a suggested method may or may not be feasible and lawful. Before one embarks on a particular course of action, it is prudent, perhaps mandatory, to seek competent and expert legal, tax, and accounting counsel.

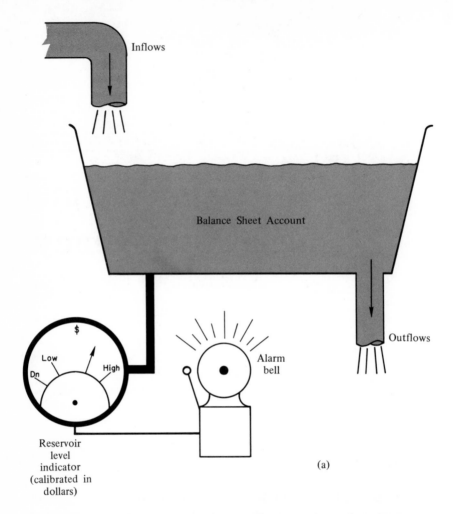

FIGURE 7-1(a).   The reservoir analogy to the cash balance sheet account. Inflows and outflows occur and affect the level in the reservoir. The measuring instrument indicates the height of the fluid in the reservoir and is calibrated in dollars. An alarm bell rings if the fluid level is too high or if the storage tank is running dry.

bring fluid into the reservoir. Some of the entering fluid comes from a recirculation; some comes from sources outside the system.

Also shown in Fig. 7-1(a) are a metering device and an alarm. If the fluid level is too high, too low, or if the tank is dry, a warning bell rings, and some form of remedial action is called for.

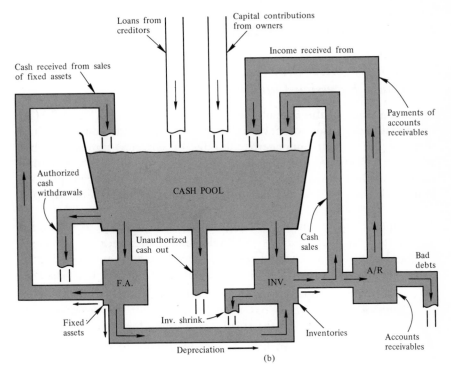

FIGURE 7-1(b). The hydraulic model of flow of funds through the firm.

Somewhat more detail is shown in Fig. 7-1(b). Funds entering the reservoir are labeled: capital contributions from owners, loans from creditors, income from cash sales, cash received from sales of fixed assets, and income received from payments of accounts receivables. Outgoing funds are labeled: funds used for purchase of fixed assets, funds used for acquisition of inventories, funds used for authorized withdrawals (e.g., dividends, debt service, taxes, etc.). Also shown are three kinds of unauthorized outflows; unauthorized cash withdrawals, bad debts, and inventory shrinkage.

Reasoning from the hydraulic analogy, we see that liquidity refers to the adequacy of the funds level in the storage tank (cash account). If the level fluctuates and periodically the tank runs dry, or if it is actually empty, the company is suffering from insufficient liquidity. On the other hand, when the fluid level is too high in relation to the cash needs of the firm, the company has excessive liquidity. Both conditions are undesirable, but in different ways. Insufficient liquidity is life-threatening. Excessive liquidity is not, but it can have some unwanted effects.

COPING WITH EXCESSIVE LIQUIDITY

How Negative Growth Can Cause Excessive Liquidity

As a study of the flow of funds models in Figs. 7-1(a) and 7-1(b) reveals, liquidity rises whenever cash inflows exceed cash outflows. In a negative-growth situation nearly all rates of flow are diminished, but when the inflow rates exceed the outflow rates, the funds in the cash and cash equivalent accounts rise. Many special conditions can produce liquidity increases while the firm undergoes a retrenchment. For example:

- Alpha Corporation goes through a partial liquidation. It sells off a part of its plant, reduces production rates, cuts back on purchases and inventory levels, and reduces employment. While reducing its scale of operation, it remains profitable and its cash balances rise.

- A shrinking company owns considerable real property which it no longer uses but which has risen in value over the years because of inflation. It sells off the surplus real estate for cash.

- A vertically integrated firm decides to dispose of its raw material fabrication and components assembly plants and confine itself to sales of private-label merchandise. The proceeds of the sale produce large cash balances.

- Beta Corporation owns and operates over five thousand leased departments in large discount houses and department stores. Its management decides to sell off half of its leased departments to its employee managers. A large finance company arranges for the financing and Beta finds itself cash rich.

- The shrinking firm has a patent on a valuable invention, but because of the ill health of its chief executive and the unwillingness of his oldest son to enter the business, the owner decides to sell off the rights. He receives a large cash payment plus a guaranteed royalty for at least ten years.

- Because of a war emergency, the machinery and equipment lying idle suddenly rise in value far beyond their value to the owners. The firm sells off this equipment.

- Because of the death of one of the company's founders, this privately owned firm decides to sell off the division formerly managed by the deceased executive. Because it is very profitable, it brings an excellent price.

— Delta Corporation has been cutting back operations and reinvesting released cash in commodity contracts. A prolonged strike in a producing country causes a worldwide shortage and a spectacular price rise. Delta Corporation has a windfall profit on its contracts.

— Zeta Company is in a steep decline because its top executives have been drawing very large salaries. When Zeta defaults on its bank loans, the bank puts its own man in as president. The new chief executive fires the old managers and sues them for damages. They agree to settle for a large sum. Without the load of executive salaries plus the cash settlement, the profitability rises and cash flow increases substantially until the company has a large cash surplus.

— RST Corporation has been shrinking in size because of declining profitability and reduction in working capital. They need an infusion of capital but have been unable to interest private investors. Because of a sudden upsurge in the Dow Jones Industrial Average and a wave of speculative fever, a small underwriter agrees to sell RST shares to the public. They issue 200,000 shares at $7.50 per share, and the issue is snapped up overnight. The proceeds to RST are over $1,250,000, about three times their former net worth.

Dangers and Temptations Inherent in Excess Liquidity

Although having too much cash is infinitely more pleasant than having too little, excessive liquidity has its dangers and temptations that are detrimental to the well-being of the firm. A number of reasons are illustrated by the following cases.

ATTRACTION TO CORPORATE RAIDERS.   Gamma Corporation is a publicly owned firm whose executives and directors own only 15 percent of the outstanding common stock. Because the stock market is in a deep slump, Gamma's shares sell at less than book value per share. Gamma sells off a profitable division and finds itself very cash rich. When the annual report is released and distributed to shareholders and security analysts, an investment group known to be corporate raiders makes a tender offer to Gamma's shareholders that Gamma's directors believe to be much below its true value. Because of the excessive liquidity, Gamma becomes a prime target for cash-hungry corporate raiders.

LOW RATE OF RETURN ON TOTAL ASSETS.   Theta Corporation has large cash balances that it prudently keeps invested in low-yield treasury securities. Although Theta earns a good return on its operating assets, the aggregate return on investment is degraded by the earnings dilution by low-yield treasuries. The Dow Jones Industrial Index shows a steady rise, but Theta's shares fail to participate in the general rise.

SECTIONS 531–37 PENALTIES.   Sections 531–37 of the Internal Revenue Code provide for stiff penalties for unreasonable accumulation of earning for the purpose of avoiding income taxation of shareholders' dividends. Theta Corporation hoards its cash and pays little or no dividends and finds itself threatened with the Sections 531–37 penalties (up to $100,000, 27½ percent; over $100,000, 38½ percent).

INVITATION TO ADVENTURE.   The devil finds works for idle hands and for idle funds, too. Because of the low earnings potential of safe, liquid, marketable investments, Theta Corporation's management finds itself under pressure to put idle funds to work. As a result of such pressures, Theta's management becomes receptive to all kinds of harebrained and marginal investment proposals that it would have found unacceptable under more normal conditions.

TEMPTATION FOR PROFLIGACY.   Theta's executives and directors are overcome by a general feeling of affluence and prosperity because of the large, unused cash balances. They vote each other generous expense allowances and company-paid junkets, and other extravagances grow increasingly frequent. Lost completely is the lean and hard frugality that contributed so heavily to Theta's growth and successes of earlier years.

Using ROI Computations To Avoid Imprudent Investments

The fact that a firm has generous cash balances does not lessen the need for rigid financial discipline. Investment proposals should be given the same close scrutiny and be subject to the same critical standards whether funds are plentiful or scarce.

A set of techniques widely used by financial analysts involves the computation of investment quality, setting a minimum standard of acceptance, and then ranking the surviving proposals by investment merit. Although the actual details of the computations are performed by specialists, usually with the aid of a high-speed computer, each manager should have good familiarity with the logic underlying return-on-investment (ROI) analysis.

The ROI method is a way of comparing cash inflows and outflows (the time value of money being taken into account) for pairs of alternatives, e.g.:

1 / Make no changes versus Adopt a proposed investment.

2 / Adopt project A versus Adopt project B.

3 / Make no change versus Drop project C.

4 / Adopt project D versus Drop project E.

After estimating the inflows and outflows and discounting them all back to the same instant of time (usually the time the project begins), the internal rate of return is computed. When multiple investment alternatives are being evaluated, only projects that have rates of return equal to or exceeding the minimum standard are given further consideration. The others are rejected. Because projects have inflows and outflows over an extended time horizon, and the estimated values are subject to forecasting error and other kinds of risks, some allowances must be made for risk and uncertainty factors.

Return-on-investment methods are by no means infallible, because the future flows are subject to many imponderables. However, using the method does allow for dispassionate appraisals of project merit free from the inevitable distractions of departmental politics, favoritism, and other intangible considerations. The method should not be used as a blind substitute for the exercise of good executive judgment, because monetary return on investment can never be the sole determinant of overall worth of important projects. But, skillfully applied and intelligently interpreted, ROI methods can serve to bolster and refine executive decision-making capabilities. Moreover, the ability to quantify the monetary aspect of a project provides statistical support for reports and oral presentations without which the audience would have to rely on the personal persuasive powers of the project's supporters.

Methods for Reducing
Excessive Liquidity

A certain firm's leaders do not wish to invest its surplus funds in projects aimed at future growth of operations, and their best estimates indicate that the excess funds are not needed to finance ongoing operations. They seek alternatives to the conventional, low-yielding, short- and intermediate-term portfolio of money market instruments. Depending upon the outcome of careful ROI analysis, there are several possibilities.

REPURCHASE LONG-TERM DEBT AT A DISCOUNT.   Firms that issued long-term debt in the form of straight bonds, convertibles, and subordinated debentures at times when market rates of interest were abnormally low by present-day standards, see the market prices of these obligations at extraordinarily low levels. Many of the so-called "junk" bonds and debentures traded on the New York and American Stock Exchange in the years 1973–75 sold at discounts from face value of over 60 percent. For example, the bond prices listed in *The New York Times* of June 22, 1975 showed the following (for a $1000 unit):

Ampex conv. 5¼s 1994	$465.00
Consolidated Edison 9⅛s 2004	800.00
Eastern Airlines conv. 5s 1993	382.50
Gulf & Western conv. 5½s 1993	738.75
Lockheed conv. 4¼s 1992	430.00
Lykes Youngstown 7½s 1994	676.25
Rapid American 6s 1988	372.50
Reliance Group 9⅞s 1998	605.00
Whittaker Corp. conv. 4⅛s 1988	433.75

Of course, many of these securities were selling at cut-rate prices because the companies have insufficient liquidity, but even for firms with superior financial strength but low current earnings, the bonds were selling at deep discounts. Thus, if the bond indenture permits, the company whose debt is selling at big discounts has an opportunity to repurchase a portion of the outstanding obligations and to see their balance sheets take on a healthier glow (lower debt-to-equity ratio).

Even firms that are severely restricted from repurchasing their own debt out of surplus funds may have the right to do so for sinking-fund or debt-retirement purposes. The indenture terms may give the company the option of making a sinking-fund payment in cash or by delivering debt instruments of equivalent face value (not market value). Or a firm that is required by contract with its trustee periodically to retire a percentage of an outstanding debt issue may have the option either of using the call provision (with a small penalty over par) or of repurchasing an equivalent dollar face value in the open market.

REPURCHASE OF OUTSTANDING COMMON OR PREFERRED STOCK. Every share of stock in the hands of an outside investor represents a permanent lien on the firm's present and future earnings. When this company's shares are selling at abnormally low prices in relation to earnings, return on total assets, and book value, they represent an unparalleled repurchase opportunity for the issuing firm. Reducing the number of outstanding shares in public hands has many advantages, including:

1 / Lowered stock registration and transfer fees.

2 / Lowered cash dividend payout.

3 / Lowered communication expenses, fewer copies of annual reports, interim reports, and proxy statements to be mailed directly or through stockbrokers.

4 / Greater relative power for inside shareholders.

5 / Less vulnerability to corporate raiders.

6 / Treasury stock available for stock purchases by employees, executives, merger negotiations, private investors.

Ultimately many firms may wish to repurchase all stock owned by public investors and thereby to "go private" (the reverse of "going public"). This course of action has the special advantage of allowing for greater managerial flexibility and freedom from constraints imposed by stock exchange listing requirements and Securities Exchange Commission regulations.

DISTRIBUTIONS TO SHAREHOLDERS.   When it becomes apparent that the company's return on invested cash surpluses is consistently smaller than its shareholders could obtain for themselves in other ways, there is a strong argument on grounds of equity and economic logic in favor of returning the extra funds to shareholders. Income tax considerations will have a major influence on both the timing and size of such payments. Only if, in the end, the payout alternative proves to be advantageous to a majority of the shareholders and to the firm's creditors should the payout be seriously contemplated.

COPING WITH INSUFFICIENT LIQUIDITY

Financial Stringency Defined

Financial stringency, a condition that results from insufficient liquidity, differs from insolvency (to be discussed in the next chapter) in that the company remains viable but perennially starved for funds. And, like a case of sustained hypertension in a person, if the condition persists uncorrected, the cumulative effects can lead to life-threatening complications. Financial stringency may be the result of a temporary imbalance between the inflow and outflow of funds or from a persistent shortage of operating capital. Referring to the reservoir models in Figs. 7-1(a) and 7-1(b), either the storage tank runs dry from time to time or there is a dangerously low level of fluid.

As the reservoir model implies, the cash inadequacy can happen for several reasons:

— Inability to obtain adequate credit accommodations from banks or other lending agencies.
— Undercapitalization, excessive trading on the firm's equity.
— A large portion of the firm's new worth is tied up in fixed assets and other nonliquid resources.
— Slow payments of accounts receivables; too many overage accounts.
— Excessive losses from bad debts, inventory shrinkages, and unauthorized cash withdrawals.
— Slow inventory turnover, too large an accumulation of unsalable inventories, safety stocks too high.
— Insufficient gross markup on goods and services offered for sale; expenses exceed income; price cutting.
— Slackening in the volume of sales.
— Imprudent cash dividend payouts and poorly planned debt service payments.

Relieving Financial Stringency

The details of a program for amelioriating the difficulties caused by financial stringency depend, of course, on the specific set of conditions faced by the firm at the time. In general, however, the program must have these aims:

— If the level of funds in the cash reservoir fluctuates from too much (or enough) to too little, to fill in the gaps by skillful management of inflows and outflows.
— If the level of funds in the cash reservoir is dangerously low for a long time, to increase inflows, decrease outflows, or a combination of the two, and to obtain thereby a higher and more satisfactory average level.

RAISING CASH FROM SALE OF FIXED ASSETS.   When a company has a large percentage of its capital tied up in fixed assets, its management may find it prudent to release these funds for working capital purposes. This goal can be achieved in a number of ways:

— Sell off idle or underutilized assets for cash.

— If assets are still needed, arrange a sale-leaseback deal with investors or a leasing company that leaves the company in possession of the assets and also provides it with a large cash infusion.

— If the assets are fully paid for, arrange for a long-term mortgage. If already mortgaged, refinance to stretch out the date of maturity and to reduce the monthly payments.

— Instead of owning the fixed assets and having them on the premises for the purpose of securing the services the assets provide, purchase these same services from outside vendors and sell off the company-owned assets for cash.

— If additional fixed assets are needed, buy them on an extended payment plan; lease in place of buying; obtain the assets on short-term, month-to-month rental plans; pay for the services of the assets on a royalty basis—so much per unit of service.

INCREASING THE ACCOUNTS PAYABLE FLOAT.   One form of corporate balance sheet is shown in Table 7-1. Lines 1 through 16 make up the asset section; lines 17 through 28, the liabilities section; lines 29 through 35, the capital section.

A useful way of interpreting the asset section is to think of it as "This is the total capital used in the business." The liabilities, reserves, and capital section are interpreted as, "These are the monetary values of the contributions to the total capital made by the various classes of contributors." According to this reasoning, the accounts payable account represents the contributions made by vendors to the capital used by the firm.

Viewing the statement in this manner makes clear the fact that, in a going concern, the vendors supply *permanent* capital. It is true that any single item that goes into the accounts payable account is extinguished in a relatively short time, but there are both inflows and outflows to and from the accounts payable reservoir [similar to the cash reservoir of Fig. 7-1(a)]. The level in this reservoir at any instant of time is called the *accounts payable float.*

One way to increase the capital available for use in the business is to raise the relative proportion of contributions to capital made by vendors; that is, to increase the accounts payable float, not by purchas-

TABLE 7-1
FORM OF A CORPORATE BALANCE SHEET

XYZ INCORPORATED
BALANCE SHEET AS OF
DECEMBER 31, 197_

Line			
1		ASSETS	
2	CURRENT ASSETS		
3	Cash in banks	$XXX,XXX.XX	
4	Short-term investments	XXX,XXX.XX	
5	Accounts receivables	XXX,XXX.XX	
6	Inventories	XXX,XXX.XX	
7	TOTAL CURRENT ASSETS		$XXX,XXX.XX
8	NONCURRENT ASSETS		
9	Fixed assets (cost)	XXX,XXX.XX	
10	less Accumulated depr.	(XXX,XXX.XX)	
11	Net fixed assets	XXX,XXX.XX	
12	Investments in subsid.	XXX,XXX.XX	
13	Security deposits	XXX,XXX.XX	
14	TOTAL NONCURRENT ASSETS		$XXX,XXX.XX
15	OTHER ASSETS		$XXX,XXX.XX
16	TOTAL ASSETS		$XXX,XXX.XX
17	LIABILITIES, RESERVES, AND CAPITAL		
18	CURRENT LIABILITIES		
19	Accounts payable	$XXX,XXX.XX	
20	Notes payable	XXX,XXX.XX	
21	Accrued liabilities	XXX,XXX.XX	
22	Prepaid items	XXX,XXX.XX	
23	TOTAL CURRENT LIABILITIES		$XXX,XXX.XX
24	NONCURRENT LIABILITIES		
25	Long-term debt	XXX,XXX.XX	
26	Reserves (prepayments)	XXX,XXX.XX	
27	TOTAL NONCURRENT LIABILITIES		$XXX,XXX.XX
28	TOTAL LIABILITIES		$XXX,XXX.XX
29	CAPITAL		
30	Common stock	XXX,XXX.XX	
31	Preferred stock	XXX,XXX.XX	
32	Paid in surplus	XXX,XXX.XX	
33	Retained earnings (restricted)	XXX,XXX.XX	
34	Retained earnings (nonrestricted)	XXX,XXX.XX	
35	TOTAL CAPITAL		$XXX,XXX.XX
36	TOTAL LIABILITIES, RESERVES, AND CAPITAL		$XXX,XXX.XX

ing more materials, goods, and services than needed, but by slowing the rate of outflow from the account by delaying payments.

Outright delinquency is undesirable and is recommended only as a last resort, because such delayed payments cause loss of cash discounts. However, a planned program of slower payments can often be arranged with vendors, because many suppliers use liberal credit as a part of their marketing mix (as an inducement to do business with them rather than with their competitors).

Some firms, even the largest and best financed, try shortcuts with cash discounts. Practices that in earlier days would have been considered sleazy and marginally ethical have become commonplace. For example:

— Alpha Corporation pays bills having terms 2 percent 10, net 30 in 15 days and still deducts the discount. Many vendors overlook the delayed payment. Those that insist on full payment carry the unearned discount on the books as unpaid accounts receivable, but, after dunning the customer unsuccessfully, write the amounts off as uncollectable. Alpha tries paying in 18 days, then 20 days, then 25 days until the vendor's protests indicate that Alpha has gone too far. Then they backtrack to a late payment policy that the vendor will tolerate.

— Beta Corporation buys large dollar amounts of materials from many suppliers. A supplier that has a small percentage of Beta's purchases asks the purchasing agent what it can do to get a larger piece of Beta's business. Beta's purchasing agent suggests that terms of ⅓ 30 days, ⅓ 60 days, and ⅓ 90 days would be irresistibly attractive. This is too much for this vendor to bear, but they offer the terms 2 percent end-of-month (E.O.M.) instead of 2 percent 10, net 30. Thus, Beta can still earn the 2 percent cash discount if it pays for shipments by the tenth of the following month, allowing for a 30- to 40-day grace period. (Or perhaps it pays on the fifteenth of the next month?)

— Gamma Corporation is annoyed by the fact that the date from which discounts are computed is the date of invoice and not the date of receipt of shipments. It asks its vendors to allow for shipping delays and to adjust the date of invoices accordingly. The vendors agree and Gamma has several extra days to earn the cash discount.

ACCELERATING THE ACCOUNTS RECEIVABLES AND INVENTORY TURN-OVER RATES.   Although financial analysts prefer to consider accounts receivables and inventories as current assets, by which they mean temporary capital, in a sense, these items are no more temporary than fixed assets. It is true, as was the case for accounts payables, that a particular item becomes extinguished as it passes through the accounts receivables and inventory reservoirs. However, in a going business, there are *always* accounts receivable and inventory floats, and these are just as permanent as are fixed assets.

Liquidity can be increased if the distribution of accounts numbered 3, 4, 5, and 6 of Table 7-1 are apportioned so that account 7, total current assets, contains a greater proportion of cash and near-cash items relative to accounts receivables and inventories.

Techniques companies have used to raise their liquidity by lowering the two floats include:

— Taking title to goods at their own loading dock instead of at the supplier's.°

— Lowering the levels of safety stocks by buying from more reliable and nearby suppliers.°

— Taking in merchandise on consignment and paying for it only after it is sold.°

— Shortening the production cycle by reducing the degree of vertical integration.°

— Selling off slow-moving items at cut prices.°

— Subletting space within the firm's plant for vendors to do finishing operations, materials being delivered without delay to the production line.°

— In a retail establishment, using leased departments with rentals including percentages of leasees' sales income.°

— Sell accounts receivables to factoring firm or finance company as soon as the obligation is created.†

— Weeding out slow-paying accounts and selling for cash on delivery only, or a combination of cash in advance and cash on delivery.†

THE CASH BUDGET AS AN EARLY-WARNING DEVICE.   The cash reservoir models of Figs. 7-1(a) and 7-1(b) are stop-motion, pictorial representations of a cash budgeting procedure. In a typical cash budget, all items of cash inflow and outflow are tabulated for a sequence of discrete times. A simplified cash budget sheet is shown in Table 7-2. The net cash balance (line 4) tells the management what the cash level will be in the

° Lowers inventory float.
† Lowers accounts receivable float.

TABLE 7-2
CASH BUDGET FOR OMEGA CORP. 1972 AND 1973
(BY CALENDAR QUARTERS) (SIMPLIFIED)

LINE	CASH ITEMS * ($000)	For the Calendar Quarter Ending							
		3/31/72	6/30/72	9/30/72	12/31/72	3/31/73	6/30/73	9/30/73	12/31/73
1	Receipts	$12,000	$21,000	$31,000	$35,000	$22,000	$18,000	$12,000	$45,000
2	Disbursements	16,000	23,800	31,400	46,200	16,200	8,600	16,000	16,200
3	Gain or (loss)	(4,000)	(2,800)	(400)	(11,200)	5,800	9,400	(4,000)	28,800
4	Cumulative gain or (loss)	(4,000)	(6,800)	(7,200)	(18,400)	(12,600)	(3,200)	(7,200)	21,600
5	Amount of loan needed to maintain minimum balance of $5,000	9,000	11,800	12,200	23,400	17,600	8,200	12,200	0
6	Incremental borrowings (repayments)	9,000	2,800	400	11,200	(5,800)	(9,400)	4,000	(12,200)

* Cash balance at beginning of 1972 is assumed to be zero.

cash reservoir in the absence of borrowing on the designated dates (assuming, of course, that the flows are as indicated). If the cash balance is negative at any time, a means for restoring the balance to a positive value must be devised. Bank borrowing may be the answer, but only if the budget figures show that the funds will be available to repay the loans on the maturity dates. If such is not the case, other means for obtaining cash must be devised.

Many lenders insist on seeing a cash-flow projection similar to that in Table 7-2 before they will approve a loan. The loan executive of the bank is more favorably inclined toward the borrower who can show exactly how and when the loan can be repaid. Running to the bank on the day the company's checks are returned marked "insufficient funds" for a short-term loan does not leave a favorable impression on the loan executive. More than likely, the loan request will be turned down unless there are extenuating circumstances (such as uncollected funds or a bank error).

TAKING IN ADDITIONAL INVESTORS.   If all other methods for restoring liquidity fail, and the company has favorable prospects, the best alternative remaining is to bring in additional permanent capital. Such an act will raise the amounts in lines 25, 30, and 31 (possibly 32 as well) of Table 7-1.

If the firm is privately owned, it has two alternatives: (1) to sell equity, debt, or combinations to private investors, or (2) to make a public offering of debt or equity securities. Which of the two is the preferred method depends upon the availability of private financing and the accessibility to the public markets. Both forms have their own particular advantages and disadvantages, and both should be explored before a choice is made.

Firms that do not have good prospects for growth or survival usually find it impossible to bring in outside capital, except at prohibitive cost. If the firm cannot restore its lagging liquidity by generating funds internally, then its only alternatives are a partial or full liquidation to rescue the remaining capital for the owners, or to seek some form of corporate reorganization that will allow the firm to continue operations. Although it is common practice to resort to reorganization under the protection of the bankruptcy statutes only *after* the firm has sunk into the quicksand of insolvency, there is absolutely no reason why a suitable arrangement cannot be made *before* that unhappy event occurs. In fact, a satisfactory arrangement with creditors is much more feasible if the chances for survival are favorable than if the outlook is bleak.

SELECTED REFERENCES

BIERMAN, H., et al., *The Capital Budgeting Decision.* New York: The Macmillan Company, 1972.

Cash Management. Chicago: The First National Bank of Chicago, 1975.

STETTLER, HOWARD F., "Break-even Analysis: Its Uses and Misuses," *The Accounting Review,* Vol. 37 (July 1962), pp. 400–463.

TAYLOR, GEORGE A., *Managerial and Engineering Economy: Economic Decision Making* 2nd ed. New York: D. VanNostrand Company, 1975.

Chapter 8

Financial Crisis
and Insolvency

COPING WITH INSOLVENCY

Insolvency and Financial
Embarrassment

In its broadest sense, without any adjective modifier, insolvency means that the firm is unable to discharge its current liabilities in a timely fashion. The rates of inflow and outflow in the cash reservoir are such that the reservoir is, or is about to run, dry. Thus, insolvency (sometimes also called financial embarrassment) is insufficient liquidity carried to its logical conclusion. Insolvency is an intermediate stage between financial stringency and formal bankruptcy.

Insolvency in the *equity* sense simply means that a firm with positive net worth (book value of assets exceeds book value of liabilities) cannot meet its financial obligations as they become due. Insolvency in the bankruptcy sense means that the firm has negative net worth (the book value of its liabilities exceeds the book value of its assets) in addition to being unable to pay its current bills.

The distinction between the two types of insolvency can become blurred when different methods for valuing assets are employed. The typical balance sheet values are based upon the "going concern" worth. If the firm does not continue its operations, many of the asset values drop, and this causes an equity insolvency to change into the more malignant type. For example, a manufacturing firm has a large inventory of component parts made to its own special specifications. Although the cost of these items is $1,000,000 and the inventory would have this value if the firm continued in business, the parts have no value to anyone else. Thus, if the firm were to discontinue operations, the $1,000,000 valuation would be reduced to scrap value, possibly $1000. This fact alone could switch a positive net worth to negative. In addition to inventories, many balance sheets carry such items as good will, organization expense, prepaid insurance, research and development, etc., the values of which would drop much below book if the firm ceased operating.

Although an insolvent firm is in a precarious state, steps can often be taken to halt the deterioration and restore it to a more viable condition. Insolvency does not inevitably lead to the demise of the firm, although many companies that reach this state do not survive.

STAGES OF AN INSOLVENCY.   A wise man once said, "There are three stages in an insolvency: (1) when it actually happens, (2) when the management discovers that it has happened, and (3) when the firm makes a public admission of the fact."

The equity type rarely comes as a surprise to anyone. The most prominent symptom is the inability to pay the company's bills on the due date. First there is a slowness, missing discount dates; then comes lateness; then, delinquency. The process takes a long time, and by the time the company is totally mired in its state of financial embarrassment, the facts are well-known to everyone in the firm, in the trade, and in the financial community. The existence of credit reporting services such as Dun and Bradstreet prevents equity types of insolvencies from being kept secret.

The bankruptcy type of insolvency is harder to detect, and it fits the wise man's epigram. At which particular point in time the firm's net worth becomes less positive, goes through zero, then into the negative region is impossible to tell. The main difficulties arise from two sources: (1) the fact that full and complete accounting of the firm's condition takes place no more than once a year, and (2) the errors and uncertainties in the valuation of assets and liabilities are substantial under the best conditions, but when management tries to hide the true facts, valuations become increasingly unreliable.

AVOIDING ACTS OF BANKRUPTCY.   If there is to be any hope of rescuing the insolvent firm from death and dissolution, it is critically important that the authorized representatives of the present owners maintain their control of the firm's destiny. If they lose their grip on the firm's helm, disaster in the form of loss of the owners' equity in the business is virtually inevitable. "Don't give up the ship" must be the overriding philosophy at this critical juncture in the firm's life.

There are a number of acts, which, if detected, are considered prima facie acts of bankruptcy and may allow creditors to petition a court to judge the firm as involuntarily bankrupt.*

— Transfer and concealment of assets with intent to make them unavailable for the satisfaction of creditors' legitimate claims.

— Granting preference to one creditor or class of creditors to the detriment of others.

— Allowing liens against the firm through legal proceedings which, if executed, would constitute a preference.

— Making a general assignment of assets to the benefit of creditors.

— Permitting the appointment of a receiver or trustee to take charge of the firm's property.

— Making a written admission of inability to meet obligations and a willingness to be adjuged bankrupt.

There is one act of omission that can precipitate a financial crisis. If the firm has long-term debt in its financial structure and the debt agreement provides that the entire unpaid balance becomes due if an interest or sinking fund payment is in default, deferred liabilities are transformed into current liabilities. In such an event, the size of the current liabilities is magnified to a degree that makes meeting them impossible.

Emergency Measures To Stave Off Disaster

It is always better to recognize the potential for disaster and to take timely and appropriate action before a true crisis develops. If this

---

* Application and interpretation of these six acts are highly technical, and any matters relating to them should be dealt with by the firm's legal counsel.

can be done, the price exacted will be less onerous. But, up to the very end, efforts can be made to convert a critical, life-threatening condition to one that is merely serious, but stable. A number of measures that should be considered follow.

DEUX EX MACHINA.   In old-time movies and melodrama, a common plot device is to place the hero (or heroine) in a seemingly impossible, life-endangering situation, and then, at the time when his (her) situation seems hopeless, as if by miracle, a rescuer appears. The beleaguered management of the threatened company cannot wait passively in hope that the United States Cavalry will come to its rescue. Rather, they must search for one or more private investors who might be willing to save the company from bankruptcy. The stockholders will be required to give up a portion of their equity in the foundering firm; just how much depends upon the specifics of the rescue negotiations, and how desperate the company's condition is at the time.

If the firm is publicly owned, this form of rescue is more complicated, because the interests of public as well as inside stockholders must be protected. However, the Securities and Exchange Commission can be expected to be reasonably sympathetic to a plan that will save the public stockholders' equity.

REVALUATION OF UNDERVALUED ASSETS.   Firms that have been in business for a long time often have assets that have been fully depreciated and are carried on the books at zero or very low value. In some situations, particularly with real property, the current market value may be very much larger than the book value. If the undervaluation of this property causes the firm's net worth to be very small, zero, or even negative, some immediate relief can be had by revaluing the property closer to its current worth. To achieve this bookkeeping change, the company's accountant may wish to increase the fixed-asset valuation and make a corresponding adjustment to the capital surplus account. If there is any question about the size of the adjustment, the services of a reputable appraisal firm should be obtained to aid in making the revaluation.

If the revalued property can then be sold or mortgaged, immediate cash can be released for current operations. If not, then at least some time has been bought by avoiding the negative net-worth type of insolvency.

INFORMAL ARRANGEMENT WITH MAJOR CREDITORS.   A meeting is called of all major creditors for the purpose of obtaining temporary relief from financial pressures. The company's managers present a workable plan to the creditors that convinces them that the company can survive and prosper once again if the plan is adopted. Such plans usually involve converting short-term into deferred liabilities, thus relieving the immediate pressures for meeting current payables.

Since creditors are usually rational people and have no desire to kill off a good customer, they are amenable to any plan that recognizes the legitimacy of their claims but allows the firm to continue as customers for years to come. The important ingredients in any plan of continuation is that it be thoroughly convincing and well presented.

Informal arrangements with creditors can take several forms: (1) extension of the payment dates, (2) composition (partial or full forgiveness) of indebtedness, (3) combinations of the two foregoing, and (4) exchange for equity.

EXTENSION.   An agreement is made for deferring the payment dates of creditors' obligations, usually for several years. A schedule for repayment is agreed upon (e.g., 10 percent per year beginning with the next year, or two years hence). Creditors agree to subordinate these deferred obligations to new current liabilities so that the company can continue in business with reasonable credit accommodations.

COMPOSITION.   Composition involves a forgiveness of all or part of the debts. The plan may involve a cash payment of x percent of the claims (where x is less than 100 percent). Some plans call for small creditors to be paid in full and larger creditors to receive pro rata shares of reduced percentages.

Creditors are willing to compromise their claims in this way if by doing so they believe that the company will continue to be a good customer. Also, some firms prefer to write off as bad debts any excessively over-aged receivables, so agreeing to a partial forgiveness allows them to recover immediately part of a written-off bad debt.

COMBINATION OF EXTENSION AND COMPOSITION.   In cases where the cash available is insufficient to make immediate payment under a percentage forgiveness, because of the necessity for paying off small creditors in full, the large creditors should be asked to defer the amounts remaining after forgiveness. The effect of their acceptance of both extension and composition is to clean up the balance sheet. A large portion of the current liabilities is wiped out, and the part that remains is transferred to the deferred liabilities section. Thus, the current ratio (current assets/current liabilities) and the quick ratio (cash + near cash + receivables/current liabilities) both improve, and the credit worthiness of the firm is restored.

EXCHANGE OF DEBT FOR EQUITY.   Another alternative arrangement with creditors which has the effect of wiping out the debt altogether is to exchange their claims for common or preferred stock. The creditors surrender their immediate claims in exchange for a hope that someday they will receive more than their money back because the revitalized firm's shares rise in market value. Just how many shares or what proportion of the total equity the creditors receive is a matter for negotiation. In some instances, the creditors may insist that they have the right to designate one or more of their number as members of the company's board of directors so that they will have representatives to watch over their interests.

CHAPTER XI PROCEEDINGS; DEBTOR IN POSSESSION.   When all attempts at achieving a satisfactory informal arrangement fail, and creditors file suit in the courts to obtain payment of the amounts due them, the last resort of the company is to seek the protection of the courts under Chapter XI of the Federal Bankruptcy Statutes. (This is a highly technical procedure that requires the guidance of competent legal counsel. All that can be done in this brief section is to touch on the general purpose of the act without giving any of the legal details.)

By seeking the protection of the court, the company is able to prevent any single creditor or combination of creditors from seizing the assets of the firm through execution of a judgment award by the courts. If such protection were not obtained, a single creditor, upon obtaining a judgment against the firm, could employ a marshall or sheriff and have this functionary seize enough of the company's property to satisfy the judgment.

When actions of this nature become public knowledge, other vendors are likely to cut off all credit accommodations and insist on cash on delivery or even cash in advance of order.

A Chapter XI action, with debtor in possession, does not require the approval of 100 percent of the creditors. A simple majority of each class is sufficient to approve a plan of continuance. If the plan submitted by the company's financial officers seems reasonable to the court, it may allow the company's management to continue operating the firm without the direct supervision of a court-appointed receiver.

The principal disadvantage of the Chapter XI proceedings over the informal arrangements is the great expense involved. An informal arrangement does not necessary involve extensive legal work by high-priced lawyers. The creditors meet among themselves and appoint a committee from among their number who usually agree to serve without fee. Occasionally, a man from one of the credit reporting agencies is asked to serve as committee chairman or executive secretary for a modest fee. Thus, informal arrangements are *much less* expensive to arrive at, to monitor, and to terminate. Formal petitions and involvement of the courts can be devastatingly expensive.

If the court grants the petition, the debtor remains in possession, all past trade debts are subordinated to the cash needs of current operations. The firm may have to pay cash for all of its requirements, but if suppliers are willing to grant new credit, the new obligations have precedence over the old.

Another important advantage of the informal arrangement with creditors is the fact that less publicity is given to such matters. The financial and local press are more likely to report filings of formal petitions of bankruptcy than news of informal meetings of creditors. Parties whose business it is to know about the financial condition of the firm have the means for keeping informed, principally through the credit reporting services, through their banking connections, and through the industry grapevines. Confidentiality is easier to maintain with informal arrangements, because credit information is circulated mainly among paid subscribers and parties with a need to know.

The requirements of the stock exchanges and the Securities and Exchange Commission are a great deal more stringent for formal bankruptcies. Trading in the company's securities is suspended, special code letters are assigned to the newspaper listings, and other warnings to potential and current investors are disseminated. With the informal arrangement, such draconian measures can be avoided either partly, or altogether. Proper notifications are required to the stock exchanges and the S.E.C., but the reporting requirements are not nearly so severe.

EVENTS THAT CAN PRECIPITATE A FINANCIAL CRISIS

Just as a person weakened by a prolonged, debilitating illness can be carried off by an infection that would cause him no harm if he were in good health, so can a financially weakened firm be destroyed by sudden happenings it could easily cope with in normal circumstances. The following are a few examples of events that could easily provide the last straw for a tottering company.

— A large customer with many unpaid invoices files a petition of bankruptcy and offers ten cents on a dollar to all unsecured creditors.

— A company in a seasonal business has inventories that fluctuate over a wide range over the year. The all-risk insurance policy on the inventory requires monthly reporting of monetary values. In order to save on premiums, the company consistently underreports on inventory values. A fire destroys the warehouse and all of its contents, and the insurance is too low to cover the loss.

— The company invests its seasonal cash surpluses in short-term treasury bills and commercial paper. Upon presentation of the documents for collection, payment is refused because the serial numbers reveal that some are forgeries and others are stolen property. The executive who manages these transactions has been on vacation in South America and is two weeks overdue.

— The company maintains large distributor inventories with absolute price protection. Because of a technological breakthrough by a large competitor, there is a large price break—to about 25 percent of former prices. The company is required to refund large amounts of money to its distributors or to accept merchandise back for credit at the old, high prices.

— The company is defendant in a multimillion dollar suit for product liability involving deaths and injuries from fires caused by its products. It loses the suit and waits for its insurance company to pay the money ordered by the court. The insurance company fails to pay and files a petition of bankruptcy.

— A supervisory employee of a company that makes ammunition for the United States Army confesses that he has participated in a plot to falsify quality assurance data. A large quantity of defective material was shipped, and several deaths of military personnel have occurred directly traceable to the defective materials.

— The company designs, manufactures, and sells a complex machine used in conjunction with electronic data processing equipment. It sells 100 of these machines per month in its home territory. Although there are servicing problems, the annual service agreements paid for by each customer cover the costs adequately. The company is acquired by a large conglomerate, and a new president is installed. He arranges to sell 2000 machines to a large multinational firm with sales offices in the United States and Latin America. Because of the rush in increasing production rates and in filling this large order, there are many built-in defects in the machines. Besieged by a flood of service calls, the company's service department suffers a total collapse. Bills for air travel mount, and customer complaints rise in frequency and anger. Finally the multinational corporation suspends payment and demands the right to return all of the machines for credit and full refund.

— Because it has been found guilty of practicing racial and sexual discrimination, this firm has been ordered to make a large cash payment to all employees who can sustain a claim of damages because of discrimination. The company is unable to pay.

— The company suffers large losses from speculation in commodities, gold, and foreign currencies.

— Zeta Corporation takes a fixed price contract and, because of strikes, design errors, and rising costs of labor and materials, suffers large losses.

— Omega Corporation makes a public offering of its shares. After the offering is completed and the funds received from the sale are committed, a stockholder sues for rescission of the sale because of alleged fraudulent representations in the prospectus. The court orders the company to refund the money to the many stockholders who ask for their money back.

— A large investment in a foreign operation becomes worthless because a revolution in the country leads to expropriation with little likelihood of compensation.

— A company sues another for patent infringement. The defendant firm files a countersuit for antitrust law violations. The counterclaim prevails.

— Theta Corporation maintains large inventories of oil and other liquids in storage tanks. When the auditors make a spot check of the contents of the tanks, they find that many of them contain sea water.

EARLY-WARNING SIGNALS

An insolvency can often be avoided if early warning of danger enables the interested parties to take timely and appropriate remedial action. But, for many reasons, the true facts about the firm's condition may be withheld or falsified by managers fearful of losing their jobs, or paralyzed by fear and indecision. It is not unknown, in such precarious situations, for stockholders, directors, creditors, employee representatives, suppliers, and customers to be misinformed about the true condition of the firm. Good news is usually freely available, but who loves the bearers of ill tidings?

What is needed, therefore, is a set of clues that the parties with a large stake in the firm's welfare and survival can use to test, from time to time, the condition of the firm. Some of the tests listed below can be made by using data in financial statements; some require information not readily available through public sources. If actual published information does not suffice, careful interrogation of persons who have specialized but fragmentary knowledge can often reveal a pattern of behavior not discernible from study of ordinary financial and accounting figures.

Financial Ratios

Financial ratios derived from the balance sheet, income and expense statement, and other financial sources can be used to judge the condition of the firm. No one ratio taken by itself is authoritative, because many unique circumstances can cause the values to give misleading indications. But if the ratios are taken in combination, patterns of decline do become apparent. Table 8-1 contains several types of ratios: activity, leverage, liquidity, profitability, and miscellaneous. The first four can usually be computed from straight financial reports; the last may involve inspection of the company's books and records.

These ratios can be used to compare the condition of the firm with itself over a sequence of time intervals (a relative ratio study), or to compare the condition of the firm in relation to its competitors or the industry as a whole. Thus, if the firm's condition deteriorates, but not as rapidly as its competitors', the comparison places the firm's condition in a different light. Or if the firm's condition seems to be improving, but slower than the industry as a whole, the improvements need closer examination.

Other Danger Signals

Although a great deal of useful historical information can be obtained from a careful examination of the firm's financial reports, the interested parties require data that can serve as both anticipatory signals and confirmatory tests.

ABNORMALLY HIGH CUSTOMER RETURNS.   Very high returns from customers, undesirable at any time, can be exceptionally harmful when the company is in a precarious condition. Such returns may be the result of bad workmanship, inferior materials, poor quality control, obsolescent designs, incorrect shipments, or many other causes. Information concerning the quantity of returns in relation to sales does not appear in the financial report until the firm issues credits or refunds *and* records these facts in the books of account. For many firms, issuing credit memoranda is a low-priority job. The time lapse between the receipt of request for

TABLE 8-1
FINANCIAL RATIOS, FORMULAS FOR COMPUTATION, AND INTERPRETATIONS

Category and Name of Ratio	Numerator and Denominator of Ratio		Determination Is Shown When This Ratio
Activity			
Inventory turnover rate	sales	inventory	drops
Average receivable collection period	receivables	daily sales	rises
Fixed asset turnover rate	sales	fixed assets	drops
Leverage			
Debt to equity	total debt	net worth	rises
Fixed charge coverage	net profit before fixed charges	fixed charges	drops
Current liabilities to net worth	current liabilities	net worth	rises
Fixed assets to net worth	fixed assets	net worth	rises
Liquidity			
Current ratio	current assets	current liabilities	drops
Quick ratio	current assets less inventories	current liabilities	drops
Instant liquidity ratio	cash and near cash	current liabilities	drops

Category and Name of Ratio	Numerator and Denominator of Ratio		Determination Is Shown When This Ratio
Profitability			
Gross profit margin	sales (cost of goods sold)	sales	drops
Net profit on sales	after-tax profit	sales	drops
Productivity of assets	income before taxes, dividends, depreciation, and interest	total assets	drops
Return on shareholders' equity	after-tax profits	net worth	drops
Miscellaneous *			
Sales expense as a percentage of sales income	total selling costs	sales	rises
Returns and allowances as a percentage of sales income	returns and allowances	sales	rises
Aging of receivables	(a) receivables over 30 days (b) over 60 days (c) over 90 days	total receivables	rises
Aging of inventories	(a) current inventories (in house less than 30 days)	total inventories	drops
Bad debts	uncollectible receivables	total receivables	rises

* Information for computing these ratios may not be available in normal financial reports.

153

permission to return goods and the actual issuance of credit memoranda may be as long as six months.

EXCESSIVE INVENTORIES OF UNSALABLE ITEMS.   Although the actual monetary value of inventories may not appear to be unreasonably high, in fact, the company may be running with abnormally low levels of salable goods, with all the problems associated with inventory stockouts. This can happen when the stockrooms are filled with unsalable, damaged, obsolescent goods, but inventories of current merchandise in high demand are totally depleted. The people in the sales department are running around trying to expedite customers' orders. The factory is working overtime because every order is a rush. Goods are shipped by air at company expense because of delinquencies in delivery dates, yet the stockrooms are bulging with goods that no one wants.

AUDITORS REFUSE TO ISSUE NORMAL, UNQUALIFIED CERTIFICATION. If the company's affairs are in good order, the outside auditors will append their usual statement to the published financial statements. If they are not satisfied with the condition of the books and records, their statement will contain reservations. These qualifications must be read carefully, because they may be warnings of trouble to come.

CHANGE OF EXTERNAL AUDITOR.   When a company wishes to delay publication of bad news, one technique that may be used is to fire the auditing firm and to replace it with a new firm. The new firm is no more likely to issue misleading statements than the discharged auditing firm, but it does take the new people more time to complete their examination of the books, records, and inventories. The analyst should be particularly alert and suspicious when the firm discharges a well-known auditing firm and replaces it with a small, little-known firm.

CHANGE OF BANKS.   When the firm has been refused loans by its banks, its managers may seek to retaliate by withdrawing its funds and placing them in another bank. Changing banks, by itself, is not necessarily a noteworthy event, but such an action is consistent with impending trouble, too.

SUDDEN DISAPPEARANCE OR SUICIDE OF KEY EXECUTIVE.   Executives operate under great pressures in negative-growth situations, and they do have personal problems that may have nothing to do with the company's affairs. But an executive who has betrayed the trust of the firm in his integrity or personal honesty may decide to escape. His choice may be to leave town without letting anyone know of his destination, taking along some company funds to tide him over until he can establish a new identity. His choice may be to escape into mental illness. Or he may take his own life. Any of these events call for a closer scrutiny of the company, because they may indicate trouble is impending.

AUDIT CONFIRMATION TESTS INCONSISTENT WITH BOOK ACCOUNTS. When the company's auditors make their confirmatory tests of inventories, accounts payable, accounts receivable, cash balances, contents of investment accounts, etc., they usually find the accounts in good condition. If there are discrepancies, the differences are usually due to bookkeeping or other human errors. However, if there has been a major defalcation, this is the time it is likely to be discovered. All discrepancies should be carefully followed up, because they may be signals of bigger losses.

MONITORING CUSTOMER ACTIVITY.   If the firm has a few large customers on which it relies for a large percentage of its sales, a change for the worse in the customer's situation is ultimately reflected in the firm's condition. Purchases may be reduced, bills may remain unpaid, or goods already manufactured to customers' special requirements may be refused or returned.

CONTROLLER UNAVAILABLE TO SUPPLIERS.   An early sign of financial stringency is the case where suppliers call the office of the controller to find out why their invoices remain unpaid. If there is an error, the controller is usually available to receive telephone calls. Even if there is a temporary shortage of funds, the controller or his deputy usually field the suppliers' inquiries. But when they are unavailable and do not return telephone calls, the red flag of danger must be raised. Of course, the controller may have suffered a severe case of laryngitis, or he may be on vacation, but his failure or his deputy's failure to show normal business courtesy should be interpreted as a warning.

THE COMPANY'S CHECKS ARE RETURNED MARKED "INSUFFICIENT FUNDS."   Mistakes do happen in the best-run banks and accounts payable departments. With modern cash management practices, many firms do keep very low cash balances in their checking accounts. Computers do make errors. Therefore, a check returned with the mark "insufficient funds" is not a perfect indicator that the maker is in deep financial trouble, but such an event is a very positive danger signal that must never be ignored. If a satisfactory explanation is offered and the event does not recur, it may have only been the result of an unfortunate error.

Key People Resign. Many competent people with highly marketable skills have the sensitivity of a canary bird in a coal mine. They have the ability to sniff out impending trouble before it becomes known to anyone else. The fact that these key people leave may serve to hasten the time of trouble because of the loss of their valuable services, because it may take a long time to replace them, and because they take along know-how that in a competitor's hands reduces the firm's comparative advantage.

Watching the Stock Transfer Sheets. Every publicly owned company receives stock transfer sheets and up-to-date lists of shareholders from its registrar and transfer agent. These records of stock transfers can provide valuable insights about the kind of persons, firms, and institutions that are buying and selling the company's shares. Large-scale accumulations and distributions can be detected from a study of these transactions before the results become public knowledge. A large-scale flight from the company's stock by people who are highly knowledgeable about the company's outlook should be interpreted as a warning.

Insider Transactions. Taken by themselves, insider transactions in the company's shares are not valid indicators of the firm's financial prospects. Executives buy and sell their shares in the firm for so many diverse reasons that no inferences can be drawn about their motives. However, insider transactions examined in the light of other information may serve as one more missing piece in the metaphorical jigsaw puzzle, which then reveals hitherto obscured information.

General Economic Conditions. Healthy, well-managed firms are usually able to weather economic storms with little long-term damage to their survival prospects. However, a firm already weakened by poor financial condition may not be able to survive any more adverse developments in the economy or in its industry.

Selected References

Altman, E. I., *Corporate Bankruptcy in America*. Lexington, Mass.: D. C. Heath Co., 1971.

Credit Research Foundation, *Cash Management Handbook*. Homewood, Ill.: R. D. Irwin, 1965.

Foulke, Roy A., *Practical Financial Statement Analysis*, 4th ed. New York: McGraw Hill Book Co., 1957.

HELFERT, ERICH A., *Techniques of Financial Analysis,* rev. ed. Homewood, Ill.: R. D. Irwin, 1967.

HUTCHINSON, G. S., *Why, When, and How to Go Public.* New York: President's Publishing House, 1970.

KELLY, A. J. et al., *Venture Capital: A Guidebook for New Enterprises.* Boston, Mass.: North East Regional Commission, 1971.

RING, ALFRED A., *The Valuation of Real Estate.* Englewood Cliffs, N.J.: Prentice-Hall, Inc., 1965.

MITCHELL, W. E., "Cash Forecasting: The Four Methods Compared," *The Controller,* Vol. 28 (April 1960).

STANLEY, D. T. and M. GIRTH, *Bankruptcy: Problem, Process, Reform.* Washington, D.C.: Brookings Institution, 1971.

STAPLES, FREDERICK, *Auditing Manual.* Thiensville, Wis.: Counting House Publishing Company, 1972.

WALTER, JAMES E., "Determination of Technical Solvency," *The Journal of Business,* Vol. 30 (Jan. 1957) pp. 30–43.

Chapter 9

Evaluation
Techniques

A MULTIPLE CRITERIA
EVALUATION PROCEDURE

The multiple criteria evaluation begins with a set of items, subjects, or alternatives along with a set of evaluation criteria. The output of the procedure is a ranking of the items by figure of merit. (F.O.M.) The sequence of steps is as follows:

— Prepare a list of the items to be evaulated.
— Identify the criteria by which the items are to be evaluated.
— Assign numerical weights to the criteria to reflect their relative importance in the particular evaluation.

158

— Prepare the outcome matrix.

— Prepare the valuation matrix.

— Compute the figures of merit (F.O.M.) for each candidate, using the weighted sum of the evaluation points for each.

  F.O.M. = Σ (u_{ij}) (w_j) for each of i candidates on j criteria

— Using figure-of-merit numbers, arrange the items in rank order of desirability.

To illustrate the way the various steps are performed, a numerical example is presented.

A MULTIPLE CRITERIA EVALUATION EXAMPLE

In this example, the Hard Times Company has decided to make a substantial staff curtailment. HTC's personnel director is a very sensitive man and hates to treat anyone unfairly. He knows that the staff reduction must be done, but he would like to do it as fairly as he can—fair to the company, to the employees bidding for the fewer remaining jobs, and to the persons who will remain with the firm. As a model of how to proceed, he asks his staff assistant to prepare a procedure to be used in deciding who goes and who stays. As a trial, the assistant focuses on one job category, office supervisor. There are ten persons who hold the rank before the staff cutback and there will be only three positions left after. The problem is to arrange the ten candidates in rank order of merit so that the three top contenders can be identified.

STEP 1. PREPARE A LIST OF THE CANDIDATES TO BE EVALUATED. These persons are the candidates for the three office supervisor positions (in alphabetical order):

CANDIDATE	NAME	CANDIDATE	NAME
1	Betty Abelson	6	Roberta Franklin
2	Arthur Blair	7	William Goldman
3	Mary Clarkson	8	Allan Holden
4	Peter Davis	9	Patty Iverson
5	Harry Evans	10	Lois Judger

STEP 2. IDENTIFY THE CRITERIA BY WHICH THE SUBJECTS ARE TO BE EVALUATED.   HTC's personnel people chose the following criteria:

CRITERION	NAME OF CRITERION
1	Level of competence and experience in particular job
2	Employment record (absenteeism, merit ratings, etc.)
3	Earnings on most recent assignment
4	Debt of loyalty owed by firm to employee
5	Effect on morale if this person is terminated
6	Future value of employee to firm (versatility)
7	Hardship to employee if terminated
8	Length of time with firm in this or other positions

STEP 3. ASSIGN NUMERICAL WEIGHTS TO THE CRITERIA TO REFLECT THEIR RELATIVE IMPORTANCE.   This step involves a sequence of sub-steps:

3a / Rank the criteria in order of importance to firm.

3b / Assign any number from 0 to 100 to each criterion to reflect its importance relative to all higher and lower ranking criteria; assign higher number to more important; lower number to less important.

3c / Compute the sum of these relative importance numbers; let sum = R.

3d / Divide each of the numbers assigned to the criteria by R; the result for each is the numerical weight w_j.

3e / Compute the sum of the w_j's; the sum should equal 1.000.

3f / Round off the w_j's to two significant figures.

As applied to the HTC problem, the results are as shown in Table 9-1.

STEP 4. PREPARE THE OUTCOME MATRIX.   The outcome matrix is a simple tabulation of the objective scores earned by each candidate on the eight evaluation criteria. The rows of the table correspond to the candidates; the columns to the criteria. The matrix cell, the intersection of a row and a column, is the score for the candidate on the specific criterion.

The cell entries are objective scores, but they need not be numbers. Any numerical or nominal scale can be used.

For the HTC example, the scales used are either actual numbers

TABLE 9-1

RANK ORDER NUMBER	CRITERION NUMBER	RELATIVE IMPORTANCE NUMBER I	NUMERICAL WEIGHT $I/R = w_j$	NUMERICAL WEIGHT (ROUNDED)
1	1	100	0.2128	0.21
2	6	80	0.1702	0.17
3	2	70	0.1489	0.15
4	4	60	0.1277	0.13
5	8	50	0.1064	0.11
6	3	40	0.0851	0.09
7	7	40	0.0851	0.09
8	5	30	0.0638	0.06
Sums		$R = 470$	1.000 (check)	1.01 (check)

(e.g., dollars for criterion 3; years for criterion 8) or nominal scales which convey the quality or degree in a multi-interval scale (e.g., exceptionally fine, very good, quite good, good, neutral, poor, very poor, exceptionally poor). Table 9-2 contains the outcome matrix for the ten candidates.

STEP 5. PREPARE THE VALUATION MATRIX.   This step is a little more difficult than the previous step, because it involves translating the objective scores into valuation scores. Using the desirability of the outcome from the company's viewpoint, assign numerical scores to each cell, using a scale of 0 to 100. Higher desirability gets higher scores, lower desirability, lower scores.

In order to avoid the problem of double weighting of valuation scores, a leveling subprocedure is followed. The scores in each column are totaled, and each cell entry in the column is divided by the column sum, then multiplied by 100. Expressed in mathematical language:

a /   Enter valuation score for the ith candidate on the jth criterion; this is the score u_{ij}.

b /   Compute the sum of each column; this is

$$\sum u_j$$

for all values of i and one value of j at a time.

c /   Divide u_{ij}/u_j for each value of i.

TABLE 9-2

THE OUTCOME MATRIX FOR TEN CANDIDATES FOR POSITION OF OFFICE SUPERVISOR AT HARD TIMES CORP.

CANDIDATE'S NAME AND NUMBER	NOMINAL OR NUMERICAL SCORES ON THESE EIGHT CRITERIA							
	1[a]	2[b]	3[c]	4[a]	5[d]	6[a]	7[a]	8[e]
1. Abelson	V.H.	Q.G.	10.5	V.L.	N	V.H.	V.H.	5
2. Blair	Q.L.	E.G.	11.5	V.L.	N	N	Q.H.	6
3. Clarkson	Q.L.	Q.G.	9.5	V.H.	V.U.	N	N	2
4. Davis	N	N	14.5	Q.H.	Q.U.	V.L.	N	12
5. Evans	N	N	12.5	V.L.	Q.F.	V.L.	Q.L.	9
6. Franklin	Q.H.	N	8.5	N	N	Q.L.	E.H.	1,9
7. Goldman	E.H.	Q.G.	14.5	Q.L.	Q.U.	Q.H.	Q.H.	14
8. Holden	E.H.	V.G.	16.5	Q.H.	V.U.	N	N	20
9. Iverson	V.H.	N	10.1	N	N	N	Q.H.	4
10. Judger	V.H.	Q.P.	8.2	N	N	Q.L.	Q.L.	1,6

[a] Exceptionally, very, quite, high; exceptionally, very, quite, low; neutral.
[b] Exceptionally, very, quite, good; exceptionally, very, quite, poor; neutral.
[c] Thousands of dollars per year in payroll cost.
[d] Exceptionally, very, quite, good; exceptionally, very, quiet, poor; neutral.   neutral.
[e] Years (and months if needed to break tie).

d / Enter the leveled cell entry u_{ij} into the valuation table. Check sum of column entries should equal 100.

e / Enter the criterion weights in a row below the last candidate's valuation scores.

The data from Table 9-2 transformed into leveled valuation scores are shown in Table 9-3. Note that where two candidates earned the same scores on the nominal scale, a finer discrimination is possible when numbers are assigned. This was done for the data in Table 9-2 based upon differences in the candidate's raw data.

Table 9-3 also contains the figures of merit computed from the weighted sums of the entries in each candidate's row along with the associated rank order numbers. Note that Goldman ranks first; Holden, second; Abelson, third. If the top three scores identify the successful candidates, those persons would be retained and the others terminated or placed elsewhere.

It is quite possible that the candidates chosen by use of this procedure may not be the ones that would be selected by using the ordinary intuitive methods. If such is the case, there are several possible reasons for the discrepancy:

— The weights assigned to the criteria are not the true weights.
— Other important criteria were left out of the procedure.
— The valuations of the outcome scores do not accurately reflect true valuations.
— The evaluators have a different risk-attraction, risk-aversion function that the weighted sum of the points implies.

There is nothing inherently sacred in the choice of the weighted sum of the points rule for combining valuation points into a figure of merit for each candidate. It is equally possible to use the weighted product of the points, the weighted square root of the sum of the squares, etc. However, each of these rules for combining the partial valuation scores implies quite different attitudes toward risk and profile scatter in the candidate's valuation score sets. A detailed discussion of these various combining rules is beyond the scope of this book.*

* For the reader who wishes to pursue the matter further, a detailed analysis of the combinatorial problem is contained in Allan Easton, *Complex Managerial Decisions Involving Multiple Objectives.* New York: John Wiley & Sons, Inc., 1973.

TABLE 9-3

VALUATION MATRIX OF SCORES FOR TEN CANDIDATES FOR POSITION
OF OFFICE SUPERVISOR AT HARD TIMES CORP.

Candidate's Name and Number (i)	Valuation Scores on These Eight Criteria (j)								Figure of Merit	Rank
	1	2	3	4	5	6	7	8		
1. Abelson	11.8	10.4	10.5	6.1	8.7	16.3	13.2	8.9	11.2	3
2. Blair	5.9	15.2	9.6	7.1	8.7	10.2	11.6	9.7	9.7	7
3. Clarkson	5.6	11.2	11.6	16.2	13.0	10.2	8.3	5.6	9.9	5
4. Davis	7.4	8.0	7.6	14.1	10.4	6.1	8.3	13.8	9.2	8
5. Evans	7.4	7.2	8.8	6.1	7.0	6.1	6.6	11.3	7.5	10
6. Franklin	10.3	8.8	13.0	10.1	8.7	8.2	14.9	5.2	9.8	6
7. Goldman	13.3	12.0	7.6	8.1	12.2	14.3	11.6	14.9	12.2	1
8. Holden	14.0	12.8	6.7	12.1	13.9	10.2	8.3	17.8	11.5	2
9. Iverson	11.8	8.0	10.9	10.1	8.7	10.2	10.7	8.0	10.1	4
10. Judger	12.5	6.4	13.5	10.1	8.7	8.2	6.6	4.8	9.15	9
Criterion Weights (w_j)	0.21	0.15	0.09	0.13	0.06	0.17	0.09	0.11		

OTHER EVALUATION TECHNIQUES

Cost-Benefit Analysis

Cost-benefit analysis (abbreviated CBA) is a method for comparing the merits of alternative projects, programs, or actions when both the costs incurred and the outcomes can be expressed in monetary values. This technique involves a careful enumeration of all costs and benefits (also disbenefits) expected and computation of a ratio of net monetary value of benefits to net monetary value of costs. The relative worths of alternatives are determined from a ranking by the cost-benefit ratios.

Although it is customary to require that the cost-benefit ratio (actually benefits/costs) be substantially greater than one before an action can be considered for adoption, there may be instances where a choice must be made from among undesirable options. Then, although none has a ratio greater than or equal to one, the action with the highest ratio may be selected as the least undesirable.

Since costs and benefits usually take a number of different forms, it is customary in using CBA to try to make them all commensurate by reducing them to monetary values, no matter how difficult that task might be. Also, since many projects or actions incur costs and produce benefits at more than one point in time, it is customary to translate all to a common point in time—usually the present—through use of present value computations.

Complex projects usually produce costs and benefits for many persons and interest groups. To do a really comprehensive study, the costs and benefits to all affected parties ought to be considered. Typically, however, such thoroughness is exceptional. The CBA is performed from the viewpoint of the sponsor, and all subsidiary effects are left out of the computation altogether, or perhaps assigned to a catch-all category named *spillover effects.*

A CBA is one of the best ways for anticipating conflicts that usually erupt when one group receives the benefits from an action and another pays the costs. The daily newspapers carry stories regularly about such protests. Inequities of this sort can cause unexpected trouble for the firm, unless some kind of compensatory action can be added to the program to equalize the cost-benefit allocation.

Cost-benefit analysis has been used in the public sector for the evaluation of complex military, highway, waterway, and urban planning projects. It can also be used for actions of lesser magnitude such as evaluating the results of alternative direct response advertisements.

As a matter of fact, almost every rational person uses CBA, albeit in crude mental approximation, when he compares the worth of what he will receive in relation to what he must give up to obtain the benefits. What is lacking in the mental approximation is the actual quantification.

Since CBA depends heavily upon the ability to quantify costs and benefits, the technique loses power if important elements, such as collective benefits, noncompensatable disbenefits, etc. cannot be expressed in monetary terms. It is simply not true that everyone and everything has a price. In such cases, another technique called cost-effectiveness analysis (abbreviated CEA) may prove useful.

Cost-Effectiveness Analysis

Cost-effectiveness analysis is a procedure in which alternative means for attaining a clearly defined objective are compared. The purpose of a CEA is to discover the alternative action that will attain the stated objective at least cost, or, conversely, will maximize performance at a given level of cost. The result of a CEA is a numerical ratio having the dimensions: units of performance per dollar of cost.

Although some objectives may be impossible to quantify, it is frequently possible to devise a surrogate indicator that reflects the degree of objective attainment. The indicator must be a valid measure of the underlying objective, but its validity need not be 100 percent.

For example, a marketer with a fixed number of dollars to spend on an advertising campaign has as his overall objective to maximize the sales income from advertising, but he knows that this may not be feasible to quantify, because other factors than advertising affect the sales results. So he compromises by devising an indicator of campaign effectiveness, the *reach* of the media combinations available to him for the money he has to spend. What he looks for is the best combination of media, frequency, and message timing to maximize the audience exposure to his sales message. Or, alternatively, for a given reach, he would like to find the combination that will result in the least cost.

Although this advertising manager's purpose may be the same as the fellow who uses CBA for evaluating alternative direct response campaigns, that is, to translate advertising outlays into sales, direct measurement of the ultimate goal is not possible for many kinds of advertising. Thus, CEA is used in place of CBA.

When an activity will have both costs and results spread out over time, it is customary in CEA, too, to discount the cost back to a single instant in time, usually the present. The choice of an annual rate of interest to be used is not always a simple matter, but can usually be decided upon in the specific problem context.

When comparing the cost effectiveness of a family of alternative actions, it is not always necessary to quantify the numerator (the effectiveness measure of goal attainment). All that is necessary is to be able to express the relations: greater than, less than, or equal to.

Then, if cost can be held constant for a pair of alternatives, the one with the larger numerator is the preferred option. Conversely, if the goal attainment criteria scores for two alternatives can be held constant, the costs can be compared, and the one with the lesser cost found.

Thus, CEA can be used in instances where quantification on cardinal, interval scales is not feasible. All we really must know is, for a given cost, is one alternative better than, lesser than, or equal to another? Or, for two equally effective alternatives, which has the lesser cost? And, if we can perform a pair-by-pair comparison of the cost effectiveness of alternative actions, we can usually do a complete ranking job through the process of successive elimination analogous to the elimination procedure used in tennis tournaments.

Alternative Viewpoints in Negative Growth Situations

It is customary in designing change programs for the designer to give greatest weight to his client's viewpoint. If the client is a business firm, the change manager tries to arrive at a compromise among the conflicting interests of his immediate superiors, the company as a whole, the stockholders, and perhaps, the welfare of the particular organizational component of which he is a part.

Viewpoint can be important when there is a great deal at stake. A change that does not make disproportionate changes in the costs and benefits applied to the various interest groups that operate within and outside the firm is more likely to find easy acceptance than one that disturbs the equilibrium. If one group seems to be given an advantage over another, open conflict may be the result. It is not sufficient to focus on the overall good. All interests must be considered. This point is illustrated in Fig. 9-1. The large circle represents the gains made by the firm as a whole by a change. Note that the net benefits are equal to 50 units. Interest group A gains 40 units; group B gains 60 units; group C loses 50 units. Although the net gain for the company is 50, the gains and losses within the firm are unbalanced. We can expect Group B to be happy. Group A will be unhappy because it did not do as well as B. Group C will be very angry because it loses. If it has the power to disrupt or sabotage the change, C will do so.

One important principle can be inferred from the foregoing exam-

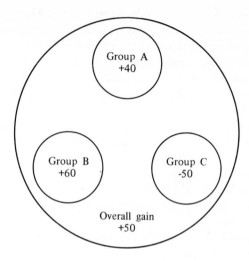

FIGURE 9-1. Circle diagram illustrating the relationship between interest group gains and losses in relation to gains for the firm as a whole.

ple. If one group gets benefits and another pays the costs, there is a built-in pressure leading to overt or covert conflict. Only equitable distribution of gains and losses can be depended upon to hold conflict to a minimum.

It is virtually impossible in a negative-growth situation to leave everybody better off at S_f than they were at S_i. To do so would be a major miracle. But what can often be done is to share the disbenefits of the change equitably. In some instances, equality in distribution of disbenefits is a better course than having some benefit and others suffer losses. Equality of sacrifice in a crisis often brings out the best in people. A distribution seen as inequitable provokes conflict and protest that can lead to damaging strife and disruption.

SELECTED REFERENCES

BELL, CHAUNCEY F., *Cost-Effectiveness as a Management Tool.* Santa Monica, Calif.: The Rand Corp. Doc. #2988, Oct. 1964.

EASTON, ALLAN, *Complex Managerial Decisions Involving Multiple Objectives.* New York: John Wiley and Sons, 1973.

MACCRIMMON, K. R., *Decisionmaking Among Multiple-Attribute Alternatives: A Survey and Consolidated Approach.* Santa Monica, Calif.: The Rand Corp. Doc. #RM-4823-ARPA, Dec. 1968.

McKEAN, R. N,. *Efficiency in Government Through System Analysis.* New York: John Wiley and Sons, 1958.

PREST, A. R. and R. TURVEY, "Cost-benefit Analysis: A Survey," *The Economic Journal,* Vol. LXXV, No. 300 (Dec. 1965), pp. 683–735).

QUADE, E. S., *Cost-Effectiveness: An Introduction and Overview.* Santa Monica, Calif.: The Rand Corp. Doc. # P3134, May 1965.

PART III

IMPLEMENTING NEGATIVE GROWTH PROGRAMS

Chapter 10

The Implementation Phase

Good ideas and good intentions do not lead inevitably to good results. One need only study the disappointing results of many of the well-intended programs for lifting the poor from poverty authorized by the United States Congress and carried out by successive national administrations to become convinced of the wisdom of Hazlitt's proverb:

> There's many a slip 'twixt the cup and the lip

and Robert Burn's observation:

> The best laid schemes o' mice and men
>   Gang aft a-gley
> And lea'd us naught but grief and pain,
>   For promis'd joy.

After the choice of action programs has been made, there comes the time for competent execution. It is here, in the implementation phase, where the best-intended plans go astray; where Murphy's Law—"If anything can go wrong, it will"—invariably applies.

THE ENVIRONMENT OF THE IMPLEMENTATION PHASE

Between the time that the negative growth program is conceived and the sequence of times that it is carried out to its conclusion, the firm's environment will have changed, too. If the environmental changes prove to be substantial, the details of the implementation plan will have to be altered accordingly.

However, rather than using a pure trial-and-error approach to implementation planning, a practice that usually requires an inordinate amount of scarce managerial time, a better approach is to do some forecasting before putting the implementation plans on paper. Of course, no amount of forecasting can totally eliminate the need for periodic adjustments in the implementation plan. But in cases where the environment changes in foreseeable ways, substantial economies of scarce managerial time can be achieved with a small effort at preplanning.

Although the relevant factors concerning the firm's environment will vary from situation to situation, the following list may be helpful in identifying the important aspects of the firm's external environment:

— Behavior of competitors in response to firm's changes.
— Behavior of customers in response to firm's actions.
— New technological developments.
— Interest rates and the state of the capital markets.
— Availability and price trends for basic materials.
— Import and export trade trends and legislation.
— Personal income and consumer buying expectations.
— Wage, salary, fringe-benefit trends.
— Employment and unemployment trends.
— Changes in local, state, and federal taxation.
— Changes in community attitudes.
— Legal developments (antitrust, consumerism, etc.).
— War and peace developments.
— Demographic factors.

Some of the foregoing environmental factors change so slowly that, in the short run at least, they can be thought of as being invariant. Others change from week to week, but in ways that are predictable. For example, the United States Congress may be considering important legislation that could have a major influence on the well-being of the firm. Although it is never certain what Congress will do, or when it will act, the effect of the legislation, if enacted into law, can be factored into the change plan.

Forecasting Methods

Everyone does some forecasting, because everyone makes decisions that will have their consequences at a later time. Most people do their forecasting intuitively, using whatever information is available to them at the time. Business executives are no exception to this rule. However, when matters of importance are involved, many businessmen prefer to have their intuitive predictions bolstered with formal forecasts made by persons trained in the art.

Since no one can really know what will happen in the distant future, it is usual to sort the environmental factors into three basic categories: certain, risky, and uncertain. By certainty is meant that one is willing to act as if he knew what the state of the environment will be. Everyone recognizes that errors are possible, but if the certainty condition exists, the likelihood of serious error is small.

Risk is different in the sense that we are willing to act as if we knew the probability of an event's happening. In actual fact, it will either happen or not happen. But, over a long chain of events, we act as if we knew the relative proportion of happenings and nonhappenings.

In the case of uncertainty, we admit to ourselves that we have no idea what will happen, nor is it possible to find out. We know that we must maintain the utmost flexibility because one event is just as likely, or unlikely, as another.

Under the certainty assumption, plans can be made with a high degree of confidence. Under risk, alternative plans may be necessary to cope with the situation that may or may not happen. Under uncertainty, we plan for the greatest flexibility; that is, we proceed on a trial-and-error basis.

Reasoning from the foregoing, we say that forecasting begins with a belief that the environment is characterized by either certainty or risk. Since, by definition, uncertainty is unknowable, forecasting has no place in such situations.

THE PERSISTENCE MODEL.   This method of forecasting is based upon the assumption that what is now happening will continue to happen. For example, we know that a particular machine is capable of producing 5000 pieces of work per hour. It has always done so, so we predict that it will continue to do so in the future. Of course, everyone knows that from time to time the machine breaks down, but with good preventive maintenance, these breakdowns can be held to a very low frequency.

THE TRAJECTORY MODEL.   The environment is changing, but the rate of change is known, and we believe that that rate will not change materially. For example, the population on earth is growing at a rate that will cause it to double every 30 years.

THE CYCLICAL MODEL.   Certain phonomena occur in cycles, and we assume that they will continue to exhibit cyclical behavior. For example, stock market prices change in a cyclical manner.

THE ASSOCIATIVE MODEL.   We believe that the phenomenon under study has shown a high degree of positive correlation with another observed or measured phenomenon—for example, forecasting sales of luxury goods from changes in discretionary income.

ANALOG MODELS.   We believe that the phenomenon under study obeys certain mathematical laws. By discovering the nature of the natural or mathematical laws, we can make reliable forecasts.

FAMILIAR COMBINATION OF CIRCUMSTANCES MODEL.   We believe that we can detect striking similarities between the current situation and ones that we have knowledge of from the past. Since we know how the past events worked out, we forecast that the present situation will work out in the same way.

IDENTIFICATION OF CAUSES MODEL.   If we can discover the underlying cause of a phenomenon, we can make good predictions of how a particular environmental factor will be affected by a change in the causative factor. For example, sales calls result in sales to customers.

INFERENCES FROM A SMALL SAMPLE.   Although we cannot get all the evidence needed to make a reliable forecast, we believe that the smattering of evidence we do have is sufficiently representative to justify making a forecast.

THE ADAPTIVE MODEL.   We begin with a forecast made with our favorite model. As time goes on, we compare the forecasted events with those that actually happened. Periodically we update the forecast until a pattern of over- or underpredicting emerges. From a study of the forecasting errors, we can refine the methods used.

THE BACKWARD-LOOKING MODEL.   We devise a method of forecasting and test it by seeing how well it reproduces the past. If it does a good job of reconstructing the past events or state of the environment, we make predictions about the future with greater confidence.

THE JURY OF INFORMED OPINION MODEL.   We ask a number of well-informed people or people expert in a certain field what they believe will happen, and we accept their opinions as our forecast.

THE NOSTRADAMUS MODEL.   A well-recommended prophet, seer, or clairvoyant is consulted, and his (or her) forecast is accepted as plausible. Although this model does not work well in societies that place little stock in the predictions of such persons, it may work remarkably well in societies that believe in their prognostications. Thus, the forecast becomes a self-fulfilling prophecy, because people often act on the basis of what they believe to be the truth and not on the objective truth.

CONTROLLED IMPLEMENTATION

One way of controlling the progress of the negative-growth program is to construct a detailed plan, indoctrinate all the departmental managers in the objectives and procedures of the program, and let it fly, hoping that everyone will do his job exactly as expected. In general-systems parlance, this is an example of open-loop control or "free flight."

A second way of controlling the progress being made is to use periodic control with feedback, a modified closed-loop procedure. Such a control procedure is shown in flow-chart form in Fig. 10-1.

The output of the system being observed is monitored on one or more criteria. Their readings are compared, criterion by criterion, with the standards established by the plan. If the deviation of the criteria scores in comparison to the plan is excessive, timely and appropriate action is called for. If no one deviation falls outside of the tolerable bounds, another set of observations is made, and this subroutine is repeated over and over again until the change process is completed.

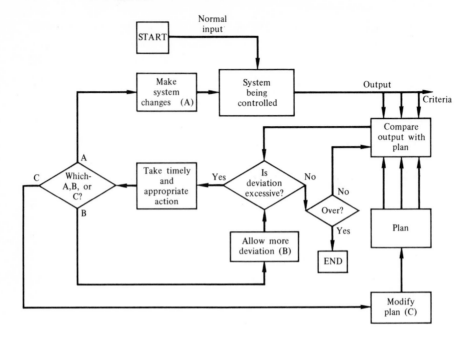

FIGURE 10-1.   Control model.

If timely and appropriate correction was called for by the control model, there is a choice of three types of corrective action:

1 / Make changes in the system to bring it into conformity.
2 / If the system cannot respond or the changes required are too costly, change the plan.
3 / If the foregoing are not feasible, relax the tolerance on one or more of the criteria so that the deviations will no longer be excessive.

A control system such as is shown in Fig. 10-1 can be applied to each organizational segment undergoing change, and to the firm as a whole.

MONITORING THE CHANGE PROCESS

As the firm goes through its retrenchment, from its initial to its final size, its component parts, too, undergo alterations. A few of the organizational segments must shrink disproportionately; others shrink proportionately; some remain relatively unaffected; others may even grow larger because of reallocation of resources.

Whichever happens, the firm's management cannot leave the program implementation to chance, nor can it allow the firm to drift. Proper, detailed planning, control, and coordination are needed to guarantee that all parts of the organization follow predetermined paths, in correct time sequence, so that they all make their contribution to the end result. The planning for the implementation phase can be broken up into several steps.

STEP 1. SPECIFICALLY, WHICH FUNCTIONS OR ORGANIZATIONAL SEGMENTS ARE INVOLVED IN THE CHANGE?   As an answer to this question, prepare a complete table of organization by activity area, departments, and functions. Those components that will be unaffected by the change can be shown in rough form, but the parts that will be affected should be shown in full detail. If the chart becomes too unwieldly, separate charts should be prepared for each organizational component. Examples of activity areas are production, marketing, research and development, and finance and control.

Figure 10-2 shows a condensed table of organization for a highly centralized, multiplant industrial firm. The arrows indicate the three plants that will be shut down and disposed of. The check marks indicate those segments of the firm that will probably be affected by the plant shutdowns and will probably have to undergo negative growth. The numbers indicate the size of the employment rosters for the segments. By shutting down the three plants, the firm's operations roster will shrink from 23,850 (operatives, supervisors, support personnel, and managers) to about 11,650 (a drop of 12,200 persons).

Before the initiation of the negative growth program, the headquarters staff consists of 595 persons, which includes all officers, staff specialists, and employees, down to sweepers and clerks. The sales force in the four regional divisions approximates 610 persons, including salesmen, sales administrators, and other clerical workers.

Figure 10-3 shows more detail for the organizational segment under the jurisdiction of the Vice President for Personnel and Industrial Relations located at headquarters. Also shown are the numbers of employees engaged in each of thirteen functional departments. Not shown in Fig. 10-3 are the numbers of persons engaged in personnel work in the eight plants who report directly to the plant general managers but who look for standards and guidance to the headquarters people engaged in their specialty.

STEP 2. SPECIFICALLY, WHAT IS THE TIME SCHEDULE FOR THE

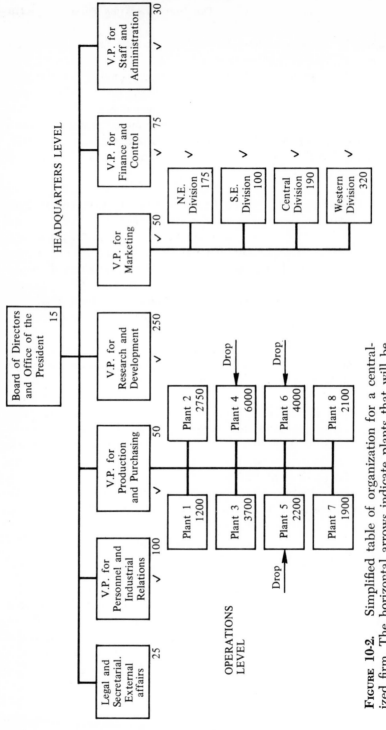

Figure 10-2. Simplified table of organization for a central-ized firm. The horizontal arrows indicate plants that will be disposed of. The check marks indicate segments that will un-dergo negative growth. The numbers indicate the size of the employment roster for that segment.

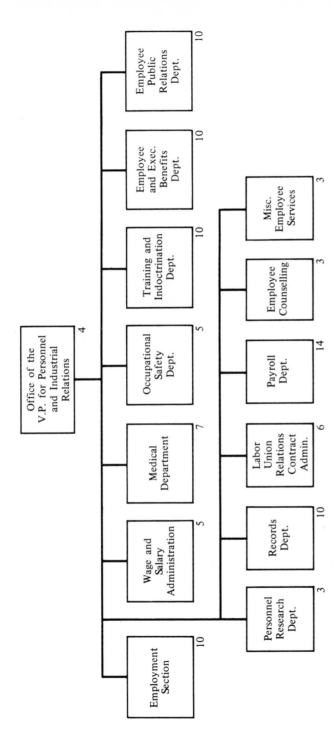

Figure 10-3. Breakdown of the functions of the headquarters staff under the jurisdiction of the Vice President for Personnel and Industrial Relations. In addition to his headquarters responsibilities, each departmental manager has general supervision over his opposite numbers in the company's plants. Numbers show the number of persons in each department located at headquarters only.

CHANGES?   The timing may be determined by factors beyond the control of the firm's management, but usually, an alert management can anticipate events with sufficient precision that it can remain the master of the firm's destiny. If that is the case, then a schedule of changes can be established. The change can be accomplished in one sudden swoop (the "earthquake" technique), or it can be accomplished in stages. Which pattern is used depends upon the specific set of facts that control the situation.

For the example shown in Fig. 10-2, we assume that the curtailments will take place as follows:

1 /   Plant 4: shutdown starts January 15, ends February 15.

2 /   Plant 5: shutdown starts March 15, ends April 15.

3 /   Plant 6: shutdown starts June 15, ends July 15.

4 /   Sales force reductions start June 15 and are completed by September 15.

5 /   Layoffs in the Personnel and Industrial Relations segment start March 14 and should be completed by year's end.

6 /   Layoffs in other affected departments are substantially at the same rate as for the sales department.

STEP 3. SPECIFICALLY, WHAT WILL THE FIRM BE LIKE AT THE COMPLETION OF THE NEGATIVE GROWTH CHANGE PROCESS?   At this stage in the planning process, the best one can do is to establish the end-of-change condition of the firm in broad-brush strokes. Questions like these are asked and answered:

—   What will be the annual sales rates?

—   How many plants will still be operating?

—   How many customers will we continue to serve?

—   How many employees will we still have?

Stage 3 is merely a rough before-and-after estimate. The firm's managers know where they stand at the initiation of the change. Wishful thinking aside, they estimate where they can realistically expect to be at the end of the change.

STEP 4. SPECIFICALLY, WHAT CRITERIA AND MILESTONES ARE TO BE USED FOR MONITORING THE PROGRESS OF THE CHANGE?   Both for the firm as a whole, and for each of its segments, monitoring criteria and checkpoints in time are established with detail sufficient to enable those in charge of each segment to monitor the change process.

Some of the criteria that can be used are:

1 / Number of employees in each job category.

2 / Breakdown of income and expense by relevant category.

3 / Total number of units of output (product or services).

4 / Total numbers of units of input handled.

5 / Output quality.

6 / Inventory levels.

7 / Quantities of fixed assets (e.g., equipment, machines, furniture, etc.).

8 / Total financial assets used by the segment.

9 / Absenteeism, number of grievances, employee turnover.

Of course, the specific nature of the activity determines the actual criteria that should be used for monitoring purposes.

The criteria having been established, the next task is to assign the initial, final, and interim values expected for the criteria. If possible, fixed checkpoints in time should be used for monitoring, reporting, and control purposes.

A particularly useful display technique for assembly and monitoring the performance and progress of a segment is the Gantt chart shown in condensed form in Fig. 10-4. The rows of the Gantt chart correspond to the criteria used; the columns correspond to the milestones (times), and the cell entries to the planned numerical values of the criteria at each milestone. A parallel set of cells can be supplied to permit entering the actual criteria scores.

The Gantt chart is used to compare planned progress with actual performance. If the change goes according to plan in all segments and on all criteria, no alarms need be raised. However, if the performance is at variance with the plan, timely and appropriate corrective action may be called for.

The Gantt chart of Fig. 10-4 shows the staffing criterion scores for the personnel segment of the firm illustrated in Fig. 10-2 and 10-3. Note that as the staff curtailments proceed in the plants, the work loads of the various departments change. For example, the employment section with the task of aiding employees in finding new jobs takes on a few extra employment counsellors. The training and indoctrination section is given the task of retraining many high-seniority employees that are being transferred to other jobs vacated by people of lesser seniority.

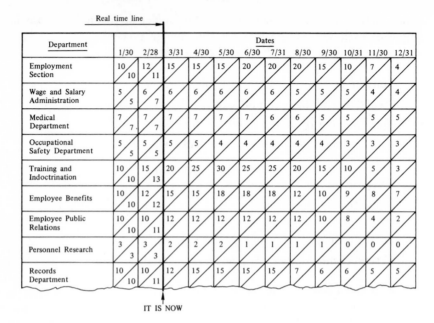

Real time line

Department	Dates											
	1/30	2/28	3/31	4/30	5/30	6/30	7/31	8/30	9/30	10/31	11/30	12/31
Employment Section	10/10	12/11	15	15	15	20	20	20	15	10	7	4
Wage and Salary Administration	5/5	6/7	6	6	6	6	6	5	5	5	4	4
Medical Department	7/7	7/7	7	7	7	7	6	6	5	5	5	5
Occupational Safety Department	5/5	5/5	5	5	4	4	4	4	4	3	3	3
Training and Indoctrination	10/10	15/13	20	25	30	25	25	20	15	10	5	3
Employee Benefits	10/10	12/12	15	15	18	18	18	12	10	9	8	7
Employee Public Relations	10/10	10/11	12	12	12	12	12	12	10	8	4	2
Personnel Research	3/3	3/3	2	2	2	1	1	1	1	0	0	0
Records Department	10/10	10/11	12	15	15	15	15	7	6	6	5	5

IT IS NOW

FIGURE 10-4.   Staffing chart for the Personnel and Industrial Relations Division (upper left-hand part is planned value; lower right, actual value).

Thus, the work load of this department rises during the actual factory layoffs. The employee benefits department's work load rises, too, because it must handle severance pay, vested rights to pensions, transfer of insurance benefits from company-paid group-life to employee-paid insurance, and many other similar tasks.

Although in the interim phases of the change program some personnel departments and sections show a rise in employment, by the end of the year all are below their initial staffing levels as of January 1. By the end of the year, the nine departments shown in Fig. 10-4 have experienced a drop in personnel from 70 to 33.

Although it is not shown in any of the figures, the sales department, the production and purchasing department, and the others marked with checks in Fig. 10-2 would undergo corresponding staff curtailments.

STEP 5. WHICH INDIVIDUALS ARE TO BE ASSIGNED THE RESPONSIBILITIES FOR STEERING EACH SEGMENT AND SUBSEGMENT THROUGH THE NEGATIVE GROWTH CHANGE PROCESS?   Usually the responsibility for monitoring and steering the segment through the change process is assigned to the manager in charge. Each manager reports to his superior. This simple arrangement may not be workable if one of the persons to be discharged is the manager of the particular segment. In such cases, it may be better to make the leadership change at the beginning so that the new manager can approach the task with a free mind.

STEP 6.   In accordance with the management by exception principle, each segment manager has his end and interim goals as specified in the criteria scores. He ought also be given some leeway in the form of numerical tolerances or deviations within which he has the freedom to operate. If, for any reason, the performance deviates more than the tolerance, he is required to call this fact to the attention of his superior as soon as the manager discovers the excessive deviation.

STEP 7. WHAT ORGANIZATIONAL ARRANGEMENTS ARE MADE FOR CO-ORDINATING AND CONTROLLING THE OVERALL PERFORMANCE OF THE FIRM? Regular interim reports of progress and deviations should be made and distributed to a prearranged list. Periodic committee meetings can be held in which managers meet to discuss their progress, the obstacles they face, the miscalculations embodied in the change plans, any plan modifications that seem necessary, plus any other matters deemed necessary for smooth implementation.

THE HIERARCHY OF IMPLEMENTATION PLANS.   As the seven steps discussed above imply, the full set of implementation plans make up a hierarchy. At the top of the ladder is the overall plan for the firm as a whole. Then there are the plans for the major organizational segments as wholes. Each of these will also include plans for its component parts, and so on down the line until every organizational segment that will be affected by the negative-growth change process is covered by a plan of implementation.

Obviously, in a real change situation, some short cuts can be used, particularly with lower-level units. Also, for tactical reasons, it may be unwise actually to commit all plans to writing. This is especially true when it is necessary to keep the change plans secret. Because of the many possible breaches of security possible with written plans, however desirable they may be, putting plans into written form may not be prudent.

However, in a large, complex organization, the risk of bad mixups grows if the plans are kept in the heads of just a few people. Memories fail; semantic confusions abound; errors are covered up. Thus, the executive in charge is faced with a tradeoff decision. On the one hand he risks premature disclosure of details; on the other hand, he risks defective implementation because of lack of specificity in plans, difficulty in securing accountability for unwritten plans, and greater opportunity for errors and outright misfeasance, malfeasance, and nonfeasance in execution.

DOWNWARD COMMUNICATION POLICY

Because the implementation phase of the negative growth program is likely to be one filled with anxiety and stress for all participants, downward communication policy takes on special importance. What should the management's policy be? What are its alternatives? Consider these two extremes:

1 / Tell everyone in the firm everything there is to know except possibly for those few bits of information that must be kept confidential.

2 / Tell only those very few things each person must know in order to do his particular job, and nothing more.

What are the consequences that can be expected from either policy?

Before attempting to answer this question, it is necessary to consider first the nature of the communication networks in the typical firm. All firms have two communication networks: the formal and the informal. The formal channels are controlled mainly by members of management; the informal are controlled mainly by employees (both supervisory and nonsupervisory).

Formal communication networks are used by management to promote its own aims for the company. They send messages, either written or verbal, down the organizational hierarchy for the purpose of enhancing productivity and promoting effectiveness.

Informal networks have a completely different aim. Employees use the informal channels to keep themselves informed about matters that affect their well-being and that help them to protect themselves against the capricious exercise of managerial power. Therefore, the informal communication network is aimed at defense and not at all at enhancing organizational efficiency. Whatever may be the communication policy of the firm, through the interplay of the formal and informal communication channels, the organization's participants work very hard at keeping themselves informed of whatever they believe they ought to know.

SPECULATION ON THE EFFECTS OF POLICY 1.   When the firm uses policy 1 and makes full information available for everybody in the organization, there is very little information gathering work for the informal organization to do, because the burden of generating and circulating information is taken over by the formal organization. However, if this policy is carried to its logical extreme, there is so much information issued each day that members suffer from information overload. Desks are piled high with unread memoranda and reports. Hardly anyone knows what is and what is not important.

Because of the unending flood of information, a well-developed informal organization devotes itself to the task of interpretation and anticipation. Persons who develop skills in knowing what is and what is not important, or who know when something important is in the communication pipelines, find themselves in positions of power and prestige in the organization.

SPECULATION ON THE EFFECTS OF POLICY 2.   If there is an information drought, the informal organization's urgent task is to obtain the necessary information by whatever means it can devise. Key people with access to critical information leak the data in exchange for power, prestige, deference, and, perhaps, more tangible rewards. The rumor mill is active, and all kinds of tricks are developed either for getting information directly from a reliable source or for obtaining clues that allow reasonable inferences on what is going on and is about to happen.

FURTHER SPECULATIONS.   In the case of policy 1, little effort is required of the informal organization for gathering useful information. But with policy 2, a great deal of effort and time must be spent in gathering, passing along, discussing, and interpreting information obtained through leaks and guesses.

In the case of policy 1, the firm incurs large expenses for writing, typing, copying, transporting, reading, and filing away written matter. For policy 2, much less time and money are expended on preparation and transmission of written materials, but a lot of company-paid time is used by employees in discussion and exchange of information.

Which policy is the better? Part of the answer lies in the choice of managerial style of the firm's executives. If they wish to appear open and outgoing with their subordinates, freer rather than restricted access to information is indicated. If, on the other hand, they elect to be closed-mouth and unforthcoming, less information passes through the formal channels and more through the informal route.

There is still no conclusive research to support a definite conclusion about whether or not the firm's employees are adequately informed under either policy extreme. Perhaps the amount of good and useful information in circulation will be just as large under either policy, but the relative burdens placed on the formal and informal channels differ markedly.

If a retrenchment is carried out over a short time span, both the formal and informal networks are seriously disturbed. However, since the informal organization is probably the more flexible of the two, management need not fear that its people will be shamefully uninformed if it temporarily neglects feeding the formal channels. Only a naïve management will believe that the organization's members will allow themselves to remain uninformed for long about the things that affect them in an important way.

During the implementation of a program of negative growth, many employees leave the company, some voluntarily; others are terminated. When this happens, there is a great danger that trade and business secrets will be jeopardized by employees carrying off copies of confidential documents. If there are many documents, memoranda, and reports circulating around the company, it is much too easy for some to be taken away. This danger tends to support a restrictive communication policy, at least when layoffs are imminent.

Another fact that suggests a restrictive rather than an open policy is the large difference between what the employees want very much to know and the kind of information management issues in the name of efficiency. Management may sincerely believe that it is being open and forthcoming by placing large amounts of operational information in the formal network, when, in fact, most of the employees and supervisors have their minds on quite different subjects. Under such conditions, much of the information regularly supplied under policy 1 is ignored, and as a result the money spent in the name of full and free communication is partly wasted.

SELECTED REFERENCES

BENNIS, W. G. et al., *The Planning of Change.* New York: Holt, Rinehart and Winston, Inc. 1969.

BOCCHINO, WILLIAM A., *Management Information Systems: Tools and Techniques.* Englewood Cliffs, N.J.: Prentice-Hall, Inc. 1972.

CARROL, S. J., and H. L. TOSI, JR., *Management by Objectives: Applications and Research.* New York: The Macmillan Company, 1973.

CHASE, ANDREW, B. JR., "How To Make Downward Communication Work," *Personnel Journal* (June 1970), pp. 478–483.

ENRICK, NORBERT L., *Market and Sales Forecasting*. San Francisco, Calif.: Chandler Publishing Company, 1969.

GEMMIL, GARY, "Managing Upward Communication," *Personnel Journal* (Feb. 1970), pp. 107–110.

Long Range Profit Planning. N.A.A. Research Report #42, New York: National Association of Accountants, 1964.

O'CONNELL, J. J., *Managing Organizational Innovation*. Homewood, Ill.: R. D. Irwin, 1968.

READ, W. H., "Upward Communication in Industrial Hierarchy." *Human Relations*, Vol. 15 (1962), pp. 3–15.

STEINER, GEORGE A., *Top Management Planning*. New York: The Macmillan Company, 1969.

STRONG, E. P. and R. D. SMITH, *Management Control Models*. New York: Holt, Rinehart and Winston, 1968.

Chapter 11

Human Factors
and Stress

INTRODUCTION

Why should the business executive accept human factors as a matter of concern equal to, if not greater than, his concern for the management of economic resources? When he accepts the proposition that he must give a large part of his time and energy in dealing with human problems, does he not run the risk that he will confuse his role with that of a social worker?

If we think of the business firm, not as a piece of personal property that the owners (through their agents) can do with as they please to achieve their personal aims, but as a coming together of many interest groups, we can gain a better insight into the answers to the two questions posed above. According to this view of the firm, the chief executive and his team of helpers manage the coalition of interest groups so as to achieve a reasonable compromise of the benefit-contributions mix due to and from each.

Thus, the executive team (an interest group itself) mediates the demands made on the firm by:

— customers
— suppliers
— employees and their unions
— creditors of all classes
— stockholders of all classes
— governments on all levels
— the local and regional communities
— prospective and former employees
— families of employees
— competitors
— industry and trade associations
— criminal elements in the community

Each of the foregoing interest groups have claims on the business firm. Some are legitimate (stockholders' claims for dividend income, creditors' claims for repayment of debts, employees' claims for just compensation, etc.); some are illegitimate and must be combatted. Some are urgent and pressing and, therefore, must be assigned high priority (e.g., customer shipments, meeting a payroll); others are less pressing and need not be given high priority (employment opportunities for graduates of local high schools). Each group has the potential for making a contribution (good or bad) to the continued well-being of the firm. Viewed from this perspective, the economic resources under the control and trusteeship of the firm's executives are but a means to the end of serving (or frustrating) the interest groups, and are not an end in themselves.

The combination of interest groups that make up the firm's legitimate and illegitimate claimants can be divided into two large classes: internal and external. This chapter is devoted to examination of the response of the internal constituencies to the stresses imposed by negative growth and to their responses to the fact and threat of change. Later chapters deal with the responses to negative growth of external groups and how managements can cope with these reactions.

Management's Attitude Toward Change

Management perceives the change process as essential to the continued well-being of the firm. They recognize, however, that they will encounter some reluctance on the part of the firm's employees to cooperate enthusiastically with the change program. This sluggish response to management's logic is given the name, "resistance to change"; many articles have been written on the general topic of "overcoming resistance to change." Resistance to change, in the management's view, arises either from employee misunderstanding of the obvious merits of the change, or from the management's inability to "communicate" with the employees. "If only they can be made to understand the objectives of the proposed change, we're certain we can persuade them that it's to their best interests," the firm's executives reason.

As a practical matter, employees see organizational change in a totally different light than does the management. To the employees, change can be a real threat to important values. Thus, management commits a serious error if it views resistance as being pathological and unwarranted and something to be explained away. Management also commits a serious error if it believes that its perceptions of the benefits and disbenefits of a change for employees are correct, and the employee's perceptions, misguided.

Management will be better able to cope realistically with the human response to change if it accepts the fact that the employees probably understand the effects of the change on their well-being better than does the management. Employees know when they are being hurt; they know what is good and bad for them. They are not likely to respond in a favorable manner to an emissary from top management who tries to convince them that black is white, that bad is good, and that falsehoods are the truth. Employees do not take kindly to being treated as recalcitrant children who must be taught what is good for them. They do not react favorably to well-intended lectures that reveal that the lecturer is completely out of touch with the realities of the work environment and to the real effects of change for the people directly affected by it.

COMMON HUMAN REACTIONS TO CHANGE

Shock of Disaffiliation

Many psychologists believe that man, being a social animal, has a strong affiliation need. For example, one of the cruelest punishments that can be inflicted on a misbehaving prison inmate is to place him in solitary confinement, where he is deprived of all human contact for an extended time. Thus, to deprive a person of the opportunity for making satisfying human contacts is to deprive him of the ability to satisfy one of his basic human needs.

People find the opportunity for satisfying their affiliation need in a number of ways. They have human contact within their family situation (if they have a family to go home to); they meet with people in social activities (e.g., parties, congregating in the local tavern, etc.); they have human contact in their work situation.

The work environment in which the employee spends a large part of his week (eight hours a day, five days a week) provides him with multiple opportunities for satisfying his need for affiliation. Not only is there the face-to-face interaction with fellow employees, with customers, suppliers, etc., but the money he earns allows him to go places to meet other people in a more congenial atmosphere.

A retrenchment presents the employee with several kinds of threats to his ability to satisfy his affiliation need. He may be separated from the firm altogether, so he loses good friendly contacts; he suffers a loss of income, which curtails his opportunities outside of his job. If he still remains with the firm, but is transferred to another job, he finds that his social relationships with his fellow employees have been disrupted and he is isolated until he can make new contacts in the changed work place. If the new position places him in a group that has close social relationships, he may find it difficult if not impossible to break into that impermeable group. Even if the particular employee does not have his job and place of work changed but his fellow employees are moved away or terminated, the satisfying work and social group that aided so much in satisfying his feeling of belongingness is shattered. In this sense, organizational change causes the employee to see himself as worse off.

Rising Anxiety Levels

Fear, a distressing emotion, is aroused by the perception of imminent danger to the person, of pain, or of loss of something believed to be very valuable or dear. By definition, fear is associated with a recognizable threat. Fear has survival value, because it stimulates defensive measures designed to protect and defend the threatened person against imminent danger of harm or loss.

Anxiety, on the other hand, is a generalized anticipatory form of fear, in which the true nature of the threat is not yet apparent. Anxiety results from mental pictures of dangers that have not yet materialized, but which might some day appear. Anxiety may have survival value if the anticipation of danger turns out to be fully justified. But when one builds defenses, time and again, against threats which never materialize, anxiety can cause large wasteful expenditures of mental and physical energy.

Free-floating anxiety is the name of the generalized, anticipatory fears completely unassociated with any real, perceivable threat. It is accompanied by general forebodings of disaster, with pessimism, and with constantly mobilized bodily defenses. Free-floating anxiety can have destructive effects of mental and physical health and at the very minimum is a major cause of fatigue. An analogy is a fire department that spends its working day responding to false alarms. When a real fire alarm rings, the firefighters are exhausted and can hardly cope with the real dangers to property, human life, and their own physical safety.

If the popular psychological literature is any guide, virtually every person alive today suffers from free-floating anxiety. Are there not enough threats to our sanity and safety? Think of the atom bomb, radioactive leakage from nuclear reactors, bacteriological warfare, pollution of the air and water supply, eavesdropping by wire tappers, violations of individual privacy and freedoms by use of centralized data banks, the threat of famine from food shortages and an inability to feed a rapidly growing population. Add to these global threats the danger of annhilation by automobile accident, cancer and heart disease, food poisoning, building collapse, and random violence by crazed bomb throwers and political terrorists.

If these real and imagined dangers are not enough for the average company employee to bear, a program of negative growth will pile more threats upon already overburdened anxiety-prone individuals. Some will be strong enough to carry the additional burden; others will not. Those unfortunate individuals, already on the verge of breaking, will either crack up or seek some form of escape from the overwhelming pressure.

More specifically related to the work situation, employees' anxieties can be expected to shoot up in intensity when presented with any combination of the following job-related dangers:

— Loss of satisfying social relationships

— Loss of money income

— Loss of prestige at work and in his social and family milieu

— Loss of opportunity for advancement

— Loss of security in his old age

— Loss of stability and certainty in his life

— Loss of satisfying ways to spend his time

— Loss of specific company-paid benefits

— Loss of control over his personal destiny.

It is inevitable that the employees, managers, and executives of a firm that is ripe for a substantial retrenchment will be suffering from elevated levels of free-floating anxiety. As the necessity for a contraction in size of the firm becomes increasingly apparent, the generalized anxiety is transformed to actual fear of specific dangers.

A humane management will seek to minimize the human cost associated with these elevated anxiety levels. Objective fear, stimulated by known dangers and imminence of loss of valued things and relationships, is easier to cope with than vague anxiety. Doing something constructive to rescue one's self, and to reduce the impact of losses, is less damaging to physical and mental health than allowing one's self to become paralyzed into inaction, or to develop symptoms of psychosomatic or mental illness in a futile and self-defeating attempt to escape from reality.

BEHAVIOR SUGGESTIVE OF STRESS OVERLOAD.   As anxiety levels rise, more and more employees and managers can be expected to show signs of stress overload, occasionally through unusual or even bizarre behavior.

— Gamma Corporation manufactures fine furniture sewing machine cabinets, but business has been declining in the face of cut-price foreign competition. Frank X, Gamma's star salesman, returns to the head office every Saturday to fill out his expense vouchers and arrange for special customers' orders. Frank arrives early one Saturday morning, walks into the factory and sprays fifty finished cabinets with fire-extinguisher fluid and sand from fire pails. The factory manager, who happens to arrive just as Frank is putting the fire pails and extinguishers back on their hangers, is horrified by the damage Frank's action has caused. To protect Frank from being discovered, the factory manager calls his cabinet finishers in to work and has all of the damaged cabinets refinished by Monday morning.

— Anthony P is production foreman of an electrical appliance assembly plant. Anthony is known throughout the compony for his good nature, his willingness to stop and swap jokes with other managers, and above all for the wonderful rapport he has with the female assemblers who comprise 95 percent of the work force. Anthony's friends notice that he is going through a change of personality. Instead of being his usual smiling self, he flies into rages and shouts at everyone in his vicinity. Instead of joking chitchat with the factory women, he scowls at them, mutters under his breath, and sometimes calls them by uncomplimentary names.

— Harry Y has always been a decisive person. His subordinates marvelled at Harry's ability to make difficult choices quickly, without evidence of strain or vacillation. Recently, Harry's decisiveness has vanished. Not only is he unable to make the simplest decisions, but even after deciding, he changes his mind over and over again. If the decision is a difficult one, he may procrastinate until the pressure for action builds up to an intolerable level and calls for action from a higher authority.

— Charles L, General Sales Manager, has been missing too many days' work. He disappears for a week at a time and no one, even his wife, knows where he goes. One day, the president receives a telephone call from the local police precinct saying that a man named Charles L (so identified by a business card in his wallet) has been arrested for public intoxication upon the complaint of a motel manager.

— Marty J, a man of robust health, is taken away by ambulance to the local hospital, suffering from a hemorrhaging stomach ulcer.

— Thomas P, a group product manager, has been complaining that everyone in the company is plotting against him. He has prepared a long bill of particulars, all of the incidents proving that the people in the company are "out to get him."

— Mary Q is the executive secretary of the personnel director. She is a woman of middle age, but she is proud of her smooth skin and trim figure. She is known to go for ballet lessons and to spend many hours making her own clothes. Mary has a companywide reputation for cleanliness, stylishness, and meticulousness of dress and grooming. A few weeks after Mary learns that her boss is being terminated, she appears depressed. She comes to work in wrinkled clothes, her stockings show holes, her hair is bedraggled, and instead of smiling to everyone she meets, she whines and complains.

— Peter M is a hard-driving junior executive who has his eye on a top job in the company. He receives a promotion to the rank of Assistant Vice President for Finance and Divisional Comptroller with the understanding that he is next in line for the full vice presidency. As an economy measure and because he is showing signs of increasing dissastisfaction with company policy, Peter's boss is fired and Peter is elevated to the coveted position. After three weeks on the job, Peter develops severe abdominal cramps and is diagnosed as having a serious case of ulcerative colitis.

— Albert Z works in the purchasing department as assistant to the Director of Purchasing. One of his jobs is to take care of the breaking in of new buyers, assistant buyers, expediters, and clerks. Albert knows more about the workings and history of the purchasing department than anyone in the company, including his boss. Albert has always been a willing teacher and a fountainhead of information. He has received numerous written commendations from top buyers on his helpfulness and cooperation. A rumor filters through the department that the firm is planning to go out of the fabrication part of its business and that a number of the people in the purchasing department will be let go. Albert undergoes a change in personality. He is no longer outgoing and free with information. He becomes morose and secretive. Before long, he refuses to tell anyone the right time. When asked for information he would have given freely a few months earlier, Albert just grunts and grimaces and gives a nonresponsive reply.

Miscellaneous Social and Cultural Responses

Observers who have studied the organizational change process have formulated a number of useful generalizations:

1 / Organization change can be done more smoothly if the employees have personalities high in flexibility and low in rigidity.

2 / An organization is a complex, interlocking system of learned behavior. Breaking up that system of habitual, preprogrammed behavior is not easy, and putting a new one together quickly and at low cost is harder still.

3 / Offers for all employees, supervisors, and managers to participate in the change implementation phase will reduce unpleasant feelings of helplessness and the anger at being manipulated by remote, powerful, malignant, and invisible forces.

4 / Employees and work groups look not only at what happens to them, but also at what happens to others. They judge both the absolute and the relative desirability (or lack of same) of what is asked of them.

5 / In general, both low- and middle-level managers and employees harbor deep suspicions and mistrust for top management. Part of this is bound up in their cultural inheritance, the so-called "rank-and-file complex." Part of the hostility arises from the bad press business has received in recent years. Part is based upon bad experiences almost everyone has had in his business life; the bad is

more likely to be recalled in times of stress than the good. No amount of "sweet talk" or appeals to rational thought will ever succeed in dispelling completely that ingrained suspicion of management's motives in ordering a retrenchment.

6 / Although change is more likely to be unwelcome rather than greeted with pleasure, if conditions are intolerable enough, almost any change will be perceived as an improvement.

7 / The survivors of a large staff curtailment will have deep guilt feelings about the departed. The more survivors rejoice that they were not fired, too, the deeper and more intense will be the guilt. For many persons, guilt changes into self-hate (I did that rotten thing, so I must be no good); self-hate, into anxiety (because I'm bad, I deserve to be punished by God or by fate); anxiety, into anger at those who provoke the guilt (who the hell are they to make me feel so bad?).

8 / When a manager's range of responsibility is reduced as, for example, when he has fewer subordinates to supervise, or his segment of the operation accounts for fewer dollars than before, or when he finds himself one more layer away from the top, he has a feeling of being diminished as a person. His organization status both within the firm and among other comparable firms is lowered; lower status brings lower prestige, lower power, and a general diminution of ability to obtain his just share of the world's goods.

9 / "This time, I survived; next time it may be my turn" is a theme that runs through the survivor's mind. He watches how the persons terminated are treated. He knows that the company will treat the survivors well, because it still needs them. But how do they treat the people they no longer need? That, in many employees' minds, is the acid test of good character.

WHO HAS POWER OVER WHOM?

Top-Down Power

According to traditional theory, managerial power and authority flows from the top of the hierarchy, down the line, to the bottommost layer. The closer a line position is to the top layer, the greater is the power of the holder of the position over lower-level employees.

The power a superior has over his subordinate is far from absolute, even in the most authoritarian organizations. The superior's power is constrained by organizational policy, by informal precedents, by operation of common and statutory law, by custom and culture, and by contract. When the power differential between superior and subordinate is recognized by both as thoroughly legitimate, the top man's authority is exercised and accepted without stress or conflict.

Typically, the superior has more than tacit acceptance of the leadership-followership roles reinforcing his power. He may exercise it in a number of ways, for example by:

— Initiating action for the subordinate.

— Controlling and monitoring performance.

— Demanding and receiving reports of actions taken.

— His ability to manipulate the system of rewards and punishments.

— His ultimate power to hire and fire subordinates, so long as he follows the rules laid down by contract or custom.

Of course, every superior is also the subordinate of someone higher up on the hierarchy. According to this view, each manager is a transmission medium for the flow of authority from the top to the lowest level of the firm's formal organization.

Bottom-Up Power

Each organization has a dual nature: its formal and its informal. Top-down power is an aspect of the formal; bottom-up power, of the informal. The following propositions describe the operation of bottom-up power:

ACCESS TO KEY PEOPLE.   Employees who have access to key people have more power than those who do not have such access. Think of the executive secretary who may earn a much smaller salary than a manager in her superior's department, but who exacts deference (and generous Christmas gifts) from members of the department because of her easy access to the department head. She knows when her boss is in a good mood and can be asked for a raise in salary. She knows when he is in a bad mood and should not be approached.

ACCESS TO IMPORTANT INFORMATION.   Access to important information increases power; failure of access lowers power. If a subordinate has information sources essential to his superior's success but not generally available through formal channels, the subordinate develops power over the superior. Example: a sales clerk has a friend in a competitor's sales department and can get advanced knowledge of the competitor's minimum bids on contracts.

LENGTH OF SERVICE.   The longer an employee works for a firm, the greater the likelihood is that he will have access to key persons and important information. Thus, a long-time employee will have power over his newly appointed superior, who may try unsuccessfully to have his powerful subordinate discharged.

AMOUNT OF EFFORT.   The more effort an employee is willing to put into his job, the greater power he will have over other employees. Conversely, the lazier the supervisor, the more likely it is that an energetic subordinate gets power over his boss. The indispensable employee makes himself so by extra diligence so that his boss finds that he cannot get along without him. The boss gets used to doing less work and places more and more reliance on his irreplaceable assistant.

CUTOFF POWER.   Employees whose jobs place them in strategic positions where they can cause total disruption of an operation have power over their superiors. A clear example is the teamsters, who can shut a company down by refusing to move goods to customers and blocking the receipt of incoming materials.

DISRUPTIVE POWER.   The ability to assure smooth performance places the subordinate in a powerful position. For example, a smoothly operating plant gets a new general manager. During his first week on the job, there are several wildcat strikes, quality of product deteriorates, and customer shipments are misdirected. Back at headquarters, the new man's boss wonders if putting the man there was not a mistake. By withholding smooth performance the lower-level employees are telling the new man who's really the boss of the operation.

BLACKMAIL POWER.   If the executives of the firm commit illegal acts and employees find out about those acts, the employees will have power over the executives and the company. Such employees may do nothing but wait until the time is ripe for action; they may try blackmail immediately; or they may take their special knowledge as a license to themselves engage in illegal activities without fear of punishment.

Top-Down and Bottom-Up Power
in a Negative Growth Situation

When layoffs, reassignments, and demotions are the order of the day, holders of top-down power undertake the change-planning process, using management's efficiency logic. People are shuffled around, with the best interests of the company as the paramount consideration. In the absence of bottom-up power, there would be no one to challenge management's right to act as if it were sole judge of what is best for the company.

As a practical matter, however, employees with the less formal, but nontheless real, bottom-up power will not allow themselves to be moved about like pieces on a gigantic chess board. Even before the change program is implemented, the invisible bottom-up power is made visible; the implicit is made explicit; the subtle is made obvious.

Faced with the realities of the countervailing informal power, managements rethink their change strategies, introduce the so-called "resistance to change" phenomenon into their calculations, and do what they have to do the best way that they can. The employees who find themselves in jeopardy because of the retrenchment plan, present their I.O.U.'s, show their teeth, take off the velvet gloves, and in other unmistakable ways bring to bear their accretions of bottom-up power.

EXHAUSTION OF STRESS ADAPTATION
CAPABILITY

It has been known for a long time that stress overload can cause harmful psychological and physiological changes in humans. The normal person has a capability for adapting to occasional stress. For example, if a person is confronted with great physical danger, certain chemical changes occur within his body. There is a rush of adrenalin to give him a quick burst of energy for flight or fight. His blood clotting factor may rise, so that if his skin is punctured, life-endangering loss of blood can be averted; his bowel contents may become liquified, so that if the abdominal wall is punctured, the wound is less likely to result in deadly peritonitis. His blood pressure rises.

When the danger is overcome or goes away, new chemicals flush away the stress-induced changes, and the body chemistry of the organism returns to its quiescent state. This process can be repeated as many times as necessary for the safety of the person without doing any permanent harm, so long as the *stress adaptation capability* (S.A.C.) remains intact.

There is a good deal of evidence that each person has a nonrenewable bank of S.A.C. that he can draw upon all of his life until it is exhausted. Because S.A.C. is an incredibly complex combination of chemical reactions, no one can be sure which components wear away first. Thus, the S.A.C. exhaustion will be different for each person, because he had different S.A.C. at birth and used it up under different conditions.

When the S.A.C. components are exhausted, the body can no longer respond to overstress as it did before. One of two things may happen: the chemicals produced by the normal stress response are there, but the flushing-away antagonists are absent; or the S.A.C. chemicals are exhausted. In either case, the body loses its resilience and ability to undo any harm caused by stress overload.

For example, in the presence of extreme danger, the body produces a large quantity of clotting factor. But the antagonist is not supplied later to flush it away, and the blood has an excessive level of clotting factor. This abnormality can produce a thrombosis, which can lodge in the legs and produce phlebitis or in the heart to produce a coronary thrombosis. Under normal conditions, danger was met with elevated blood pressure to assure rapid and plentiful supply of glucose to the brain and muscles. After S.A.C. is exhausted, the blood pressure elevates, but the antagonist is lacking, so the blood pressure remains at the high level and causes sustained hypertension.

Exactly which diseases are the result of S.A.C. exhaustion is not known, but there is evidence that many psychosomatic ailments such as gastric ulcers, ulcerative colitis, coronary thrombosis, arthritis, phlebitis, and hypertension may be related to the inability of the body to respond properly to stress overload.

There are two kinds of stress that the body copes with regularly: situational stress and stress from free-floating anxiety. The former is normal stress, and in the absence of the latter, the S.A.C. may be sufficient to protect the person from damage. There are exceptions, of course, because some people encounter tremendous stress in their lives that prematurely exhausts their S.A.C. For example, in World War II, bomber pilots were relieved after fifty missions over enemy territory. The theory behind this policy must have been that after fifty missions, the pilot would have burned out his store of S.A.C. and thereafter he would be a danger to himself, his crew, and to his associates. Also, exhaustion of S.A.C. must have been behind what in World War I was called "shellshock," and in World War II, "battle fatigue."

The main feature of situational stress that makes it tolerable is that it goes away. The same cannot be said about stress induced from free-floating anxiety. If the anxiety level is elevated, the body is always mobilized for flight or combat, and the S.A.C. is exhausted prematurely. That is why free-floating anxiety is so damaging to health.

Since the study of human response to stress is still in its infancy, we do not know how to measure the levels in the S.A.C. reservoir, and we do not know how to monitor the rate of outflow. Therefore, we can only speculate and develop a tentative hypothesis that seems to fit the facts as we know them.

We postulate (that is, we assert without offering proof) that every normal person is born with a supply of S.A.C. (this allows for the possibility that a certain percentage of persons have less than the normal quantity at birth). If the S.A.C. is distributed throughout the population in the same proportions as other attributes, we speculate that the distribution follows the bell-shaped curve. Some people have smaller amounts of S.A.C.; some have abnormally large amounts; most fall within a so-called normal range.

The people with abnormally low S.A.C. can go through life without any unusual health troubles, as long as they are protected from sustained overstress. If they are subjected to stress overload for too long as time, they are the early casualties. Such a person might fall apart at a young age from the death of a parent, or from other highly stressful events. On the other end of the distribution, we find the supermen and -women, the people with so much S.A.C. that they can bear more stress overload than any normal person. (We should get our leaders from this segment.)

Between these two extremes, we find the normal range. Persons who are faced with high stress overload and have a high level of free-floating anxiety suffer early breakdowns in health. If their free-floating anxiety can be eliminated or reduced substantially before S.A.C. exhaustion happens, the damage can be put off for years.

Thus, if we accept the speculative S.A.C. model, we accept as plausible the proposition that every person has his (or her) breaking point; every person can reach a point where his (or her) S.A.C. becomes exhausted. Therefore, every person can suffer serious mental or physical deterioration if his (or her) life or work situation involves sustained stress overload after S.A.C. exhaustion has taken place.

As it applies to the retrenchment process, the possibility of causing sustained stress overload is very real. In a working population (and we include management, professional, and executive personnel in this category) we can expect to find a significant number of persons who are close to S.A.C. exhaustion or who have already crossed over. These are the people who are in real jeopardy from the great stresses caused by a negative-growth program.

If the shock is too great, if the anxieties are too high, if the pain and suffering are too great, casualties are inevitable. People with reserves of S.A.C. will bring themselves closer to exhaustion; those on the border-line or over the line will suffer *real* damage to their physical and mental health. A sensitive, compassionate management will try to moderate the pressures on the change participants to minimize the harm done to them. Only the out-and-out sadist will use this time to deliberately heighten tensions, because to do so is to endanger the lives and health of innocent people as surely as would planting infectious bacteria in their food and water. Not everyone would succumb, but the persons with S.A.C. ex-haustion will be harmed; possibly very seriously harmed.

RELOCATION STRESS

Census figures reveal that Americans are a geographically mobile people. In fact, the average American moves his place of residence four-teen times during his lifetime compared with eight times for the average Briton, and five times for the average Japanese. The United States Postal Service estimates that close to forty million Americans change their addresses each year. Data accumulated by the American Telephone and Telegraph Company and large electric utilities across the land confirm the high frequency of residential relocations obtained from census data. This constant moving about of families has prompted sociologist and author Vance Packard to call the United States "a nation of strangers."

Corporate personnel from supervisors to top executives move, either because their companies transfer them to other jobs or because they leave one position in favor of another. When the employee is the head of a fam-ily unit, the move involves more than change of residence. Also involved are taking children out of school, making new friends, growing accus-tomed to new surroundings, and, perhaps, substantial changes in cul-tural opportunities.

Each change of place of residence is stressful for every member of the family, but the one who carries the greatest stress overload is the woman of the household. It is she who must make the living arrange-ments, see that the children are properly settled, suffer the intense lone-liness of living among strangers, try to pick up the threads of a disrupted social life.

The husband is protected from these stresses because of his deep involvement in his work and the contacts he has with his fellow employ-ees and other persons he meets in the course of his work. However, he shares his wife's distress through the close interaction with all family members. Thus, each member of the family affects every other member, and when one faces emotional difficulties, all others are affected, each in his or her own way.

As in the cases of other situational stresses people encounter in their lives, relocation stresses can be the proverbial straw that breaks the camel's back. For persons who already live on a knife edge of emotional instability, the pressures associated with relocation can cause them to go over the line into mental or physical breakdown.

A large-scale corporate retrenchment usually involves many personnel reassignments. Some are minor, from one floor of the building to another. A few may require more travel time for driving to work. Others may make it necessary for managers to move their homes to other cities if they wish to remain with the firm.

Managers and their families differ in their ability to cope with the stress of relocation. Families that have gone through a recent change of location are believed to be less likely to adapt easily to another change. In general, the more changes a family has gone through, the less able it will be to cope with one more.

The company executives who have the task of moving people around like pieces on a chessboard tend to focus principally of overall efficiency of operation. The general sales manager says to himself, "We have a weak spot in the Kansas territory; we're overstaffed in New York. I think I'll shift Bob Keefer to Kansas." Bob Keefer may be delighted with the new assignment, but if his wife is a native New Yorker, moving to Kansas will be more than normally stressful.

The decision to transfer executives to other cities ought to be treated as a multiple criteria problem that takes into consideration both company efficiency and the mental and physical health of the manager and the members of his family.

SELECTED REFERENCES

ARGYRIS, CHRIS, "Human Problems with Budgets," *Harvard Business Review*, Vol. 31 (Jan.–Feb. 1958).

DOHERENWEND, BARBARA S. and BRUCE P., *Stressful Life Events: Their Nature and Effects*. New York: Wiley Interscience, 1974.

GORDON, RICHARD L. and KATHERINE K., and MAX GUNTHER, *The Split-Level Trap*. New York: Bernard Geiss Associates, 1961.

MECHANIC, DAVID, "Sources of Power of Lower Participants in Complex Organizations" in W. W. Cooper, et al., *New Perspectives in Organizational Research*. New York: John Wiley and Sons, 1964, pp. 136–149.

MENNINGER, KARL, *The Vital Balance: The Life Process in Mental Health and Illness*. New York: The Viking Press, 1963.

PACKARD, VANCE, *A Nation of Strangers*. New York: David McKay Company, Inc., 1972.

SELYE, HANS, *Stress Without Distress*. Philadelphia, Pa.: J. B. Lippencott Co., 1974.

Chapter 12

Ethical
Considerations

CORPORATE SOCIAL RESPONSIBILITY

Responsibility Models

Do business firms have any compelling responsibilities other than
to avoid breaking laws and to honor their contractual commitments?
Clearly, when the firm accepts a customer's purchase order, it is obligated
to supply the goods in question with proper regard to quality and delivery
dates. The firm is bound, legally and morally, to pay its taxes, its bills to
vendors, wages and salaries to its employees, rents on its leased premises,
etc. But does it have responsibilities that go beyond the terms of the
contractual agreements and the legal constraints imposed on it?

No unanimity can be found in the business community on answers
to these questions. Scholars and practitioners disagree, and opinions range

from emphatic negatives to idealistic affirmatives. The range of views of the contenders can be encapsulated in the following models:

1 / The societal model

2 / The owner's interest model

3 / The one-big-family model

4 / The responsibility of power model

5 / The supplier of services model

6 / The defensive model

7 / The economic function model

8 / The idealistic model

THE SOCIETAL MODEL.   Advocates of the societal model assert that the economic needs of a society can be satisfied in any number of ways: through a socialist, communist, or capitalist system, along with variations. A form of economic organization best for one people may not be best for others. The private-property, free-enterprise system found in the United States is just one way that the needs of the American people can be met.

Thus, there is a form of contract between the society and the components of the economic system which implies that so long as they efficiently meet the people's needs, they are encouraged to continue in their method of operation. If, at any time, the business components fail to perform in the best interests of the society as a whole, changes will be made. The actual process of change is diffuse and inchoate, but changes are inevitable when the business sector fails to meet the demands made on it.

According to this view, business leaders must keep asking themselves, "Are we serving society's best interests at the same time as we serve our own?" If, in the best objective sense, the answer is yes, the business firm and the system as a whole are meeting their social responsibilities. If not, behavior must be changed until the answer becomes affirmative, because punishment of the offenders will surely follow.

If individual firms act in ways that detract from the overall efficacy, it is necessary for the preservation of the ongoing system that the offenders be identified, cautioned, punished, or rehabilitated. To fail to take action or to cause corrective action to be taken is to shirk one's responsibility to the efficient serving of society's needs. Continued failure to meet those needs is a danger to all, because society must then adopt new and changed forms of economic organization.

According to the advocates of the societal model, therefore, by acting with the best interests of the society foremost, business leaders ensure the continued preservation of the free-enterprise system. By failing to act so, they threaten the stability of the system. As a corollary, some sacrifice of the firm's unbridled self-interest may be called for because the overall welfare of the society has top priority.

The role of the central government, under the societal model, is to act on behalf of the people and that part of the business community that performs well, and to take remedial actions against the persistent offenders who allow self-interest to take precedence over the public interest. All economic behavior must meet the acid test of societal benefit.

THE OWNER'S INTEREST MODEL.   This model is exclusively self-centered. The persons who provide the entrepreneurial and financial input to the firm run it to suit their own interests. The firm is a means to narrowly defined ends such as: to make a profit for the owners, to provide the owners with a socially acceptable way to exercise the hunger for power over others, to build a large estate, to create conditions that will enable owners to elevate themselves to a higher social niche, and others.

If any thought is given to the welfare of other persons or parties, it is only in the self-interest context. The owner reasons, "I may have to give these people something in order to get them to do what I want them to do, but I'll give them the absolute minimum I can get away with."

Extreme advocates of this model accept the credo, "There's a sucker born every minute." Every person is an object for exploitation. The owner begrudges anything he must give up to obtain the things or services he requires.

More enlightened advocates of the owner's viewpoint are willing to be more generous and have a longer time horizon, but their motivation is still the same. They still ask, "What is there in it for me?" Perhaps they are less grasping and more polished in their dealings, but their underlying motivation does not differ in kind, only in degree. All behavior is gauged by the self-interest measure. Whether or not the steel fist is covered with a velvet glove, the operative philosophy is, "This is my (our) company and I'll (we'll) do with it as I (we) damned please!"

THE ONE-BIG-FAMILY MODEL.   According to this model, the managers, employees, suppliers, and customers are all viewed as members of an extended family. The nuclear family, the insiders, control the firm's wealth and activity, but they have a paternal interest in welfare of the more distant relatives (employees, etc.). Who is and who is not considered to be members of the quasi-extended family differs from organization to organization. Some closed companies consider only top-level executives as worthy of family treatment. Others include all managers.

Still others include "loyal" (usually this means nonunion) employees as being entitled to membership.

At the extreme, the one-big-family model merges with the view of the organization as a coalition of interest groups. Each legitimate claimant's interests is considered, and the firm's management tries to make equitable demands on each group in exchange for the benefits each realize from their participation in the firm's activities.

For the one-big-family model, the operative philosophy is: "There's enough for everybody, if everybody carries his own weight."

THE RESPONSIBILITY OF POWER MODEL.   This model is more applicable to large powerful firms than to small ones. There is a rule of the sea that holds that each vessel is responsible for any damage done by its wake to smaller boats. Thus, the large powerful ships, by their very nature, have the potential to do harm to smaller boats, even though the larger one merely carries out its normal routines.

When a firm is large and powerful enough, every one of its actions affects other firms and people, whether or not the large firm intends that to happen. Thus, according to this model, bigness carries special responsibilities for not harming the smaller, weaker company or group.

By like reasoning, when a large powerful entity has the capability to prevent a wrong from being perpetrated and it fails to act to prevent the wrong from being done, it is being derelict in its duty. It is just as if a policeman sees a child being beaten by a gang of teenagers, and he knows that the child's life is in danger, but he turns away and ignores the happening. That policeman would be committing a sin of omission. So, according to the responsibility of power model, to fail to take action when one has the obligation and power to prevent harm being done to weaker firms or groups is to commit the sin of omission. The powerful have the obligation to take extreme care not to do injury to the less powerful, even though the particular action, taken out of the power context, might be perfectly moral and acceptable.

THE SUPPLIER OF SERVICES MODEL.   The modern version of this model is the so-called "total marketing concept." All of the human, financial, and economic resources of the business firm are to be mobilized to serve the needs of its customers. It is a cardinal sin to be "product oriented" instead of "customer oriented." The latter leads to profits; the former, to failure.

The supplier of services model is outward-looking. The interests of the customers take precedence over other interests. The operative philosophy here is "We'll take care of our customers, and they'll reward us with their loyalty and patronage."

THE DEFENSIVE MODEL.   The emphasis on the defensive model is preventing the firm from accumulating enemies who may some day do it harm. Money is donated to neighborhood organizations so if there are any disturbances, the firm's property will be spared. The company tries to develop a good corporate image, because it fears that it may be damaged if it fails to do so.

THE ECONOMIC FUNCTION MODEL.   Stated in its simplest form, this model is based upon the concept that when a firm produces its products for sale and makes a profit for its providers of capital investment, it is carrying out its mission and social function. This model is derived from the Adam Smith idea of the "unseen hand" that guides an aggregation of profit-seeking firms into producing social and economic benefits for the entire society, merely by paying close attention to their own affairs.

IDEALISTIC MODEL.   According to the idealistic model, each business firm has the duty to make a worthwhile contribution to the improvement of the quality of life of the society. It may do this commendable task by making donations of funds to worthwhile social, cultural, and educational causes. The firm seeks to be a good corporate citizen, and its managers see themselves as leaders in the improvement of the society and its institutions.

Sethi's Three-State Classification

A detailed tabulation of corporate social responsibility and behaviors associated with several theories is shown in Table 12-1. This table presents three attitudes toward social responsibility: proscriptive (thou shalt not!), prescriptive (thou shouldst), and anticipatory-preventive, plus these behavioral dimensions:

— Search for legitimacy
— Ethical norms
— Social accountability
— Operating strategy
— Response to social pressures
— Activities re governmental actions
— Legislative and political activities
— Philanthropy

TABLE 12-1 *

A THREE-STATE SCHEMA FOR CLASSIFYING CORPORATE BEHAVIOR

DIMENSIONS OF BEHAVIOR	STATE ONE: SOCIAL OBLIGATION PROSCRIPTIVE	STATE TWO: SOCIAL RESPONSIBILITY PRESCRIPTIVE	STATE THREE: SOCIAL RESPONSIVENESS ANTICIPATORY AND PREVENTIVE
Search for legitimacy	Confines legitimacy to legal and economic criteria only; does not violate laws; equates profitable operations with fulfilling social expectations.	Accepts the reality of limited relevance of legal and market criteria of legitimacy in actual practice. Willing to consider and accept broader—extra-legal and extra-market—criteria for measuring corporate performance and social role.	Accepts its role as defined by the social system and therefore subject to change; recognizes importance of profitable operations but includes other criteria.
Ethical norms	Considers business value neutral; managers expected to behave according to their own ethical standards.	Defines norms in community related terms, i.e, good corporate citizen. Avoids taking moral stand on issues which may harm its economic interests or go against prevailing social norms (majority views). Individual managers responsible not only for their own ethical standards but also for the collectivity of corporation.	Takes definite stand on issues of public concern; advocates institutional ethical norms even though they may seem detrimental to its immediate interest or prevailing social norms.

Dimensions of Behavior	State One: Social Obligation Proscriptive	State Two: Social Responsibility Prescriptive	State Three: Social Responsiveness Anticipatory and Preventive
Social accountability for corporate actions	Construes narrowly as limited to stockholders; jealously guards its prerogatives against outsiders.	Construes narrowly for legal purposes, but broadened to include groups affected by its actions; management more outward-looking.	Willing to account for its actions to other groups, even those not directly affected by its actions.
Operating strategy	Exploitative and defensive adaptation. Maximum externalization of costs.	Reactive adaptation. Where identifiable internalize previously external costs. Maintain current standards of physical and social environment. Compensate victims of pollution and other corporate-related activities even in the absence of clearly established legal grounds. Develop industry-wide standards.	Proactive adaptation. Takes lead in developing and adapting new technology for environmental protectors. Evaluates side effects of corporate actions and eliminates them prior to the action's being taken. Anticipates future social changes and develops internal structures to cope with them.
Response to social pressures	Maintains low public profile, but, if attacked, uses PR methods to upgrade its public image; denies any deficiencies; blames public dissatisfaction on ignorance or failure to understand corporate functions; discloses information only where legally required.	Accepts responsibility for solving current problems; will admit deficiencies in former practices and attempt to persuade public that its current practices meet social norms; attitude toward critics conciliatory; freer information disclosures than state one.	Willingly discusses activities with outside groups; makes information freely available to public; accepts formal and informal inputs from outside side groups in decision making. Is willing to be publicly evaluated for its various activities.

Dimensions of Behavior	State One: Social Obligation Proscriptive	State Two: Social Responsibility Prescriptive	State Three: Social Responsiveness Anticipatory and Preventive
Activities pertaining to governmental actions	Strongly resists any regulation of its activities except when it needs help to protect its market position; avoids contact; resists any demands for information beyond that legally required.	Preserves management discretion in corporate decisions, but cooperates with government in research to improve industrywide standards; participates in political processes and encourages employees to do likewise.	Openly communicates with government; assists in enforcing existing laws and developing evaluations of business practices; objects publicly to governmental activities that it feels are detrimental to the public good.
Legislative and political activities	Seeks to maintain status quo; actively opposes laws that would internalize any previously externalized costs; seeks to keep lobbying activities secret.	Willing to work with outside groups for good environmental laws; concedes need for change in some status quo laws; less secrecy in lobbying than state one.	Avoids meddling in politics and does not pursue special interest laws; assists legislative bodies in developing better laws where relevant; promotes honesty and openness in government and in its own lobbying activities.
Philanthropy	Contributes only when direct benefit to it clearly shown; otherwise, views contributions as responsibility of individual employees.	Contributes to noncontroversial and established causes; matches employee contributions.	Activities of state two, *plus* support and contributions to new, controversial groups whose needs it sees as unfulfilled and increasingly important.

* **Source:** S. Prakash Sethi, *Dimensions of Corporate Social Performance: An Analytical Framework For Measurement and Evaluation.* Working Paper #2. Berkeley: University of California, Institute of Business and Economic Research, 1974, pp. 18–19.

Company! Do No Harm!

The fact that a firm is profitably offering superior goods and services at reasonable prices and may, therefore, be performing a socially useful function does not necessarily mean that it is behaving in a socially responsible manner. If it acts this way, and in addition contributes generously to social uplift programs, it may still fall far short of behaving with social responsibility. In the longer view, social responsibility implies that, at the same time that this well-meaning firm make its unquestionably worthwhile contributions to society, it must *do no harm*—negligently, purposely, inadvertently—through acts of commission *or* omission.

Many of the current theories of social responsibility neglect the do-no-harm imperative. One executive touts the positive societal values of his firm's programs, but ignores totally the harm that his firm might be doing in its day-to-day work. Another executive directs public attention to the extra good things his firm is doing, above and beyond what is normally expected of it, from the noblest motives. Others, cynical and self-serving, say, "It's smart business to get involved in this or that charitable activity. Let's get as much P.R. mileage from it as we can." Still another executive may assert that as long as the net result is favorable—social benefits exceed social disbenefits—the firm is acting responsibly because, they say, "You can't make an omelette without breaking the eggs."

Obeying the do-no-harm imperative is not as simple as it may seem at first glance. Perhaps that is why it is so often ignored. To whom must the firm do no harm? To its stockholders? To its customers? To its creditors? To its employees? To its competitors? To its neighbors? To the nation? To posterity?

If the firm, in carrying out its normal activities, cannot avoid doing harm to one or more of the foregoing claimant groups, what should it do? Should it desist, even though in doing so, it would suffer serious economic losses? Should it continue, in spite of the harm being done, but offer, voluntarily, fair compensation to the injured parties? Should it persist in its harmful activities and then spend money on "good works" (for parties not directly injured by the firm) as a balm to the corporate conscience? Should it try to offset the damage done to the corporate image by stepping up the level of expenditure for public relations on the assumption that if people only knew how wonderful the firm is, they would surely love it more? Or should it take the hard line and deny the existence of any possibility of injury; malign the complainers as cry babies, bleeding hearts, knee-jerk liberals; counterattack with litigation, harrassment, propaganda, press agentry, lobbying, bribery; insist that the firm does so much good, that any incidental harm is trivial; threaten to move if it is forced to desist? All of these responses are possible; all have been used at one time or another by large, respectable American corporations.

Almost always, to remedy a harmful condition involves extra costs that may reduce the benefits available to the firm's other claimants. In a sense, reducing the harm inflicted on one group merely transfers the injury (by reducing the available benefits) in different form to others. How is a reasonable compromise found? Clearly, this is not an easy matter to deal with and there are no easy answers.

The Executive Conscience

Personal and business ethics are not particularly congruent. An act, moral in the business world, can be immoral in the social milieu. Acts that are moral and well regarded in the social milieu are thought of as foolish and unworldly by business people. This lack of congruity between business and personal morality is the cause of much confusion and tension.

In one's social life it is very poor taste to covet one's neighbor's wife, his property, and his domestic servants. In business, coveting a competitor's customers and his key employees is perfectly normal. To take calculated action for the purpose of wooing away the competitor's best customer and his star salesman is simply clever business tactics. To go home and try the same tactics with a neighbor's wife and maid would cause much negative comment in the community.

The law recognizes the difference between personal and business ethics in its treatment of usury. Many states place a limit of six per cent per annum as the maximum for loans to and between individuals, but there is no limit to the interest a corporation may pay. Getting together to settle private grievances is a well-tried social practice, but when two firms get together to settle their market conflicts, it is a violation of the antitrust laws. Telling outright lies to conceal vital information from outsiders is called business counterintelligence. In private life, lies and systematic misrepresentation are frowned upon.

In these and other kinds of behavior, what is moral in one system may be immoral in another. Thus, when the individual manager does something for his company, moral in the business ethic, but immoral in the social ethic, he suffers from tension unless he can split his conscience into two airtight compartments. When he tries to solve business problems with ethical concepts learned in his personal, religious, and social life, he gets himself into deep trouble, either with the law or with his superiors. With them, he runs the risk of being thought of as being a "lightweight" or being naive and immature.

The following are a few examples of situations that are moral and lawful in one system but may not be in another.

— A large lending institution and a business firm are engaged in negotiations for a substantial loan. In addition to the usual repayment schedule, interest rates, and security guarantees, the loan officer demands an "equity kicker" to "sweeten" the deal. The borrower agrees and issues shares in the name of the lender.

(*A "loan shark" lends his client money and, in addition to repayment of the principle sum plus interest, the lender demands that the client pay a percentage of his weekly earnings to the lender for the rest of the borrower's lifetime.*)

— A young man goes to a local bank for a loan to help him purchase a new automobile. The borrower signs a promissory note and gives the bank a chattel mortgage on the vehicle. The young man fails to meet his payments, and the bank repossesses the auto, sells it at auction, and later obtains a deficiency judgment for the difference between the loan amount plus costs, and the amount realized from the sale. The bank garnishees the debtor's salary.

(*The young man goes to his father for help in buying a car. The father agrees to lend his son money but insists that it be handled in a business-like fashion. He does the same thing that the bank does and the result is the same. The father wonders why his son is angry with him and why the rest of the family looks at the father with disfavor.*)

— I am ill and bed-ridden, so I ask my friend to buy a few necessities for me when he goes to the store to do his food shopping. He agrees, and when he returns with a brown bag full of groceries, he tells me how much he spent and, with thanks, I reimburse him. Later, I add up all of the prices paid for the items and note that my friend has marked up each item exactly ten per cent. I am outraged at such perfidy.

(*Alpha Corporation's president authorizes a buying office to purchase a few items for the company's account. When the bills arrive, the buying office has added a 10 percent surcharge as its fee. The bills are approved without comment.*)

— Lanny P. is the father of six children and works as a salesman for Alpha Corporation. Because business has been bad, Lanny receives a termination notice. Alpha has had to cut its sales force by fifty per cent.

(*When he arrives home and tells his wife about his lost job and the fact that the severance pay and unemployment insurance will not be enough* to cover the family's expenses, they agree that they, too, will have to cut back. Lanny tells his three youngest sons (the ones with least seniority in the family) that they will have to leave home and fend for themselves. To ease the shock on the three more senior family members, he gives each of the terminated children one week's allowance, takes away their house keys, and tells them that they must leave that very night.)

— A government antipoverty project tries to find productive work for teenagers in the community. They hit on the idea of having the young men sell newspapers on street corners. One part of the city has four busy corners at a heavily traveled intersection. Four boys are given the intersection, and they start to fight over who will have which corner. The social worker calls a meeting, and they agree to assign the corners so that each boy has a permanent assignment. If one corner is much better than another, the boy with the better corner will make side payments to the others to enable them to equalize their income regardless of the corner they drew.

(A real-estate developer is constructing four supermarket-shopping centers. He advertises the availability of four locations suited for food stores. Four applicants apply. When the applicants find out about each others' interest, they arrange a secret meeting and agree on how much each will bid for each location so that each of the four will get his first choice without having to bid up the price. The four are annoyed when the Attorney General of the state charges them with collusive bidding.)

— I am a customer of a local food market, and as I am walking around the store with my shopping cart, my foot encounters a wet slippery spot where another customer dropped a small bottle of cooking oil. I fall and break my leg. I sue the store for $100,000 and win the case, but the store owner's insurance policy covers him for only $50,000. I obtain a judgment and insist that the store owner pay me the full amount, and this causes him to declare himself bankrupt.

(I visit my brother's home and slip on his kitchen floor. I sue him for $100,000 and win my suit. I insist on receiving my money and he sells all of his assets to pay me. I insist on taking a garnishee on his salary. At the next family gathering I wonder why everyone treats me with open contempt and another brother threatens me with physical violence.)

Specific Obligations Arising from Negative Growth Situations

If, under the exigencies of a severe retrenchment, the firm's executives act exclusively in the owners' interests, they recognize only contractually and legally binding obligations. If there are any moral obligations, the decision on whether or not to honor them is made on the narrowest grounds of self-interest. In fact, in extreme cases, even contractual obligations are ignored with the statement, "If you want to collect (or force compliance), sue me." Legal constraints are skirted on the theory that "they have to catch me first." For such companies, a contract is nothing more than an invitation to a lawsuit. Their executives honor only those obligations they are forced to honor; all others are evaded.

In contrast to this extreme, but by no means unusual, attitude toward the firm's obligations, the executives may act according to the "one-big-family" model of corporate responsibility. If such is the case, they are concerned with the firm's obligations to all members of the quasi-extended family, as each is likely to be affected by the retrenchment process.

However, whether the firm's leaders act on grounds of narrow, short-term self-interest or broad, enlightened self-interest and social responsibility, a substantial retrenchment does create obligations to many affected parties, which the firm may choose either to honor or ignore, depending on its attitudes.

TERMINATED EMPLOYEES.   The depth of the firm's obligations to its terminated employees depends, in part, upon how long they have been with the company. As a general rule of thumb, the longer the term of faithful employment, the greater the firm's moral obligation.

Managers tend to think that the wages and fringe benefits the firm provides its employees in exchange for their services constitutes full and complete payment and that there are no residual obligations other than those imposed by law, custom, or contract. However, the firm does not operate in a social, cultural, or political vacuum. The collective impressions the company leaves on all affected parties can have powerful consequences for a firm that wishes to continue in business. Thus, an enlightened management, whether through self-interest, social conscience, or plain humanity, will make an extra effort to ease the burden the forced termination places on its ex-employees.

For example, in 1959, Armour and Company, one of the nation's largest meat-packing companies, found it necessary to shut down six plants (almost 20 percent of its capacity) in Chicago, East St. Louis, Columbus, Fargo, Atlanta, and Tifton. In all, over five thousand production workers were affected. Along with two unions, Armour undertook an extensive program to aid the terminated employees. Some of the joint actions were

— Counselling with respect to severance pay, retirement rights, and unemployment compensation.

— Canvassing other meat packers in an effort to obtain jobs for some of the terminated workers.

— Making arrangements with the state employment offices for in-plant vocational and aptitude testing.

— Making arrangements with local educational institutions to provide vocational training and general education.

Although none of the foregoing aids can produce jobs when none are available, the company can receive "points" with the community for trying its best to help.

Another important consideration with terminated employees is that many of them may be called back to work at some later time. Thus, if they carry a grudge against the company, they will try to "get even" as soon as they are given the chance to do so. Their opportunities for obtaining revenge as long as they are outside of the company's walls are small. But once they get back inside, their opportunities are virtually unlimited.

Terminated employees who see themselves as having been unfairly treated by the company are a likely source of bad mouth-to-mouth advertising. Such "bad mouthing" can adversely affect sales of the firm's products for years to come. In extreme cases, formal and informal boycotts are mounted. For example, for many years, there was a rumor that Henry Ford was a virulent anti-Semite who not only discriminated against Jewish workers but also contributed large amounts of money to anti-Semitic organizations. The charges against Mr. Ford were never substantiated, but many persons who were repelled by anti-Semitism expressed their revulsion by not buying Ford cars. Similar responses by ethnic groups and other pressure groups have had the effect of informal boycotts or adverse mouth-to-mouth advertising that proved very costly to counter and undo.

SUPPLIERS.   Suppliers of goods and services are viewed by many managers as quasi-employees. As long as their products and services are required by the firm, they buy. When they are no longer needed, the firm stops buying. According to this simplistic view, so long as the firm pays its bills on time, it has fully discharged all of its obligations to its suppliers.

As was the case with employees, there are moral obligations to people who have served the company faithfully and well that transcend the material exchanges. Suppliers, too, can "bad mouth" a company if they believe that they have been treated unfairly or with disregard for the niceties of good business behavior. Suppliers' salesman are notorious purveyors of industry gossip.

What does the firm owe its suppliers beyond prompt payment of invoices?

— Where feasible, advanced notice of permanent or sustained reductions of purchases so that suppliers, too, can make their internal adjustments to the loss of sales volume.

— Adequate notice of intention to cancel contracts and reasonable compensation for unavoidable losses caused by contract cancellations.

— Confidential treatment of suppliers' business, trade, and product innovation secrets.

— To neither solicit nor accept bribes or special favors; nor to imply that payment of a bribe or granting of a special favor is a prerequisite for obtaining orders.

— To afford suppliers' representatives a fair hearing of their complaints and to take prompt steps to remedy justifiable grievances.

— Not to repeatedly request bids, the preparation of which involves substantial expense, without ever intending to place orders with the bidder; to give prompt notification if the bid is not accepted, so that the supplier can release his productive capacity for other uses.

— To treat suppliers' representatives with reasonable courtesy and complete honesty; to give prompt replies to suppliers' correspondence.

— If samples are requested, to give prompt reports on the acceptability or faults of the samples.

— Not to misrepresent the quantity of the goods the company expects to buy.

CUSTOMERS.   A fine point of business ethics is revealed by the following apocryphal story: a retailer sells a customer some goods, receives a twenty-dollar bill in payment, gives the customer change for a ten-dollar bill, and puts the extra ten dollars into his pocket. The ethical question that bothers him is "Should I split the ten with my partner?"

Although the retailer considers that he has an obligation to deal fairly with his partner (after all, there is honor among thieves, too), his conception of fair dealing with the customer is different. The customer is merely an object for exploitation. He owes nothing to his customer but what the law provides and what he can get away with. Such business operators live and practice under the banner of *caveat emptor* (let the buyer beware).

Although the foregoing attitudes and behavior may seem extreme, they are far from extinct, if the evidence of governmental actions on behalf of the consumer is any guide. However, many corporation executives prefer a less exploitive business strategy, either out of enlightened self-interest, or because they accept a more socially responsible view of the duty and obligations of business firms toward their customer constituency.

What obligations do firms have toward their customers other than the obvious ones of offering safe and effective products, honestly represented, at reasonable prices, backed up by honest warranties?

— If the firm intends to discontinue a product or service offering, to give adequate notice so that the customer can cover his requirements in other ways.

— If the firm intends to discontinue a product or service, to aid the customer to obtain alternative sources of spare parts and repair and maintenance services.

— To give wholesalers and dealers adequate notice so that they can protect their interests and make internal adjustments to the changed supply situation.

— Not to enter into collusive arrangements with other suppliers in order to unreasonably raise prices.

— Not to make unannounced but major changes in product characteristics without adequate testing to see if any customers will be injured by the changes.

— Not to make improper offers to the customer's employees to induce them to take actions contrary to their employer's interests.

— Not to submit nonrepresentative samples in the hope of obtaining orders but with the intention of later substituting inferior materials or producing to relaxed specifications.

— Not to consistently overship or undership, nor to ship too far ahead or behind the agreed-upon delivery schedule.

— To keep all customers' business and trade secrets in complete confidence; with consumers, to keep their personal secrets confidential and not to use private information in a manner unintended by the customer.

— Not to spread false or damaging information about the customer's business practices, his financial dealings, or his financial health.

— Not to assist or encourage a customer's key employees to leave their jobs and go to work for a direct competitor.

THE LOCAL COMMUNITY.   When the firm undergoing a substantial retrenchment is of sufficient size to have an adverse impact on the well-being of the local community, and it wishes to act with social responsibility, it will try to mitigate the harmful impact. Alternatively, the firm may wish to act with seeming compassion for the problems of the community out of self-defense. Items:

— Alpha Corporation announces a large layoff; during the night when only a watchman is present in the plant, a gang of neighborhood youths firebomb the company's plant.

— Alpha Corporation also notices that the number of windows broken in the factory is directly related to the number of persons laid off.

— Because of the bad feelings aroused by the company's actions, when it petitions the local building department for a variance to extend its offices, an aroused group of citizens protest and try to block the variance by court action.

— Enraged citizens repeatedly park their cars in such a manner that trucks cannot pull up to the plant's gates to unload their cargo.

— The company has no friends left in the local legislature and regularly finds itself the victim of discriminatory assessments on its real estate and improvements, which it is forced to combat with expensive and time-consuming litigation.

— The company's executives find parking tickets on their cars whenever they park overtime on the local streets; they complain about police harrassment, but to no avail.

— The local fire department, building department, and department of public safety make monthly visits to the company's facilities, and there is a blizzard of complaints and violations.

— The company is victimized by vandalism and outright sabotage. Its water supply is interrupted; its telephone wires cut; its trucks damaged with impurities placed in their fuel tanks, etc.

If, after the retrenchment, the company intends to continue operations in that community, it must reckon with the fact that it will continue to draw its employees from there. Thus, the young people who constitute the bulk of potential employees will arrive at the company's employment office with preconceived impressions and prejudices. If the general tenor of their feelings is hostile, the relations they will have with the company throughout their years of employment will be tainted with antagonism and subconscious resentment that no amount of indoctrination can undo. Company officials wonder, "Why do these people hate us so? What did we do to deserve all that animosity?" They forget that when hatred of the firm becomes deeply ingrained in the local culture, it is virtually impossible to erase. Children get antibusiness bias with their mother's milk, and every action by the company is greeted with suspicion and is treated as further incontrovertible proof of the firm's venality, perfidy, and lack of caring about the people.

SELECTED REFERENCES

EELLS, R. and C. WALTON, *Conceptual Foundations of Business*, rev. ed. Homewood, Ill.: R. D. Irwin, 1969.

FARMER R. N. and W. D. HOGUE, *Corporate Social Responsibility*. Chicago: Science Research Associates, Inc., 1973.

PETER, L. J. and R. HULL, *The Peter Principle: Why Things Always Go Wrong*. New York: William Morrow & Co., Inc. 1969.

SETHI, S. P., ed., *The Unstable Ground: Corporate Social Policy in a Dynamic Society*. Los Angeles, Calif.: Melville Publishing Co., 1974.

VARDAMAN, G. T. and P. B., *Communication in Modern Organizations*. New York: John Wiley & Sons, 1973.

Chapter 13

Refurbishing the Corporate Image

WHAT PUBLIC RELATIONS CAN AND CANNOT DO

Every business problem has a public relations aspect, but no problem has a purely public relations solution. Failure to heed this simple truth leads too many corporate managements into fatuous self-glorifications, repulsive self-righteousness, and to unbelievable excesses of self-defeating phoniness. Their compulsive preoccupation with image and a corresponding neglect for the underlying realities leaves too many executives no longer able to distinguish between shadow and substance.

A legitimate and wholesome use for the tools and techniques of the public relations practitioner is to keep open the channels of communication between the company and its various constituencies. An illegitimate use of public relations is to fill these communication pipelines with conceits, deceptions, attempted manipulations of the public mind, cover-ups, and self-serving half-truths.

Instead of dealing honestly with the corporate character, executives who wish to present this or that corporate image purely by use of such superficialities as trade marks, institutional advertising, philanthropic works, colored stationery, canned speeches in praise of motherhood and patriotism and the free enterprise system, and cynical press agentry, risk projecting an image of slyness, insincerity, and underhandedness. Just calling a slick used-car dealer "Honest John, the poor man's friend" does not raise his credibility or persuade anyone that he is worthy of trust. When we meet a person who finds it necessary constantly to reassure us of his high moral character, it only makes us doubt him more. What peculiar quirk of an executive's mentality makes him believe that the kind of behavior that he would disdain as being crass, gauche, insincere, and self-serving in his personal dealings is magically transformed into something wonderful when it is done by his firm?

The corporate character and image are two closely related concepts. We observe the corporate character as if we were astronomers studying heavenly bodies through our telescopes. From our observation of the corporate character and the resultant behavior, we form the image of the firm. Since image is subjective, it is quite possible for it to be either closely or not closely related to the true character of the company. When the company deliberately or inadvertently behaves in an inconsistent manner, the image becomes blurred.

It is more efficient to project an image that is thoroughly consistent with the corporate character than it is to project a false image. It takes the highest level of acting skill to carry off a deception, and the danger of slipping is ever present. The attempt to project an image inconsistent with the firm's true character inevitably leads to confusion, mixed perceptions, and a general aura of falseness and insincerity.

Of course, if it would be damaging for the firm's public to know what the firm is really like, true and reliable communication about the firm's inner state would hardly be helpful. The temptation in such cases is to cover up and falsify so that the firm's true condition is not revealed.

Only when the firm has straightened up the internal mess can the public relations practitioner carry out his legitimate function of smoothing the way for effective, two-way communication between the firm and its various publics. Thus, the prerequisite of a sound public relations campaign aimed at enhancing the corporate image is to make the reality of the firm's character and behavior correspond closely to the intended image. Any other alternative brings out the worst in all participants, rewards dishonesty and deceitfulness, and is ultimately self-defeating, degrading, and corrosive of character.

A Parable on Truth Telling

One very hot day in June, I went to my local tavern for a cooling glass of lager. As I stood at the gleaming mahogany bar nursing my drink, I overheard a young man talking to the bartender.

"Boy, am I having a tough time," the young man said. "My unemployment insurance runs out next week. If I don't find a job soon, I'll have to go on welfare. . . . I'd sure hate to do that."

The bartender muttered something that sounded to me like, "Yeah, things are tough all over."

The young man turned to me and said, "Hey, man, you don't know where I could find a job, do you?"

"I might," I replied. "What do you do?"

"Almost anything in a purchasing department. I can buy, expedite, keep records—anything."

"What happened to your last job?"

"I was let out in a big layoff.—They said they might call me back in a few months. It's been six months and still no sign of a callback."

"What have you done about finding another place?" I asked.

"I've tried everything. Employment agencies, letters to purchasing departments, answered ads in the business section of the paper—everything."

"Any results?"

"Sure. I got lots of interviews, but no job offers."

"What's wrong?"

"I don't really know . . . I'm qualified. I have a business degree and five years of good experience. Maybe I'm too truthful."

"Too truthful?" I asked. "What do you mean by that?"

"Well, I have some faults. . . . I believe that a man should present a balanced picture—You know, good points and weaknesses. The whole picture, warts and all."

"That's very commendable. How does it work?"

"I still don't have a job," the young man said. "I know that if I lied about myself, I'd get a job offer, but I can't bring myself to do it. It goes against my upbringing. I just have to tell the truth about myself."

"Do you have one of your resumés with you?" I asked.

The young man handed me a copy of his resumé. I could see that he was well educated and had held two very responsible jobs with a prominent local firm. To have been entrusted with that degree of responsibility at his young age meant to me that he must be an exceptionally capable person. I handed back the resumé without comment.

"What do you think?" he asked eagerly.

I didn't answer.

"Do you think I ought to lie about myself—not tell them about my weaknesses?"

Now, I'm a management consultant and I don't usually give advice without a healthy fee, but this fellow seemed so lost. If he thought he needed to lie, I knew he'd bungle it. Honest people make lousy liars. And this fellow didn't have time to learn. I was convinced that if he went on welfare, it would do him permanent harm. So I violated one of my rules of professional behavior and took on his case.

"Son," I said, "do you know what psychoanalysis is?"

"Sure," he said. "You lie down on a black leather couch and spill your guts for fifty minutes for fifty bucks a visit."

"Right," I said. "And for how long does this usually go on?"

"I can't say . . . My dad went for over eight years. He said it took him that long to find out all about himself."

"O.K.," I replied. "How long have you been under analysis?"

"Me? I never went to a shrink. Why? Do you think I ought to?"

"No, that's not my point. Your dad took over eight years to find out about himself. Let me see, eight years times fifty visits a year—each visit about fifty minutes—that's twenty thousand minutes."

"So what?" the young man asked, slightly bewildered.

"So this," I said. "It took your father twenty thousand minutes to discover the truth about himself and to tell it to a psychiatrist, who had nothing else to think about during the visit. How much time have you spent in finding out the truth about yourself? And if you knew the truth, the whole truth, who has the time and patience to listen?"

I could see that I was getting through at last.

"You mean . . . ," he hesitated. "You mean that I don't really know the whole truth about myself? And even if I did, nobody would have the time to listen?"

"Precisely. And what follows from that?" I asked in my most didactic manner.

"It means that in the short time I have with an interviewer, I have to be selective about what I tell him."

"Correct—and what else?"

"Let me see. . . . If I have to be selective, I have a choice between a self-destructive or self-enhancing selection—right?"

"You're doing fine. But isn't being selective just a little dishonest?"

"Yes—well, er, er, No. How could it be dishonest? It is just as dishonest to tell all bad things as it is to tell all good things—That's right, isn't it?"

"I'd say so." I replied. "So what do you do? What criteria do you use for selection?"

"Relevancy? Not lying with the truth? Putting my best foot forward?"

"You have the idea, son. Now, how about buying me a glass of lager? I make it a rule never to give advice without some form of compensation."

Objectives of the Public Relations Campaign

The overriding goals of the public relations campaign are to convert defeat into victory, to transform a necessary retreat into a successful advance, and to move from dismantling the firm to reconstructing it.

There is no way to carry out a large-scale retrenchment without causing real injury to many persons. A program of contraction has the potential for seriously damaging the web of relationships between the firm and its constituencies—relationships that have been nurtured over the years at great expense. Good relationships inevitably deteriorate under the stresses of negative growth; poor relationships can become destructive.

Thus, an important aim of the public relations campaign is to halt the progressive deterioration of the relationships between the company and its constituencies. Having achieved that objective, the next step is to rebuild the relationships and, if possible, to make them better than before.

The actual content of the communication between the firm and its publics must be chosen with the foregoing aims in mind. But the foundation for the program must be a sequence of constructive acts so that the company can "do good and get credit for it".

There are times when keeping a low profile is the best tactic. For example, when there is an airplane crash with many deaths, the airline whose plane crashed often stops all of its advertising for a few days or weeks. The juxtaposition of claims for the joys of air travel and the tragic news of multiple deaths by fire and impact are too ironic. It is better not to call public attention to the unfortunate airline at such time.

In like manner, it may be prudent to keep quiet during the trauma of a rapid retrenchment and to conserve the funds used for public relations work. At a more propitious time, the funds can be used to reburnish the tarnished corporate image.

AN INVENTORY OF USEFUL PUBLIC RELATIONS TECHNIQUES

Techniques for Calling Public Attention to the Firm

When, in the judgment of the firm's executives, it is wise and helpful to bring the firm's name before the public, techniques such as those listed in Table 13-1 can be used. The general aim of these techniques is to associate the company name with newsworthy events, and to obtain mention of the company name and the names of its executives in the editorial columns of the local press. If the event is sufficiently newsworthy, it may deserve mention on local radio and television, too.

It is prudent to have the events listed in Table 13-1 supervised by a member of the company's public relations firm or department. These persons usually know members of the news departments of the newspapers, magazines, and radio and television stations and are more likely to secure the desired favorable mention of the company's participation. If the events are not handled by competent professionals, the press may fail to notice the happenings; if the happenings are noticed, the editors may fail to find them sufficiently newsworthy; or an overzealous reporter looking for an unusual "angle" may present the event in a light that proves embarrassing or damaging to the firm. Good publicity almost never happens by itself; it needs the skilled hand of a competent and knowledgeable public relations practitioner.

ADVERTISING VERSUS PUBLICITY.   The company's message to its target audiences can be sent through the mass media, either by advertising (paid use of the media) or through "free" publicity. Publicity is free only in the sense that the media are not paid; it is not actually free, because salaries and expenses for public relations personnel who arrange for the placement of the publicity items must be paid.

The advantage of paid advertising is that the firm can guarantee that the message will be placed exactly as it wishes and in the media it chooses. The disadvantage of advertising is that it has low credibility.

Publicity consisting of favorable mention of the company's name or reporting of the company's message in the editorial sections of the mass media has the immense advantage of having high credibility. The disadvantage of relying on this form is that the firm has very little control over the content and the timing of the publicity.

TABLE 13-1
HOW TO CREATE NEWSWORTHY EVENTS *

- Tie in with the news events of the day.
- Conduct a poll or survey.
- Issue a report.
- Arrange an interview with a celebrity.
- Make an analysis or prediction.
- Take part in a controversy.
- Arrange for a testimonial.
- Write a report or make a speech.
- Form and announce the names of a committee.
- Hold an election.
- Announce an appointment.
- Celebrate an anniversary.
- Issue a summary of important facts.
- Tie in with a holiday—national, state, or local celebration.
- Make a statement on a subject of interest.
- Make a trip.
- Bring a celebrity in from somewhere.
- Make an award.
- Hold a contest.
- Appear before a public body to testify or make a statement.
- Stage a special event.
- Write a letter.
- Adapt national survey to local conditions.
- Entertain a celebrity.
- Stage a debate.
- Organize a trade convention.
- Tie in with a "week" or "day" promotion.
- Fete an institution, such as the Bill of Rights or the Constitution.
- Inspect a project.
- Lay a cornerstone, turn over the first shovel, drive the first spike.
- Organize a tour.
- Issue a protest.

---

* Adapted from materials created by Prof. Lawrence Stessin.

Both techniques have their place; neither is inexpensive. A complete campaign will probably use both advertising and publicity in harmonious combinations under the supervision and guidance of skilled professionals.

Techniques for Aiding a Distressed Community

When the company undergoing a severe contraction is large enough that its action can have a material effect on the well-being of the local community, socially responsible behavior involves doing something to mitigate the adverse impact of a sudden rise in unemployment. Although the company cannot refrain from laying off employees, there are some things it can do to ease the shock to the community.

— Cooperate with the local authorities in trying to encourage other companies to set up operations and reemploy the laid-off employees.
— Allow the use of company facilities for a job-referral center.
— Donate surplus equipment to local educational institutions so that they will not have to purchase the material with the taxpayers' money.
— Switch some purchases made from suppliers outside of the community to firms within.
— If the firm is enjoying a tax subsidy from the local community, either in the form of real-estate tax-abatement or in the form of extra services, increase reimbursements to the community for such subsidies.

Employee Public Relations Techniques

According to S. M. Cutlip and A. H. Center, authors of *Effective Public Relations* (Prentice-Hall, Inc., 1971), there are five basic goals of employee public relations:

1 / To create among all hands an awareness of the firm's goals.
2 / To keep all hands informed of significant developments that can effect the firm and its employees.
3 / To raise effectiveness of all personnel as good-will ambassadors, on and off the job.
4 / To encourage favorable attitudes in the staff and to raise its productivity.
5 / To satisfy the desires of employees to keep informed about what goes on in the company.

Specific techniques that firms use to achieve these objectives are

- Oral, face-to-face communication between subordinate and supervisor.
- Written communication, including letters, notices on bulletin boards.
- Company policy and procedure manuals; health insurance and pension information booklets; employee indoctrination handbooks.
- Employee house organs, newspapers, and gossip sheets.
- Periodic meetings, social events, picnics, Christmas parties.
- Executive walkarounds, periodic inspections, stopping to chat with employees.
- Visibility of executives; common eating facilities; open-door policy.
- Employees' suggestion boxes; grievance procedures.
- Employee counselling; exit interviews.
- Remembrances; birthday, anniversary greetings; get-well cards; congratulations on wedding, births, promotions, special public mentions, success in extramural activities.
- Blood donor awards; community service awards; safety awards.
- Special scholarships for employees' children; science fellowships for talented high-school children.
- Farewell parties for retiring employees.
- Visiting days for employee spouses.
- Company-sponsored athletic competitions.
- Company representative attends funerals of deceased employees.
- Company-sponsored language training classes for non-English-speaking employees; citizenship training.
- Day-care centers for employees' young children.
- Welcome wagons for employees just moving into neighborhood.
- Cooperative buying groups to aid employees in saving money on food, clothing, and housewares costs.
- Voluntary payroll deduction plans to aid employees in accumulating funds for vacations, children's camps, extended leaves, etc.
- Hospital visits for employees or family members.
- Housing office to aid employees who must move their places of residence.

— Bus service so that female employees on the late shifts will not have to travel home in the dark.

— Testimonial advertisements that show employees at work.

Although many of the foregoing techniques involve substantial expense, they may produce benefits, in specific instances, that far outweigh the costs. If employees become convinced that in spite of exigencies that may require staff curtailments from time to time, the firm's management still cares for them, and is sensitive and compassionate in their dealings with employees, a good deal of the venom and hostility associated with layoffs can be avoided.

For many employees, nothing the management can or will do will overcome hatred and bitterness. They see the firm and its managers as natural enemies, just as many tenants see their landlords as greedy, heartless exploiters. The best the firm's manager's can accomplish with such people is to deny them a fertile ground for their venomous productions to take root and flourish. Fair and compassionate treatment of the firm's personnel and equitable distribution of benefits and disbenefits all can help create a favorable (or less unfavorable) organizational climate.

Although the foregoing list of techniques appears as a collection of actions to be taken by management on behalf of the employees, there is no reason why employees cannot be induced to participate in running specific activities. If their active participation can be obtained, the activities are less likely to be taken for granted and frozen into union contracts as revered "past practices" that continue long after they have lost all of their original meanings. Also, activities that are without value for the affected employees can be discontinued and time, funds, and energy shifted to more worthwhile uses.

Miscellaneous Events That Present a Public Relations Opportunity

A public-relations-sensitive firm siezes every opportunity to make a favorable impression on its publics. Examples of situations that can produce P.R. opportunities are

— A local employee receives a substantial promotion in rank.

— The company adopts an employee stock purchase plan.

— The company receives a very large order that assures continued production for the indefinite future.

— A nationally known celebrity takes a plant tour.

— The company is celebrating its twenty-fifth anniversary with a big party for its employees.

— An employee who is a rose grower wins a prize at the local, company-supported flower show.

— The company celebrates a particular date by giving several shares of stock to employees' babies born during that week.

— The company establishes a gift-matching program under which it will match any charitable contribution made by any of its employees to a tax-exempt charity.

— The company makes a gift to the local university in the name of its founder.

— The company purchases a new fire engine or ambulance for the volunteer fire department or first-aid squad.

— The company sponsors an art exhibition at the local high school and supplies funds to award prizes to the three-best-of-show local artists.

— The company sponsors a chamber of commerce affair to which it invites executives of all of the local business firms with which it does business.

— The company purchases some unused land and donates it to the municipality for use as a playground.

— Instead of using drab checks for payroll and payment of bills to local merchants, it has special, oversized, brightly colored checks printed that stand out from all other checks.

— The company is awarded a large defense contract, and a military delegation, in full uniform, visits the plant to speak to the employees.

— The local organizations for the blind, physically handicapped, and aged are given space on the exit side of the factory time clock to display their handicrafts for sale to employees during the lunch hour and at the end of the work day.

— The company purchases and installs new antipollution equipment or new safety equipment and holds a ribbon-cutting ceremony at which the mayor pushes a remote-control button to start the equipment.

AFFIRMATIVE ACTION PROGRAMS

In recent years, because of the pressure of organized minority groups and the force of the antidiscrimination laws, companies have been pressed to modify their hiring and promotion practices. In the past it seemed sufficient to take the position that the company did not discriminate on the basis of sex, age, race, or national origin and to leave it at that. Only merit and suitability for the work were the official criteria for hiring. Of course, most managements did not care if the policy was not enforced; just having a written policy seemed to be enough.

As a practical matter, ethnic, racial, religious, and sexual selection was the rule in American industry, but not because managements wanted it that way. If they were accused of encouraging systematic discrimination against minority groups, managers would protest vociferously that they did no such thing. And if given a lie detector test, almost every top- and middle-level executive with hiring power would have passed with flying colors. Discrimination was widespread because of powerful and not-so-subtle sociological forces operating in the work place.

A study of the ethnic composition of the work forces of many large business firms showed that some were clearly identifiable as Protestant companies, Catholic companies, Jewish companies. Large numbers of factories were lily white, or were remarkably homogeneous in ethnic composition.

How did it happen that in spite of a stated policy of nondiscrimination, discrimination was the rule rather than the exception? A number of factors, peculiarly American, combined to produce this phenomenon.

1 / The company opens a new factory or office facility close to, or in the midst of, an ethically homogeneous community.

2 / Most of the new hires for low- and middle-level jobs come from the local community. As a result, most of the employees are from the same ethnic group.

3 / Employees who are not members of the dominant group tend to feel uncomfortable and feel the hostility of the majority group. Before long, the minority employees leave the company. The company does not ask applicants what their religion or national origin is, because to ask such questions is not "democratic." Relatives and friends of the dominant majority find out about job vacancies from

their co-religionists in the firm and apply to fill the vacancies. Many are hired, thus reducing further the number of places held by nonmembers.

4 / When a nonmember applies for a job and is hired, he or she does not last. The personnel manager discovers that there is very high turnover among nonmembers and after a while stops hiring them.

5 / The word gets around the neighborhoods that nonmembers have no chance for success or longevity in that plant or office, so very few apply.

6 / When accused of systematic discrimination against nonmembers of the dominant ethnic group in the plant, the personnel manager is deeply insulted. To commit such an act is foreign to his character and his nature, and he is probably telling the truth as he sees it. He says, "I'd be glad to hire any _____s who apply if they are qualified, but they don't apply. And even the few who I do hire don't seem to be happy here. I never ask an applicant about his religion or ethnicity, so I have no idea what the ethnic composition of the work force is."

Similar patterns of hiring, retention, and systematic discouragement of specific ethnic groups occur in many firms and in subdivisions of the firms. It is by no means unusual to find an Italian department, a Jewish department, a Polish department, etc. in some firms. The ethnic self-selection process works without anyone's being fully aware of what is happening.

Discrimination against women and black Americans is easier to detect, because the differences are apparent to the naked eye. It is difficult to tell if the workers on a particular production line are Irish Catholics, Polish Catholics, Norwegian Protestants, German Lutherans, Jewish, or Seventh Day Adventists, but it is easy to tell if the workers are all white, all male, or all female.

Sociologists who have studied the informal but powerful forces leading to ethnic self-selection have come to the conclusion that the problem will never be solved by benevolent neglect or passive policy statements. What is needed is an active, positive, controlled policy of nondiscrimination. To achieve such a program requires racial and ethnic audits and racial and ethnic hiring goals (the word *quota* is anathema because of its bad history). The result of attempts to eliminate systematic but covert ethnic and racial self-selection is the current spate of "affirmative action programs" based on the paradox that to eliminate covert discrimination it is necessary to enforce overt discrimination with the commendable goal of achieving racial, sexual, and ethnic heterogeneity. Only through diligent application of this paradoxical policy is it possible to afford every minority group equal access to economic opportunity and social equality.

American business firms have taken giant steps in the direction of imposing affirmative action programs on their firms and in diligently enforcing those programs. Laggards have been given additional encouragement to comply by action of state and federal courts, which have assessed enormous fines and money damages against recalcitrants. As a result of governmental prodding and minority group pressures, members of formerly disadvantaged groups obtained better and higher-level jobs in government and industry than was possible under the old system.

As long as the American economy was growing and employment was expanding, it was possible to absorb the disadvantaged groups into the blue- and white-collar work force. However, with the onset of an economic downturn when it became necessary to enforce mass layoffs, the seniority principle (last hired, first fired) restored earlier patterns of ethnic discrimination, because the newly hired, formerly disadvantaged workers were the first to be fired.

Many of the organizations representing the disadvantaged groups are protesting, but at the time this book is being written, the trade union logic of honoring seniority seems to be dominant. Court tests of opposing views (seniority versus equal opportunity) are imminent. Which principle will prevail no one knows. Seniority may prevail, or a compromise may be possible, perhaps, on a case-by-case basis.

Whichever force wins, the inescapable fact is that management is caught in the middle of a lose-lose situation. The many years of utter neglect of the principle of equal opportunity by business executives whose basic philosophy was to go along with the current and not to "make waves," who were willing to allow the shadow of a nondiscrimination policy serve in place of the substance now present managements with an insoluble dilemma. Either solution is acceptable to managements, because they have no firm ideological commitment to their position. But they will not be allowed to escape. Their firms have been chosen as the battlefields on which this battle will be fought. As with the residents of all battlefields, the noncombatants take a bad beating and suffer grievous casualties.

SELECTED REFERENCES

CUTLIP, S. M. and A. H. CENTER, *Effective Public Relations,* 4th ed. Englewood Cliffs, N.J.: Prentice-Hall, Inc., 1971.

EELLS, RICHARD, "Corporate Giving: Theory and Policy," *California Management Review* (Fall 1958), pp. 37–46.

HIEBERT, R. E. et al., *Mass Media: An Introduction to Modern Communication.* New York: David McKay Company, Inc., 1974.

JONGEWARD, DOROTHY and SCOTT, *Affirmative Action for Women: A Practical Guide.* Reading, Mass.: Addison-Wesley Publishing Co., 1973.

LAPORTE, LOWELL, *Investor Relations.* New York: National Industrial Conference Board, 1967.

POWELL, REED M., *Race, Religion and the Promotion of the American Executive.* Columbus, Ohio: Ohio State University College of Administrative Science, 1970.

ROBINSON, EDWARD J., *Communication and Public Relations.* Columbus, Ohio: Charles E. Merrill Books, Inc. 1966.

VON FURSTENBERG, G. M., et al., *Patterns of Racial Discrimination* (2 vols.) Lexington, Mass.: Lexington Books, D. C. Heath & Co., 1974.

What Is Affirmative Action? Combating Discrimination in Employment. West Haven, Conn.: National Education Association (undated).

Afterword

I began this book with the thought that managers would find useful a systematic treatment of the much neglected topic: "How To Cope with the Nasty Little Problems Encountered During a Business Retrenchment." Nothing has happened to change my original purpose, but as my work and research progressed, I became convinced that managing for negative growth will occupy more and more executive time and energy as the national and international economies go through more frequent periods of instability.

Optimists believe that the 1973–1976 recession was a fleeting aberration. That recession, deeper and more frightening than any experienced since the Great Depression of the 1930's, came as an unwelcome shock to a population conditioned to think of uninterrupted economic growth as the normal condition of economic life.

I see too many disturbing factors in the present world condition to feel that continued complacency is justified. Items:

— The massive transfers of wealth from the industrialized to the O.P.E.C. nations (and soon, perhaps, to other commodity cartels) must cause severe harm to the American and other industrialized economies.

— The progressive contamination of the earth's land, water, and atmosphere will surely degrade the quality of life for our citizens, either from the bad effects on our physical and mental health, or because of higher prices for consumer and industrial goods brought about by the expensive but essential pollution-abatement efforts.

— The uncontrolled growth of world population with the ever-growing threats of famine and mass die-offs of weakened peoples will put greater pressures on the wealthier nations for some form of income equalization.

— The growing nuclear proliferation among smaller nations reduces the relative power of the larger to maintain global equilibrium. Just as the "six-shooter" served as an equalizer between the big bully and the weakling, so the possession of nuclear capability serves to equalize the power disparity between the strong and weak nations.

— Throughout the world there is a tendency toward disorder and chaos, with a breakdown in law and order and increases in both purposeful and mindless terrorism that destabilize the society.

— In the United States and other western nations, the power and increasing willingness of trade unions to make economic raids on the less organized population sectors, and the unwillingness of government officials to assert the primacy of the common good over the exercise of raw trade union power bode ill for the stability of those economies.

The net result of these destabilizing factors is that the past model of regular and largely uninterrupted economic growth and steady improvements in the standard of living is no longer a reliable guide to the future. This does not mean that all growth will cease. It does mean, however, that superimposed on the upward trend in economic activity will be wider and wider swings. Particular industries will go through their private depressions, as, for example, did the automobile industry in the years 1974 and 1975, and the residential home-building industry in recent times. Only when the wide swings in particular industries happen to coincide will the entire national economy be adversely affected, but that too can happen with increasing frequency.

Thus, although this book on managing for negative growth may seem "trendy" and a product of a recent economic downturn, in fact, I believe that the managerial skills necessary for coping with rapid retrenchments and prolonged contractions will be in great demand throughout industry for many years to come. If so, this little volume could be one forerunner of many more to come on the subject of managing for negative growth.

Index